THE VISIONARY

ROBERT DESCHARNES · CLOVIS PRÉVOST

GAUDI

THE VISIONARY

PREFACE BY SALVADOR DALI

A Studio Book THE VIKING PRESS New York

Originally published in French under the title *La vision artistique et religieuse de Gaudí*

First published in 1971 by The Viking Press, Inc.

This revised edition first published in 1982 by The Viking Press (A Studio Book)
625 Madison Avenue, New York, N.Y. 10022
Published simultaneously in Canada

Library of Congress Cataloging in Publication Data
Descharnes, Robert.
Gaudí, the visionary.
(A Studio book)
Translation of: La vision artistique et religieuse de Gaudí.
Includes English translation of: La visió artística i religiosa d'en Gaudí
by Francesc Pujols.
Bibliography: p.
Includes index.
1. Gaudí, Antonio, 1852–1926. I. Prévost, Clovis. II. Pujols, Francesc, 1882–1962. Visió artística i religiosa d'en Gaudí. English. 1982. III. Title.
NA1313. G3D413 1982 720'.92'4 82-70179
ISBN 0-670-33587-8 AACR2

Set in Switzerland Printed in Italy Bound in Switzerland

Printed in Italy and bound in Switzerland

TABLE OF CONTENTS

The Expiatory Church of the Sagrada Familia. Perspective view drawn by Francisco Valls.

PREFACE

Five principal perfidies have been perpetrated shamelessly with respect to the spirit of Gaudí by contemporary panegyrists—that is to say, by those who have not approached his work with their five senses.

1. Those who have not seen his militant vision

are traitors, because they intentionally ignored that Gaudí was an Apostolic and practicing Roman Catholic, and that his aesthetic vision was conditioned by his religious vision.

2. Those who have not touched the bony structures and the living flesh of his delirious ornamentation

are traitors, because they intentionally ignored the fundamental academicism of Gaudí's aesthetic and consequently have minimized his realistic and naturalistic conception of ornamentation. When Gaudí makes a natural cast of a tuft of grass, a donkey, a flock of fowl, or a person chosen to be Judas; when Gaudí makes use of static or instantaneous photography in connection with his structural investigations of his subjects, he applies these processes and techniques solely in the interests of a strictly Christian iconography. His aesthetic adapts itself to the traditional Christian vision in its most popular forms, relying on fables, familiar piety, and the most powerful academic iconographical source of Christianity: that which springs from remorse. This notion is more deeply rooted in the people and their folklore than are other, more highly evolved ideas, like those introduced by the Company of Jesus. Gaudí's iconographical vision is almost naïve. This naïveté is characteristic of academic realism; images are elementary, formed without innovation or complexity. If one concedes that in the *Sagrada Familia*, in which all types of academic images are intermingled, the major exaltation is that of self-reproach, one will understand why this chief creation of Gaudí is called the Expiatory Church of the Holy Family, with a meaning at once naïve and transcendent.

Gaudí uses all the sensory elements; his use of tactile elements may, in my opinion, be associated with the experiments of the Italian Futurists. For at that time, at the birth of their movement, Boccioni's tactile surfaces signaled a new sense of touch. The Futurists were even concerned with flavors! They sought to embrace everything, to reunite all sensory elements in a single creation that would be the triumph of an idea. They preferred, in sum, the cathedral to the art gallery.

Gaudí worked in the same way. I think that this is one of the reasons for the vitality and the vigor of his art. His brain was very much in touch with the tips of his fingers. As a result, he fabricated goose flesh wherever he found it to be necessary; every surface has a bristling texture; his architecture is a tactile erogenous zone that bristles like a sea urchin.

3. Those who have not heard the chromatic, glowing stridence of his color, the striking polyphony of his organ-pipe towers, and the clash of his mutating decorative naturalism

are traitors, because they intentionally ignored the essential role of color, light, sounds, and silence in Gaudí's work. The *Sagrada Familia* and all his other structures were imagined with multicolored and polychromatic surfaces. Gaudí went so far as to reclothe his roosters and hens with their red crests and all their varied colors, like the pious statues of Saint-Sulpice and following the great academic tradition of Catalan *pessebres* (popular *crèches* in which the polychromed figures are often modeled from life).

Gaudí sought to appeal to every human means of perception. He used mosaics to produce scintillating, dazzling colors. The sound of bells was one of his greatest concerns; he traveled to hear different sonorities and to study acoustics; indeed, his bell towers became organ pipes! The Façade of the Nativity is a decorative masterpiece conceived in accord with harmonic resonances. In front of it Federico García Lorca told me that he heard a *griteriá*—an uproar of sonorous cries that became louder and more strident as the façade rose toward the sky, until the sound mingled with that of the angels' trumpets in a glorious tumult that he was unable to bear for more than a few moments.

4. Those who have not tasted his superbly creative bad taste

are traitors, because they intentionally ignored the dominant role that it plays in Gaudí's art. It is a common error to think of bad taste as sterile; rather, it is good taste, and good taste alone, that possesses the power to sterilize and is always the first handicap to any creative functioning. One has only to consider the good taste of the French: it has encouraged them not to do anything!

It would be treacherous to want to complete the *Sagrada Familia* without a real ability to taste. The building should be left as it is. Gaudí himself probably would have finished it in a style completely different from his original idea. Nothing should be added for which exact models do not exist; a very beautiful porphyry column has already been executed in this manner.

I do not think that the *Sagrada Familia* can ever be completed, certainly not until a new genius appears. For this we must await the era of Aquarius, a new cultural revolution; for this we must await a genius capable of superimposing on Gaudí's art a new architectonic concept and style that we cannot foresee today. Such was the case with cathedrals that were begun as Romanesque, continued as Gothic, and completed as Baroque.

It would be treason against Gaudí's art to want or pretend to be able to finish the *Sagrada Familia* by bureaucratic methods lacking the touch of genius. It is far better for the building to remain like a gigantic decayed tooth, full of possibilities.

5. Those who have not smelled the odor of sanctity

are traitors, because they have intentionally ignored the angelic essence of Gaudí's genius. The greatest treason of all is therefore that committed by those who lack this sense of smell, those who never realized that in order to enjoy Gaudí's works, it is even more necessary to be able to breathe in its sacred perfume than to see, touch, hear, and taste.

In a similar way, perhaps—or rather, undoubtedly—in the aesthetic history of France, Ernest Meissonier and Édouard Detaille will eventually assume their places among the greatest French painters, while Paul Cézanne will be recognized as one of the most clumsy and most pernicious; and Auguste Rodin, without doubt, will be considered the most depressing impressionist in the entire history of sculpture.

On the other hand, the French sculptor Charles Richefeu (1868-1945), almost unknown today, will ineluctably compel recognition in the history of aesthetics as one of the greatest and most progressive, alongside Antonio Gaudí and Umberto Boccioni. "Long Live the Emperor," Richefeu's masterpiece, which stands within a sublime sanctuary, the Hall of Flags of the Invalides Museum, will someday be regarded as the archetype of erect vitality, and it will be compared to the most depressing of all its counterparts, Rodin's "Thinker," which is to be found just about anywhere and almost everywhere.

Those of Richefeu's sculptures which are as spiny as a pile of gesticulating crayfish, such as his "Charge of the Dragoons at Wagram," are biologically related to the *Sagrada Familia*, whose glory they share. Gaudí, ultrarealistic in his casts, lacked a Richefeu who was a master of "handmade instantaneous casts," just as Meissonier in his paintings was master of "handmade color photography."

Whether or not it uses casts, there is a whole body of art called "pop" in modern terminology, the genealogy of which is completely legitimate:

— Lysistratus, inventor of casting from nature, fourth century B.C.
— The sculpted carriages in Italian cemeteries at Palermo and Genoa, nineteenth century.
— Gaudí and the realistic sculpture of the SAGRADA FAMILIA.
— Boccioni and his "DEVELOPMENT OF A BOTTLE IN SPACE," 1912.
— Marcel Duchamp, with his "BOTTLE RACK," the first "ready-made," 1914.
— Richefeu, "LONG LIVE THE EMPEROR," 1917.
— Dali, "VENUS DE MILO WITH DRAWERS," 1936.
— Segal and pop art, today.

In the spring of 1967, on Tuesday, April 4, the great *couturier* Paco Rabane told me that the first intelligent photographs of the work of Gaudí—our Gaudí—had just been made by one of his friends. For the first time someone had made photographs of the "superacademic" aspect of his art: his casts made from nature, all the way from little dead infants as angels to the Catalonian *rovellon* mushroom, gastronomically the most positive soft-factor of Catalan mysticism. That same afternoon I received Paco Rabane's friend Clovis Prévost as a visitor; his photographs, as critiques of Le Corbusier, surpassed everything that would have most disgusted the Protestant Corbu, who, at the time of our memorable encounter in 1929 at the home of Roussy de Sales, declared that Gaudí was the manifest disgrace of the city of Barcelona. During the course of this meeting Corbu asked me if I had any thoughts about the future of his art, and I replied: architecture will be "soft and hairy," and I categorically affirmed that the last great architectural genius was called Gaudí, whose name in Catalan means "enjoy," just as Dali means "desire." I explained to him that enjoyment and desire are attributes of Mediterranean Catholicism and Gothic art, which were reinvented and brought to a state of paroxysm by Gaudí.

Toward the end of his life Le Corbusier changed his mind and finally considered Gaudí a genius; yet he did not understand the sublime, Catholic, Apostolic, Roman essence of his work, which the brilliant Catalan philosopher Francesc Pujols (1882-1962) was the first to explain in his masterly essay, "Gaudí's Artistic and Religious Vision." I proposed that my friend Descharnes write a book, that our faithful publisher Guichard produce it, and that it be a book in which this essay by Francesc Pujols (translated for the first time by me from the original Catalan) would be presented with the photographs by Clovis Prévost.

And so to conclude these "aclaratory" (from the Catalan *aclarar*, to enlighten) notes on the conception of this book, I should like to say that Pujols is the archetype of the Catalan, embodied today by myself, thanks to Gala.

SALVADOR DALI
HOTEL ST. REGIS, NEW YORK, FEBRUARY 1968
PORT LLIGAT, JUNE 1968

INTRODUCTION

From time to time in the last fifteen years Gaudí has been the subject of various treatises. The architect and his work, however, still remain unfamiliar to the public at large, and art historians have not yet fully studied his vision. Only a few concerned architects have attempted professional analyses of what they have taken to be Gaudí's message; they have brought to light all they thought necessary to find, while preferring to ignore the anecdotal academic so-called *pompiérisme* of his ornamental sculpture, which disturbed them. Enthusiasts of surrealistic emotionalism, the type who are naïve-exotic or modern-at-all-costs, did not show any interest in it either. At the time, they paid more attention to collages based on engravings from picturesque almanacs of the 1880s or preferred to admire in Gaudí's work the symbolism of his proto-abstract forms.

Today, in the midst of a flood of aesthetic experiments, as we complete the cycle from lyrical, informal abstraction, to pop and op art and the realism of the moment, it becomes at last necessary to speak about the figurative statuary of Gaudí.

This figurative statuary is, as Dali says about religious realism, "provocative to the point of uneasiness, fortunately displeasing, and in this sense immeasurably useful."

People have maintained that Gaudí's architecture resembles a meal at which the numerous courses are served on one plate simultaneously. Only robust stomachs can digest such a banquet! As Francesc Pujols has emphasized, it is necessary to recognize that Gaudí's sculpture has always been "disturbing" and has always provoked violent negative reactions among his admirers as well as his detractors. As architect Damian Carlos Bayón has written: " . . . on the other hand, he failed in the figurative sculpture of the *Sagrada Familia* to equal what he could do with inexpressive casts taken from life." And Michel Ragon: "If you take Bouguereau, Bonnat, and Boldini, melt them all together and cast the result in stucco, you will have some idea of the characters who crowd the façade of this cathedral . . . a world where ultimately only man has miscarried!"

It is of use these days to reaffirm that criteria of aesthetic judgment are relative and that we are all restrained by a culture that is out of date. What is meant by "good taste"? Isn't it more often than not sterile? In the name of what authority is it permissible to judge and condemn? Rather, we should question ourselves and search for the why and the how of a phenomenon: it exists in spite of us and cannot be ignored. We should recall Lautréamont's warning in the *Chants de Maldoror*: "Reader, pay attention to the contents of [this verse], and beware the distressing impression it cannot fail to leave, like a stigma, in your troubled imaginations."

Since everything is contained in the highly personal architecture of Gaudí, a systematic inventory and study of it would provide a remarkable course in architecture. And it is in his architecture that one must seek the message of this poet of space, light, and the curved line—the line of God. Gaudí is a great architect in the lineage:

— of the Greek gods sometimes heralded as builders: Apollo, according to verbal tradition, built on his native island the famous "Altar of Horns," with the horns of the wild goats killed by his sister Artemis;

— of the Cyclops, who supposedly invented towers;

— of Ictinus and of Callicrates, who designed the Parthenon;

- of Gothic architects such as Villard de Honnecourt;
- of Michelangelo, who, as an architect—though he called himself a sculptor—was one of the first to change the course of Western art by his belief in the organic character of architecture; Michelangelo, who introduced forms seemingly inspired by the anatomy of crustaceans into his fantastic, exciting plans for the fortifications of Florence;
- of Claude-Nicolas Ledoux, who carried to an extreme his ideas on *architecture parlante*, in which every form is intended to be symbolic of its function.

Like all geniuses, Gaudí is unclassifiable. Architecture for him was both true expression and a way of life; his inspiration derived from his solitude. He was one of the earliest who forcefully affirmed architecture as the pre-eminent art, maintaining that the organization of space controls the quality of other means of expression. He was the first who was able to impose an "author's imperialism" on the slightest detail and regulate the relation between object and environment. He became a painter, a musician, a sculptor, a cabinetmaker, an ironworker, and an urbanist. . . . He conceived architecture as a synthesis of all the arts and the architect as the "visionary seer" who alone can achieve a "total work of art." For Gaudí the treatment of architectural masses had to be plastic and inseparable from the concept of ornament, just as form is the symbol of function. In this sense Gaudí cannot be considered a functionalist, like most contemporary architects, who design "machines to live in." For Gaudí everything must give way to the inventive spirit, and only a poetic universe is habitable, because it alone gives free rein to everyone's imagination. Gaudí has opened the door to the fascinating dream described by Dali in *The Visible Woman:* "No collective effort has managed to create a dream world as pure and as troubling as those Art Nouveau buildings which, on the fringe of architecture, alone constitute true realizations of solidified desires, in which the most violent and cruel automatisms painfully betray a hatred of reality and the need to find refuge in an ideal world, the way a childhood neurosis is produced.

"Here is something we can still love: the imposing block of those delirious and cold buildings spread all over Europe, despised and neglected by all the anthologies and studies. This is what it takes to oppose our beastly contemporary aestheticians who defend execrable 'modern art'; indeed, this is what it takes to oppose the entire history of art."

Gaudí is generally associated with Art Nouveau, but this idea is more complex than it seems, for Gaudí does not properly belong to the style. In fact, he is often closer to the Mudejar style (Christian art influenced by Mussulman art in reconquered Spain of the twelfth to fourteenth centuries); a part of his work continues those historic tendencies that are characteristic of Spanish architecture. Gaudí began to build long before the advent of Art Nouveau, and he survived its decline in the rest of Europe. While Gaudí's work paralleled certain themes common to Art Nouveau, he did not make ornament into a principle by which objects are to be dressed up, as it were, to please the eye. He never allowed ornament to determine form. For him, construction should be treated in a naturalistic way—that is, conceived in such a way that it will be the expression of the forces that work within it. Doing just that, he adapted traditional materials (stone, brick, ceramics) to the exigencies of a personal style. His constructive elements are assimilated into his decorative system and become part of an organic whole. He thought that to organize space was not only to build structures but to cover them over as well, to vitalize them, and above all, to make them lose their materiality, to give them spirit with an all-embracing living ornamentation. Gaudí had an immense enthusiasm for natural forms; for him there was no transcendency other than that contained in substance itself—in this case, his native earth, the nourishing Catalan soil.

Gaudí devoted himself so fervently to his experiments and research with models that were concerned with the application of graphic statics that, going beyond the improvement of the Gothic system of construction that he was seeking, he brought new architectural forms into being.

He was the first to contribute a new solution to the problem of high naves and large halls by using the continuous parabolic vault, supported by inclined piers. All the great engineers of the nineteenth century designed structures articulated by small bays; but the French engineer Eugène Freycinet, in his hangars at Orly of 1916, used a continuous parabolic arch of reinforced concrete.

Gaudí was the first to break away from the right angle in order to give life and movement to his walls. He anticipated by several years what was to be called the free plan, by which rooms are freely and flexibly articulated one to another. The right angles, cubes, parallelepipeds, and cylinders that predominate in modern architecture are intellectual abstractions. Gaudí has shown that there is another conception of construction, that uses the observation of the structural principles of nature to stimulate creative forms as well as ornament.

In 1955 the architect José Luis Sert wrote: "Certain modern artists and engineers are making more and more specific use of light structures which resemble, in form, shells and other elements of nature. These forms, some of which are warped, are obviously going to play an increasingly important role in the future. We cannot continue to construct our cities limiting ourselves to edifices exactly like boxes, exclusively inspired by the system of the slab and the pillar. In the continuous evolution of modern architecture, it is more than likely that Gaudí's last experiments will acquire increasing value and will be more fully appreciated. Then his importance as a pioneer and a prophet will be acknowledged."

In a period when construction was most often standardized, the experimental nature of Gaudí's work is to be emphasized. He made each experiment only once and never tried it again for any later building. Each new work was a fresh experience. He was always prompted by an open mind, always characterized by a diversity of expression.

Others claim that the careful improvement of masonry constructional systems of historic styles is the greatest flaw in the work of Gaudí. "He lost interest in the new possibilities of iron, for example, and is merely the last great builder in stone," wrote the architect Bohigas, for whom such masterpieces as the *Palacio Güell, Casa Milá, Casa Batlló, Park Güell,* the *crypt of the Colonia Güell,* and the *school of the Sagrada Familia* were only manifestations of a cult of expressionism, of the drama of forms, of color and sculpture, and showed a general indifference to structure.

In response to this criticism it must be said Gaudí never resorted to technical solutions in the interests of a moral point, as did most of the architects of his time, who, moreover, to emphasize the virtuosity of their façades, covered them with pseudo-lyrical and systematic academic motifs. These architects forgot that Gaudí remained open-minded with regard to all materials, on condition that they corresponded to his vision, since for him form had to be entirely subject to expression. Therefore it is not surprising that most of the architects who have definitively opted for long, straight lines and obsessively repetitious parallels have avoided Gaudí's work and have often been his detractors. In this respect, Gaudí is the architect's bad conscience.

In his own day he was profoundly aware of the pressure of materialism and its consequences in the course of industrialization, which led to the destruction of every form of personal expression. In this sense Gaudí sought to save the traditional and vital values of craftsmanship. Gaudí's buildings are prodigious, passionate creations that can be understood only through a knowledge of his mysticism. The *Sagrada Familia* is a lyrical, supersensible monument that derives from the sensual. Gaudí, to a certain extent, was a fanatical mystic who thought that on earth he could take part in the beyond. His vision was militant.

Gaudí worked for just a few private clients. His most notable creations were: *Casa Vicens* (1883-1885), *Casa Calvet* (1898-1904), *Casa Batlló* (1905-1907), *Casa Milá* (1905-1910), and the religious buildings: the *Expiatory Church of the Sagrada Familia,* the *Episcopal Palace in Astorga,* and the *Convent of Santa Teresa de Jesus.*

It was, however, the patronage of a Maecenas that gave him the opportunity for most of his work. Count Eusebio Güell, a wealthy industrialist, owner of several important cotton mills, was his friend and admirer. In the 1880s he commissioned a considerable variety of works at the *Finca Güell,* his unfinished country estate, and then his residence in Barcelona, the *Palacio Güell* (1885-1889), and finally the *Park Güell* (1900-1914), which was conceived as an urban residential development, as well as the church of the *Colonia Güell* (1898-1914), which was a village that was meant as a residence for the workers in his mills. Eusebio Güell was a patron of artists—in particular, of painters. Gaudí compared Güell to the great Renaissance Maecenas, such as the Medicis of Florence and the Dorias of Genoa.

R.D.

Antonio Gaudí y Cornet, circa 1914. (Reus 1852-Barcelona 1926.)

The Formation of Antonio Gaudí as Architect

". . . the way an angel cooks a cathedral . . ."
(Salvador Dali)

In the warm bustle of a late spring evening we can imagine an elderly man moving away from a crowd on the Ramblas. He walks along, all alone, a slight, dark, round-shouldered silhouette. This evening, as every evening, he goes "to say a few words to Mary" in the oratory of San Felipe Neri, in the old quarter of Barcelona. But on this Monday, June 7, 1926, he is more absorbed than usual, lost in an inner reverie: the St. Barnabas tower of his "Cathedral of the Poor" is at last completed, and it is to be inaugurated on June 11, the Saint's day. Already, too, the first spire of his *Expiatory Church of the Holy Family* is aglow in the Catalan sky. He hesitates when he arrives at the Calle de las Cortes Cataluñas and stands still momentarily before crossing the street. As he steps off the sidewalk, he falls under the wheels of a streetcar that he had not noticed.

Found unconscious and placed on the pavement, the old man was taken for a vagabond: barefoot in his shoes, his face emaciated, his clothing wretched, all that was found in the worn-out jacket, held together with safety pins and bits of string, were a few hazelnuts, a gospel book, and a folded piece of paper. How was it possible to recognize the architect of a great church in this beggar with the body of an ascetic, dry as vine bark, whose finely lined face was illuminated only by his fresh blue eyes? Moved to the Gothic hospital of Santa Cruz, the architect Antonio Gaudí y Cornet was not to be identified until late that evening by his assistant, Domingo Sugrañes, and the chaplain of the church. He was to die three days later, on Thursday, June 10, at five o'clock in the evening. His was the glorious death of the poor man who had renounced elegance for spiritual purity and elevation.

In passing, we must note the curious connection between streetcars and the fate of this architect. Indeed, the first streetcar was put into actual service in the year of his birth, and a little after 1900, while he was in Majorca working on the restoration of the Cathedral of Palma, he replied to the priests who compared the tribune of his choir to a streetcar (see page 244) that a streetcar can be a very beautiful thing. However, he was never willing to give the right of way to one and often said, "It is streetcars that should stop, not pedestrians!"

Gaudí was an individual who advocated exciting, creative disorder; his death, a triumph of this disorder, was the supreme consecration of an obstinate, militant, and intransigent life—a veritable concentration of energy and passion. His death even accorded him the grace of causing confusion in all quarters. For him they changed the procedure of burial, the laws of interment, and even the sacred rhythm, creating complications from one end of the city to the other and throughout the ceremonies. By authorization of the government in Madrid and special dispensation from the Pope, Gaudí's body was interred on Saturday, June 12, in the crypt of the *Sagrada Familia*, the church on which he had worked for forty years and to which he had devoted exclusively the final twelve years of his life.

At the beginning of the seventeenth century a merchant from Auvergne, called Gaudí, settled in southern Catalonia, at Riudoms, near Tarragona. Seven generations later, in the neighboring village of Reus, on June 25, 1852, at half past nine o'clock in the morning, Antonio Placido Guillermo Gaudí y Cornet was born, the fifth and last child of a modest coppersmith.

The child grew up in the country, between the farmhouse and the forge. To him his father was the incarnation of the demiurge, with a genius for creating space, a visionary from whom he learned empiricism and perfect mastery. Gaudí said that he had a particular ability to see space because he was the son, the grandson, and the great-grandson of coppersmiths. His father was a coppersmith, as were also his grandfather and his great-grandfather. His mother's family were coppersmiths; her grandfather was a cooper, which is the same thing. A maternal grandfather was a sailor, and sailors are also people with a sense of space and situation. Gaudí said, "If I could not have been an architect, I would have been interested in shipbuilding." [1]* He had been prepared by generations of coppersmiths, who, as Gaudí pointed out, "must fashion a volume from a plate. Before starting out, the coppersmith has to have seen the whole space. All the great artists of the Florentine Renaissance were chisellers who created volumes from planes. . . . The coppersmith embraces all three dimensions and thus unconsciously has a command of space that not every man possesses." [1] How could Gaudí have not felt within himself this growing thirst for space, this urge to master it, sharpened by the atavism of three centuries?

* Figures in brackets refer to Notes on Sources (page 249).

For the rest of his life Gaudí was convinced that he had within him a hereditary sense of volume.

Gaudí spent his adolescence in Reus, the town where he was born. It was a small but active commercial city in the Campo de Tarragona, a land of wheat and wine, an ideal Mediterranean countryside, quite the opposite of northern Catalonia and its looming, mysterious mountains. Gaudí spoke of Reus as a privileged place where the influences of the sea and the mountains are balanced and enable the light to reveal the continuous truth and harmony of things, of beings, of the sun and the sky, of space. It was there that he found his mystical fervor and inspiration with regard to nature. How could he have avoided the impact of the sky and the waves of the nearby Mediterranean, which was itself so alive with eternal movement and eternal murmuring?

At school in Reus he was an undistinguished student, although he excelled in geometry, and he enjoyed his teachers only when their lectures were given in concrete terms, since he was unable to understand abstractions. He had a very personal sense of mathematics and went so far as to work out his own system of empirical geometry.

Instead of going to class, he preferred to sit by the shore and contemplate the sea, which fascinated him. The depth and movement of the water revealed to him, as in the depths of a mirror, a fluid space, rhythmic and architectonic, a dynamic both vivid and formal. The sea represented for him the only element that synthesizes the three dimensions of space, and, according to Pujols, he liked to watch it while standing up, so that he could see the sky twice, in the air and in the water. That sea, a geometrical entity, was, as he said, his real university, and the jetty his favorite classroom, for there he could breathe in the winds and look at the waves that came from the north, the east, and the south. In an interview with the journalist Vicente Salaverri in 1914 he said "It is unfortunate that Madrid is the capital of Spain. Philip II would have done better to set up his court in Seville or Valencia. (Note that I don't insist on Barcelona!) All great feats are accomplished by the sea. The sea has been and must be involved in the most stupendous enterprises of humanity." [10]

For those born in Catalonia, the Mediterranean light, "the true light," sharpens and purifies everything, makes all things incandescent, surrounds them with a halo, and invests them with a scintillating splendor through its reflection from the earth. As Gaudí has explained, "Mediterranean" means middle of the land. Sunlight of medium intensity strikes the shore at a 45-degree angle, an ideal light for defining things and revealing their forms. The Mediterranean is the place where all great artistic cultures have flourished, due to this equilibrium of light. Gaudí believed that one could see things clearly only in the lands of the Mediterranean, whereas in the north the light is hazy and objects appear to be deformed, becoming phantoms of themselves. For Gaudí, the art of the south would always be superior to that of the north because southern light clarifies nature. Northerners have an abstract spirit which inhibits their visual sense; they do not feel beauty, because they base their philosophic systems on the principle: "I doubt, therefore I am," while it would be more meaningful to say: "I doubt, therefore I know nothing," for doubt signifies the absence of reason, truth, and light. The sea and light of the Mediterranean, with its breezes and its mingled reflections, produces an admirable perceptual quality. For this reason Gaudí concluded that "reality has never fooled the Catalans: on the contrary, it has been their teacher." [3] Gaudí thought that the Mediterranean people alone were truly imaginative, the only people who had succeeded in giving form to all their desires, in crystallizing all their sensations. Every creation, for Gaudí, had to be a prophecy, a vision of the whole; the eye with its violent veracity is the master of thought. Above all, sight must be the sense of light, space, and beauty; it reveals the infinite—that which is and that which is not; the eye has power over everything. One knows and can dominate only what one can see. In order to have some knowledge of reality, there is no need to know; it is quite enough to question it incessantly and to believe our eyes. As Dali said: "I know what I eat, I don't know what I do," so Gaudí for his part was not sure what he thought, but knew what he saw. Thus we understand that Gaudí's visual empiricism was one of the fundamental aspects of his approach to art, and that he sought and found his one and only inspiration in nature.

The atmosphere in which young Gaudí completed his studies was peaceful in appearance only. He was sixteen the year when General Prim participated at Reus in the September launching of the "Revolution of 1868." Prim was already famous for his exploits during the Moroccan war of 1856. The painter Mariano Fortuny, like Prim a native of Reus, brought back from that brilliant campaign a series of drawings that helped to re-establish Moslem-derived art as the taste of the day.

Young Gaudí's fervent temperament was fired by the notion of General Prim as "the master of Mediterranean light." In the ebullient ambiance of cultural renaissance, anarchism, and Catalan anticlericalism, Gaudí went along with the liberal and libertarian euphoria. A number of critics did not fail to say later that "the monstrous work of Gaudí is but the product of this peremptory and chaotic anarchy that has always characterized that land!"

The following year Gaudí left for Barcelona, where he planned to attend the School of Architecture. At this time the new industrial aristocracy of the Catalan metropolis had ideas of transforming the city into a new Florence. The period was one of eclecticism, and it seemed the right time for the "decadent" styles to be supplanted by a new architecture.

At the School of Architecture the curriculum was based on imitating the styles of the past. Gaudí rejected this dreary approach and spent his time listening to the aesthetician Manuel Milá y Fontanals exalt the brilliant medieval history of Catalonia and defend "the excellence of Gothic architecture" against Neoclassicism.

Gaudí explored the countryside, with its landmarks and cathedrals. He could be found at lectures on history, economy, and philosophy. He had a universal curiosity. He frequented the Café Pelayo along with the anarchist poets and artists, and he participated in their blasphematory exhibitions. He read extensively and was passionately interested in the philosophies of Nietzsche and Goethe, as well as in the writings of Ruskin, whose influence was gradually reaching Catalonia, and in the workers' movement that was spreading throughout Europe. He quickly became aware that architecture must be related to social problems and reflect their trends.

As a young student he saw Gothic architecture as the ideal model to follow—for him, an architecture orchestrated and directed like a symphony, with every artisan guided by the master builder alone. And in the Middle Ages, Gaudí saw the architect as the lord of art, a combination of geometrician, sociologist, urbanist, liturgist, painter, sculptor, and designer of ornament. He was inspired by his reading of Viollet-le-Duc's *Entretiens sur l'architecture* and *Dictionnaire raisonné*, from which he remembered that "the organic architecture of the Middle Ages develops and progresses like natural forms and is based on a very simple principle which it modifies, perfects, and complicates, but without ever destroying its primary essence."

When Gaudí visited the South of France, he went to Toulouse to see the restoration of the medieval church of Saint-Sernin, recently carried out by Viollet-le-Duc. He was disappointed in the faded quality of the stone and the grayness of the stained-glass windows and found fault with the excessive linear accentuation in the caricature-like carvings. In conclusion he said: "Let's leave it—it has nothing to teach us." He affirmed that it was necessary to study the Middle Ages for their quality of common sense, that one should continue the Gothic by eliminating the flamboyant . . ." [1]

In the same way, Gaudí felt unlimited admiration for the Greeks, whose tradition he sought to keep alive, just as he considered himself the savior of the Gothic. For him Greek art let the stone, with its sensual energy and exemplary geometry, speak for itself. Gothic art, on the other hand, dematerializes stone in order to make it spiritual. The classical Greek organism and the theological system of expressionistic Gothic counter and complement one another like the body and its skeleton.

Later in his life Gaudí was to say of the *Sagrada Familia* that it was a "Hellenistic temple of Mediterranean Gothic" and that it represented the emancipation of the people.

Whereas those around him were occupied with imitations of Hellenistic, medieval, Mudejar, Celtic, and baroque styles for their external decoration and exotic ornament, Gaudí was analyzing the structural bases of these styles, the construction of their buildings, and the organization of their space—not in order to imitate them but to absorb all their characteristics in the interest of new possibilities. The period favored not only what he planned but what he managed to do, and valued the picturesque or romantic aspects of the past, which were being systematically explored: Greek monuments were being excavated and Viollet-le-Duc was restoring the Middle Ages.

At a time when the exuberant Catalans thought they could dominate the world, Gaudí alone had a genuine vision of architecture, and it was to prove itself an antithesis to the coming obsessive functionalism.

Eventually Gaudí received his diploma and was able to build. His yearning to create was shared with his entire generation of young architects, among whom he long remained the least recognized. His youthful diary is testimony that by 1878 he was mature and of strong, challenging opinions. He had precise ideas about everything, about ornament in particular, and these ideas remained constant for the rest of his life. At this stage in his development the seeds that would flourish in his work were already obvious.

The Catalan epic, composed of ancient myths, local legends, and Christian marvels, is contained in its entirety in the two masterpieces of the region's "Renaixensa": the *Sagrada Familia*, erected by her greatest epic architect Antonio Gaudí, and the *Atlantide*, a lengthy narrative by one of her greatest poets, Jacinto Verdaguer, whose second canto includes the following:

Allá d'allá, per entre falgueres gegantines,
De sos menhirs y torres blanqueja l'ample front,
De marbres sobre marbres pirámides alpines
Que volent ab llurs testes omplir lo cel pregon.

In the distance, between gigantic ferns,
Stands white the wide face of its menhirs and towers,
Alpine pyramids of marble upon marble,
Whose summits appear to pierce the sky.

CHAPTER II

Barcelona and the Catalan Renaixensa

Gaudí was thirty-one when he undertook the construction of his first major secular building: the *Casa Vicens*. He had already met Count Eusebio Güell, who was to become his patron. His career was to develop rapidly from this point. Nothing was impossible, because his native soil, which would eventually bear the profound stamp of his creative genius, was in a state of absolute readiness. As Francesc Pujols has written, "There exists between the city of Barcelona and Gaudí the unique phenomenon of a perfect convergence in time, the perfect harmony of a matrix awakened by the spirit that is destined to make it dynamic and immortal—the symbol of every Renaissance."

The arrival of Gaudí, whose boundless energy and fanaticism, as we have seen, derived from Catalonia itself, crowned a period not only of fermentation but of extraordinary effervescence. The only part of the peninsula to have followed the industrial and cultural revolution at the same pace as Europe, Catalonia, as of 1860, entered into an area of intense renewal, which was to reach its culminating point between 1875 and 1895: the rise of industry and commerce; foreign travel to Cuba, Mexico, the Antilles, and the Philippines; an increase in economic exchange with Germany, France, and England; the penetration of ideas and the dispersal of news. Moreover, money abounded and circulated in plenty.

Passionate, mobile, and eagerly receptive to all influences from abroad, Barcelona, after many centuries of repression of her language and traditions, had become intent upon her cultural awakening. This Catalan "Renaixensa" was motivated both by economic and spiritual developments and was destined to restore the entire country, accomplishing in fifty years what had taken other European nations over five centuries. The language was brought up to date, with grammar and spelling regularized; a university was created, with various faculties; and a personal, autochthonous artistic expression was ultimately achieved. Choirs, choral groups, and tourist societies multiplied, shedding new light on music, architecture, painting, and literature. In Catalonia what would have been impossible in any other province came brilliantly to life. As Salvador Dali is fond of repeating: "The Catalans do not deform reality, they transform it."

Barcelona was reborn through her rediscovered tradition and was able to absorb serenely an unlikely mixture of many new currents. At this moment of immediate transformation, all the arts underwent a fecund growth almost simultaneously: this was the unusual phenomenon of the time and constituted Catalan *Modernismo*, which is the artistic expression of the total Catalan revaluation. The diffusion and uncommon popularity of the movement can be explained through its origins in the social and political realities of the country.

Architects like Luis Doménech y Montaner and José Puig y Cadafalch were among the most effective promoters of this renaissance movement. As professors, politicians, museum directors, and masters of modern architecture, they played leading roles for more than half a century. They were elected deputies to the Cortes, presidents, in turn, of the Catalan Union and of the Political League of

The sumptuous *modernista* interior of the residence of Baron de Quadras, designed by Puig y Cadafalch; the floral decoration was meant to be "Arabo-Gothic-Ionian" in style. This photograph appeared in the *Ilustració Catalana* in 1907, with a commentary that is characteristic of the period: "The gentle Maria de Quadras, a live, palpitating flower, is surrounded by many other live and stone flowers, near her gracious mother, the Baroness, illuminating with their fresh smiles all the magnificence of this place where Catalan art vibrates in all its manifestations."

Catalonia and all the while taking on numerous other offices; they thus became intimately involved in the most intensive social and cultural movements of the time. Shortly, and with the help of the older architect Juan Martorell, they made Barcelona one of the capitals of the renaissance that is now known as Art Nouveau. According to a chronicler of the day, the city was a wilderness full of expansive fury. The immense need for new art was felt everywhere. While industry expanded and cotton mills and factories multiplied, sumptuous homes were built. There was a frenetic appetite for "consumption" unknown to any other city of the era. The people bought, renovated, innovated. They rediscovered traditional craftsmanship and they exalted ornament: mosaic, wrought iron, floral and animal decoration. Columns were draped and peopled with crustaceans. The Café Torino, a masterpiece of Art Nouveau, was built on the Paseo de Gracia. In 1908 the Palace of Catalan Music opened its doors. The work of Doménech y Montaner, it was intended particularly for concerts of the celebrated "Orfeó Català," considered "the most important European choral group." And there, the great musicians of the time performed Wagner and Beethoven. The windows and two wide curtains of crystal on either side of the hall rose from floor to ceiling. The rose-colored panes were decorated with heavy garlands of tinted glass. Also celebrated was the restaurant at the International Exposition of 1888, which was noted for its succession of volumes, its leaded windows, and the "medieval irregularity" in its use of towers. The painter Santiago Rusiñol

The Café Torino is a fine example of the *modernista* art of Barcelona. It was designed by Ricardo Campmany, who incorporated into its construction various elements by the architects Falqués, Puig y Cadafalch, and Gaudí. Located at the junction of the Paseo de Gracia and the Calle de las Cortes, the establishment was built especially as a bar to serve Torino Vermouth along with the customary beer, coffee, and the like.

is renowned in Europe for his "Gardens of the Alhambra." Poets and writers joined in the general euphoria, carrying the legendary Catalan spirit of excess to the verge of paroxysm. At the highest point of this artistic and intellectual ferment, comparable to the golden age of Catalonia in the thirteenth century, Gaudí could exclaim: "We are Catalans. We don't have to be Greeks, Gothics, or Egyptians. We must be *everything* at once!"

In this melting pot, in this climate of absolute artistic freedom, at a time when architecture was about to collapse into a terrifying functionalism, the towers of the *Sagrada Familia* were raised. One may wonder if it would have been possible for Gaudí, in another time or another city, to have so rapidly imposed his ideas.

On a visit to Barcelona the French Minister Gabriel Hanotaux said of this structure: "This immense church, not yet complete, half-alive in its overflowing art, is a perfect response to the strength, vigor, pressure, and personality of this strange city, and it was erected in a single day like a crown of Modernism on the brow of ancient Spain."

For Barcelona was not merely a source of inspiration; it was a springboard for those who sought further heights. Moreover, Barcelona offered, during those years of exaltation, the most extravagant possibilities that had ever been put at the artist's disposition. Gaudí could directly impose his conceptions, follow his own impulses, and, sometimes in spite of the traditional rules of urbanism,

The Palace of Catalan Music, by Doménech y Montaner, inaugurated in 1908. Created for the celebrated "Orfeó Català," a chorus with twenty-eight members, the Palace was an important musical center at the beginning of the century. The greatest performers came there to play Beethoven and especially Wagner. Frequented faithfully by Barcelona society, it was one of the most striking symbols of the Catalan Renaixensa.

DOMÉNECH Y MONTANER, one of the most important figures in the political and cultural life of Catalonia at the beginning of the century. Director of the School of Architecture of Barcelona, elected Deputy to the Cortes in 1901, he was also President of the Catalan Union and the League of Catalonia.

Luis Doménech y Montaner designed the large new hospital of S. Pablo, successor to the old Hospital of Santa Cruz, where Gaudí died. In this photograph the architect stands in front of the main entrance of the former.

A project by Doménech y Montaner for a "gran bazar y habitaciones" ("a large store with apartments"). The Mudejar-inspired decoration is inserted into a structure of exposed iron.

"translate," as Marcel Jean has said, "his dreams into architectural structures that have peopled the Catalan capital with fantastic creations." The city observed, admired, and . . . allowed everything. Even the ecclesiastical authorities, faced with the great church rising in front of their eyes, did not dare to interfere. Had he not concentrated all his efforts on the *Sagrada Familia*, Gaudí would certainly have rebuilt Barcelona completely, redesigned the squares and the fountains, and made mosaic pavements. And had the streets been curved and the houses designed in the image of the *Casa Milá* or the *Casa Batlló*, Catalonia as a whole would have followed and approved.

Thus the city forcefully experienced this vast modernistic movement at the beginning of the century, which alone sums up the astonishing courage of the Catalan mind. *Modernismo* was even more than a powerful urge for renaissance, coupled with an absolute desire for immediate, concrete accomplishments, in a synthesis of all the currents and all the styles of the era, mixed together, condensed, and transformed into a passionate regionalism. A positive aggressiveness underlay and reinforced its flights of fancy. An ardent desire was suddenly awakened for hegemony and universality, which had been dormant for more than three centuries. The Catalan art historian Alexandre Cirici Pellicer has written of a "vitality that lends the look of almost ferocious realism to art and literature," and which, contrary to what we may have thought, owes little to the variety of parallel movements out of which it has derived, but everything to its strong local roots. *Modernismo* symbolized an awakening and can be considered a reflection of the profound forgotten impulses that in other times gave birth to a Catalan genius like the thirteenth-century philosopher Ramón Lull. This awakening justified the attempts at the impossible and all the risks that were taken.

The *Casa Amatller*, at No. 41 Paseo de Gracia, stands next to Gaudí's *Casa Batlló*. Puig y Cadafalch combined modern techniques with the traditional Catalan ceramic and wrought-iron craftsmanship.

PUIG Y CADAFALCH, like Doménech y Montaner, was one of the masters of *modernista* architecture. A professor, a politician, and an architect, he founded museums and constructed buildings in Barcelona and throughout Catalonia. He also was elected to the Cortes and was made President of the Mancomunidad of Catalonia.

An example of naturalistic ornament. A lobster clings to the door-frame inside the *Casa Amatller*.

"*. . . these passionate men who created the Catalan* modernista *atmosphere by willfully converting Barcelona into a twentieth century Athens . . .*"

In the work of Puig y Cadafalch the influence of the Gothic and of the Middle Ages is manifest in details (such as here, in the foreground, on the house of Baron de Quadras) as well as in architecture as a whole (such as in the *Casa de les Punxes*, or "House of Points," seen in the background). His ornamental sculpture uses traditional medieval and Tudor motifs: gargoyles, niches, and window frames. This architect often gives large country homes the silhouettes of feudal castles with their keeps and bastions.

The parabolic architectural structures and geological naturalism of forms that were to flourish in the *Sagrada Familia* appear in this ▷ watercolor drawn by Gaudí for the projected church of the *Colonia Guell*. The polychromy consists of landscape colors: sand tones at the base, silvery gray farther up to correspond with the surrounding pine trees, and finally blue-green at the top uniting the building with the horizon and melting into the sky.

Following double page: The crypt chapel of *Santa Coloma de Cervelo, Colonia Güell*. In this interior view of the crypt, note the robust basalt and brick pillars and the dual system of arches that sustains the flat-brick ceiling. Photo: R. Roland

Parque Güell, entrance to portico and terrace. This giant lizard in ceramic tile (mosaic) graces the center of the stairway and serves as a water fountain.

Chapel of *Santa Coloma de Cervelo,* detail of stained and painted glass windows.

The outer wall and entrance to the chapel, with the pilasters of the chapel at left.

The Doorway of Charity. "The Annunciation."

Temple Expiatoria of the *Sagrada Familia*. The Portal of the Nativity, Doorway of Charity. "The Coronation of the Virgin."

CHAPTER III

Gaudí and the Sagrada Familia Church, 1883-1926

In this Barcelona of renovation Gaudí quickly reached prominence. At the age of twenty-one he had come to the city to study architecture, and he was never to leave. He settled there in 1873 and went away only on infrequent and short trips. His life merged with that of this city, to which he devoted all his energy, all his efforts, and all his faith.

Seldom has an architect conceived a set of works so concentrated in a single place. Had he become a painter or a musician, he would undoubtedly have moved outside the city boundaries. But being Catalan and an architect, Gaudí felt this work had to have its roots in native soil, and he began by organizing the space within the capital before even thinking of the outside world. An ancient Hindu legend describes how the god Shiva promised a reward to whichever of his two sons made a tour of the world. The first left at full speed on his peacock. The second son, who, taking small steps, merely walked around his parents, was declared the victor. The same wisdom permeates Catalonia. For a Catalan the land which gave birth to him is truly the center of the world. Recognizing the place of one's birth and glorifying it means not only touring the world but making it turn. Concentrating his creative spirit at this single center does not imply pure egocentricity. For the Catalan it is his duty and mission, in the same way as primitives guaranteed the equilibrium of the whole universe by giving prayers and offerings throughout the seasonal cycle of their sun. The wish to transform Barcelona into a capital of the arts, an Athens of the twentieth century, derived not from an urge to conquer but from a spirit of absolute conviction. It was a question of persuasion through the power of ideas alone. The objective was to convince the world of Barcelona's progress and the firm development of her history along the single axis of a vision that would not admit challenge. The writer Eugenio d'Ors wished above all that Catalonia would play a role in European thought, and he pursued that idea. Francesc Pujols himself declared he was not a Catalan separatist but rather the eager partisan of a Catalan hegemony that would soon be a reality. "Do you believe," asked Salvador Dali, "that since the earth is round, you will find landscapes everywhere? Does a round face have several noses? There are very few landscapes. They all converge here. Catalonia is the nose of the earth!"

There is no need to conquer any land other than one's own in order to prove this, no need for armed combat or other exploits: the strength of the mind is enough. This is why Catalan children are taught never to play at war and, above all, never to wield brooms as make-believe firearms. For, as they are told, "one day it happened that someone saw seven bullets shoot from a broom." In this tradition Gaudí could hope some day to see the first rays of a revitalized religion shine from his cathedral. Don José Giner de los Rios, an eminent figure in Madrid, the pontiff of the Spanish laity, came to visit Gaudí, thanked him for his welcome, and expressing his admiration, added with a subtle smile: "All this is admirable and absolutely new in architectural art . . . it is a shame this must be the last cathedral!" Returning his smile, Gaudí

The Doorway of Hope, the right side. "The Massacre of the Innocents."

The Principal Works of Antonio Gaudí

1883-1885 *Casa Vicens,* Calle de las Carolinas, Barcelona.
Highly characteristic of the influence of the Moorish Mudejar style that, in architecture, incorporates brick, polychrome tiles (*azulejos*), and ironwork.

1883-1885 *El Capricho,* the summer house of Maximo Diaz de Quijano at Comillas, in the province of Santander.

1883-1926 *Expiatory Church of the Holy Family* (the *Sagrada Familia*) in the Poblet district of Barcelona.
The architect's masterpiece.

1884-1887 *Finca Güell,* in Las Corts de Sarriá, a suburb of Barcelona.
Also of Mudejar inspiration, with brick construction and ornament. The front gate is in the form of a dragon, articulated and executed in ironwork.

1885-1889 *Palacio Güell,* Calle Conde de Asalto, Barcelona.
While the forms and structures are modern, the spirit is medieval; the exterior is severely, almost geometrically composed, the interior luxurious and magnificent.

1887-1893 *The Episcopal Palace in Astorga,* in the province of León.
The Gothic style of this building, begun by Gaudí, contrasts with the modest architectural ambiance of the town. The form is rectangular, with cylindrical towers—elegant vertical accents. This building is typical of Gaudí's "austere Gothic" period.

1889-1890 *Convento de Santa Teresa de Jesús,* Calle de Ganduxer, Barcelona.
Use of the parabolic arch and helical columns of brick. Elaborate ironwork.

1892-1894 *Casa de los Botines,* the house of the partners Fernández and Andrés, Plaza de San Marcelo, León.

1898-1904 *Casa Calvet,* Calle de Caspe, Barcelona.
The ornament shows signs of Gaudí's expressionistic naturalism; the architect also worked on the furniture and interior decoration. The baroque ironwork required extremely skillful metalworkers. Naturalistic elements, such as fruit and mushrooms, were incorporated.

1898-1914 *Church of the Colonia Güell,* at Santa Coloma de Cervelló, in the province of Barcelona.
One of the architect's great masterworks and his testament. A laboratory for his mechanical studies, and a structural experiment that he later utilized in the model for the *Sagrada Familia.* Here he created a new kind of hyperbolic paraboloid vaulting.

1900-1914 *Park Güell,* at the foot of Montaña Pelada, is now one of Barcelona's municipal parks. Representative of expressionistic naturalism and the influence of the Doric style. An attempt at landscape architecture, intended as a garden suburb conceived as part of an urban plan.

1904-1914 *The Cathedral at Palma,* Majorca.
Interior restorations.

1905-1907 *Casa Batlló,* Paseo de Gracia, Barcelona.
Called the "House of Bones" because of the building's skeleton effect on the exterior. The roof has almost a dragon-like scaly and undulating back. The most "coloristic" work of Gaudí. The interior ornamentation is remarkable.

1905-1910 *Casa Milá,* called *La Pedrera,* Paseo de Gracia, Barcelona.
The cyclopean aspect of this building suggested the popular name *pedrera* (rock quarry). The *Casa Milá* is, along with the *Sagrada Familia* and the *Church of the Colonia Güell,* Gaudí's most important work.

A pen drawing for the *Sagrada Familia,* made in 1915 by one of Gaudí's assistants, the architect Juan Rubió. In the middle is the Façade of the Nativity, which is complete today; at left, in profile, is the Façade of Glory. The central spire is to be 557 feet high.

said: "This is not the last of the cathedrals. It is the first of the second series," [6] by which he meant that the *Sagrada Familia* would shed light on the coming times with a light infinitely more powerful than that of the interrupted brightness of the first series of Gothic cathedrals. And Francesc Pujols exclaimed: "Catalonia, which has to bring the freedom of the earth and of men to all of Spain, has also the great mission of bringing the freedom of heaven to the whole world through universal science!" as he accumulated sheet upon sheet of writing, more preoccupied with the creation of the great work that would reveal the truth to mankind, than with the publication and diffusion of his manuscripts. Gaudí, for his part, accumulated stone upon stone, not doubting his ultimate goal for an instant, and maintaining that the more he saw people dying, the more he believed in immortality, and that the essential job was to build and not to have weak, unstable ideas. As Unamuno often said, "Realism is the coherence of mysticism, and one must put one's genius into the service of the most simple elements of the earth in order to transfigure them."

The Catalan is a mystic and knows that to sow his seeds in the minds of men, it is not necessary to spread his ideas through the outside world like a missionary. He must, above all, give sufficient weight to the earth that supports him. He must put his special genius into the service of the most humble elements in order to transfigure them. Thus for his gargoyles Gaudí chose not the fantastic creatures from Gothic architecture but rather simple garden snails, molded and swollen from periods of rain.

"I defy God to prove that He exists outside man's energy to draw Him out of chaos," wrote Élie Faure in his essay on the great builders. Dali has said, "This energy that Catalonia possesses and transmits without discontinuity should not be squandered elsewhere. For this reason our dry earth swarms with hidden treasures that make our region one of the least chaotic on earth." This is the principle of all alchemy—to transform base matter into pure gold, with but one difference: the aim of the transmutation is not to create a pinch of gold at the bottom of a crucible, or to transform a physical body as the tradition would have it; rather, for the Catalans, the goal was to purify their entire country as a true extension of themselves. For this reason "aurification" takes on its most real and concrete meaning in this context: the only thing that can attest to the generating transformation of immortality is the finished work that has become "alive."

This explains how Gaudí could make the *Sagrada Familia* his unique and total *raison d'être* for more than forty years; how such an overwhelming creation could emerge from his almost monastic life, made up of renunciations, severe deprivation, and asceticism; how his mind, which became increasingly sharp as his poverty grew, was applied not to his personal ambitions but always to the enrichment of his beloved city.

Because a Catalan is never really differentiated from his land of Catalonia, the force of his urge to attain maturity and autonomy is extraordinary. Like a child, he uses, for his own ends, the element of play, in its deepest sense. He will do or undertake anything in order to attract attention, astonish, or disconcert: provocation, exhibitionism, simulation, fireworks, and parades. Dali still dreams of having a house made of bread, not because he is mad but because he is a Catalan. Taken in this way, "Catalanism" involves playful activities as hermetic to an uninitiated mind as the games of a child, his screams, or his disguises: in order to prove his existence and make it manifest, a Catalan will put forth the same vital ardor, the same exaggeration, the same earnestness that a child reveals when playing, less out of passion for the game than for the meaning of his accomplishment. "The most essential thing in my life," said Dali, "is a tragic and pathetic gravitation toward immortality. Knowing one exists is a promise of glory. In order to achieve this, we possess the one ingredient in which the earth is most lacking: exaggeration."

This attitude explains those irrational acts, those most incoherent attitudes, the absolute obstinacy of the Catalan. At the time of the construction of the *Casa Milá*, which was to be one of the largest apartment houses in Barcelona, Gaudí very much disturbed the civil authorities when he ordered that one of the supports extend onto the sidewalk "like an elephant's foot." It was impossible to dissuade him. And when it was decided to eliminate the sculpted Virgin from the top of the façade, Gaudí was so disappointed that he dissociated himself entirely from the project and left his collaborator, José María Jujol, in charge of the rest of the ornamentation.

The perpetual games of the Catalans are sustained by solemnity and earnestness. In an atmosphere of constant

A portrait of Gaudí at the age of forty-eight. This pencil drawing by Ricardo Opisso is dated 1900. The architect is shown leaning on his drafting table. For Gaudí this was a period of intense activity: he was beginning his work for the *Park Güell* and spending a great deal of his time at the site of the *Sagrada Familia,* where construction and ornamentation were progressing rapidly.

improvisation great and small ideas are mingled, as well as piety and paganism, outbursts and contradictions, unreality and logic, all in incessant and spontaneous references to the nourishing Mother Earth. This goes on until they ultimately find the fixed pole that will bind, filter, and channel their pulsations, chisel and file their effervescent thoughts. "Therefore," writes Francesc Pujols, "our holy earth becomes illuminated. Thereupon occurs the miracle, the marvel: a sublime blossoming breaks forth, the masterpiece unfolds its wings."

For Gaudí this channeling axis was his absolute faith in the Catholic religion. His energy and impetuosity were suddenly concentrated on a continuously exalted and glorified Catholicism. He followed the rites to the letter, lived its liturgy with scrupulous observation, became ascetic and disciplined. As Pujols has commented, "It is as if he found in his religion the perfect balance, his own narrow mold, adapted to himself alone, which his genius had been awaiting in order to embody it even more, to descend to even further depths, to suffer even more, and to arise in even greater splendor. Thus his artistic and religious vision, cast in a single block and concentrated into four flames of fire denser than ice, will create a unique architectural phenomenon."

Gaudí was thirty-one when on November 3, 1883, he accepted the commission to supervise the construction of the *Sagrada Familia.* The sponsor of the cathedral, the publisher and bookseller José María Bocabella y Verdaguer, concerned about the influence exercised on the mind by revolutionary ideas and anxious about the moral impoverishment they signified, undertook in 1881 his vast "expiatory" campaign that was intended to lead all hearts in the right direction. He sponsored an association and a weekly bulletin that was put under the protection of St. Joseph, the patron saint of the family and of laborers. Donations were sent from the Vatican, and suddenly, upon his return from a trip to Italy, he announced the decision to build a temple dedicated to the Holy Family, with funds obtained through subscriptions, donations, and offerings and with no financial aid from the Church. Since José María Bocabella was in touch with many important figures whom he knew through publishing, by means of them he hoped to spread his propaganda into foreign countries. By the end of 1881 he bought a plot of land in Barcelona and entrusted the project to the diocesan architect F. de Paula del Villar y Lozano, who made elaborate plans for a church conceived in accordance with the neo-Gothic style of the era. A few months later, with the excavations for the crypt finished and the foundations half complete, del Villar resigned his position following a disagreement with the architect Juan Martorell, the assessor of the church. The commission was subsequently offered to Martorell, who declined it, for reasons of age and professional integrity, in favor of his young assistant, Antonio Gaudí, who accepted the offer as a miracle from St. Joseph.

Up until this time, most of Gaudí's work had been done in the studio of Eudaldo Punti, one of the most important builders in Barcelona, for whom he carried out small decorative projects. He had collaborated with del Villar at the Monastery of Montserrat, helped design a fountain

This stooped old man walking to the Oratory of San Felipe Neri is Gaudí, as he was drawn in pencil by Joaquim Renart one evening of March 1925.

GAUDÍ, THE PRACTICING CATHOLIC

". . . he who doubts is ignorant . . ."
(Gaudí)

Two religious ceremonies in which Gaudí participated in 1924. At the left, he is following the procession of Corpus Christi behind the banner of the Artistic Circle of St. Luke, of which he was a member. Below, he is kissing the feet of the Christ on the site of the *Sagrada Familia*, in front of the interior of the Façade of the Nativity. Behind him the sculptor Lorenzo Matamala stands with a bandage on his face.

in the Park of the Ciudadela in Barcelona, and decorated a pharmacy in the Paseo de Gracia. He was building a house for Don Manuel Vicens in the Calle de las Carolinas, as well as the little villa *El Capricho* at Comillas for the rich and erudite amateur collector of exotica, Máximo Diaz de Quijano. As the friend and private architect of Count Güell, he had a plan for designing a pavilion and stables on the Count's property in Las Corts, on the outskirts of the city.

Gaudí quickly became absorbed in the *Sagrada Familia.* He began by augmenting the height of the vault of the crypt and redesigning the columns. He called in Lorenzo Matamala, who was then twenty-nine years old, to supervise the sculpture of the church. "Come," Gaudí said persuasively, "come to Poblet to work with me! With the help of God we will grow old there!" [9] This in fact was to be the case, and Lorenzo Matamala, fascinated by the architect's powerful personality, never left him again and became not only the chief sculptor but the director of works at the site, and the two men grew old together.

On March 19, 1885, a mass was celebrated in the crypt at the new altar of St. Joseph. At this period in his life Gaudí, open and voluble, enjoyed fine food and affected an elegant dandyism. Wearing a short beige topcoat in the style of the day and high boots, he would visit the construction site in a carriage which he would leave only if he had to issue orders. He was not religious, but rather a pronounced anticleric, reacting against the absolutism that had been instituted by Ferdinand VII and against the Catholicism epitomized by his daughter Isabella II and the Restoration. Within ten years, however, Gaudí was to become a vegetarian who preached the virtues of austerity and poverty, and who wore a threadbare suit, traveling across Catalonia "clothed like a beggar, with his white brow covered with curly locks falling from beneath his large black hat, defying the world, yet prouder and mightier than a Moorish king," as the artist Opisso described him.

Ten years later, disappointed by the religious tepidity of his country, Gaudí was to exclaim: "The man without religion is a man spiritually ruined, a mutilated man!" In 1894 an event occurred which brought much anxiety to his entourage. Exhausted not only by the numerous projects with which he was involved simultaneously, including those at Astorga and León, but also and above all by a fast that exceeded the norms of an ordinary Lent, Gaudí was away from the construction site for several days. One Sunday his collaborators decided to visit him. As it is recounted by Opisso: "The first day of the Holy Week we were received by a young girl with

This drawing by Opisso shows Gaudí weakened by an extreme fast, as he was found by his assistants in his lodging in the Calle de la Diputación, during Lent of 1894. At this period in his life Gaudí extolled the advantages of poverty and its influence on artistic creativity. As he said, "One must not confuse poverty with misery. Being poor leads to elegance and beauty; wealth leads to opulence and complication, which cannot be beautiful."

The *Sagrada Familia* a little after 1900. Construction had begun twenty-eight years earlier. In addition to the crypt, the walls and pinnacles of the apse are completed. The Façade of the Nativity is still without its bell towers but its ornamentation is progressing.

GAUDÍ AT THE CONSTRUCTION SITE

". . . the more my body wearies,
the more my spirit is nimble and free . . ."
(Gaudí)

Gaudí himself would welcome the many eminent people, both strangers and friends, who visited the church. With informal simplicity, as shown here in a sketch by Opisso, he readily guided them around the building site. As he explained the architectural scheme of the church and the ornamental symbolism of its façade, he seemed to be discovering for himself the deeper meaning of his vision.

a melodious voice who resolutely brought us to Gaudí's room without even announcing us. As soon as we had stepped through the door, we stopped, astounded by the squalor of the room. The wallpaper was peeling, because the architect had apparently forbidden anyone to touch it. His furniture consisted of nothing but a sagging bed and an uncomfortable cane sofa which Gaudí evidently used as a night table as well as a cupboard, judging from the pile of objects displayed. . . . A small crucifix was hung on the wall. . . . "

Gaudí was in bed, completely clothed in his everyday suit, wearing his usual light brown shoes, and with his old coat thrown over him like a blanket. To quote Opisso: "All this was strange and incoherent. Nevertheless, I had never seen a look of such nobility and greatness on his face. His white hair, with its glints of russet, and his beard surrounded his head like a halo; his eyes were half-open, blue and as hard as metal; his hands, pale and emaciated, lay crossed on his chest. No curtain dimmed the daylight that poured in and gilded his face, and yet it appeared to me to be lighted by a kind of inner, supernatural light. . . ."

Outside of time, absent, Gaudí seemed to float in another realm. The architects and sculptors, who were not used to this kind of experience, did not understand, got panicky, and, afraid that his end was near, called in Bishop Torras y Bages, a friend of Gaudí's, who pleaded with him at length, but Gaudí, coming out of his meditations little by little, smiled strangely . . . and remained silent.

Gaudí was then living at 339 Calle de la Diputación, with his father and his niece, Rosa Egea Gaudí, the daughter of his sister who had died a few years earlier. He lived at that address for twenty years and then moved into a small house, designed by his assistant Francisco Berenguer, in the *Park Güell.* After the death of his father in 1906, followed by that of his friend the poet Juan Maragall in 1911, then the deaths of his great patron Count Güell in 1918 and Bishop Torras, and finally that of his niece Rosa, Gaudí languished in solitude. The head sculptor, Lorenzo Matamala, thereupon proposed that Gaudí move in with him so that he could keep him company. Soon thereafter Matamala was stricken by a cancerous condition, gradually weakened, and was confined to his home. Unable to bear complete isolation, Gaudí set up his bed, among the plans for the *Sagrada Familia,* in a room within the workshops of the church. His life was a study in rigor. He would arise at seven o'clock, take communion every morning in the parish of San Juan de Gracia, and then have a simple breakfast at the construction site: some chopped-up raw vegetables, a glass of milk with a slice of lemon in it, a baked apple, and half a tangerine. People would comment with awe and amazement, "There is the frugal man who covers his cathedral with all the eatables of Catalonia." Gaudí's reply: "Mortification of the flesh is the joy of the spirit. Sacrifice is the only act of true love; it alone can enrich, it alone can help us make our way to inner truth, a way without which there can be no true art." And he would add: "Mortification of the flesh begins with work, incessant work that is not interrupted for a single day ". . . this technique, he said, "should be learned by anyone who has no gift for what he has to do. I am the slave of no convention, I merely follow my train of thought. . . ."

Music played an important role in his life. One day, mingling in a crowd watching a procession, he declared: "There shouldn't be cordons of soldiers standing at attention at street crossings—there should be choirs!" At an early period in the construction of the church Pope Leo XIII allowed the parishioners to sing for the first time with the choir. Gaudí's enthusiasm was unbounded. He said, "The people should sing—if not patriotic hymns, at least revolutionary hymns or religious songs. And if not religious songs, then blasphemous ones. It is more than necessary that they take part in the church singing." His own ideal in music was the Gregorian chant. In 1918, when Gaudí was sixty-six years old, the Benedictine father Gregorio M. Sunyol, considered in the musical world to be one of the most eminent authorities on liturgical art, gave a series of lectures on Gregorian chants at the Palace of Catalan Music. His specialty concerned questions relating to rhythm and modality. A photograph of the time shows twenty-eight well-known figures assisting Father Sunyol; all of them were professional musicians with the exception of Antonio Gaudí and Aureli Campmany. The latter, an eminent folklorist, said, according to F. de P. Baldelló, that he "took courses in Gregorian chant, although he was not a musician, because through them he learned to dance." For his part, Gaudí would listen attentively without saying a word until one day Millet, the founder of the Catalan

Chorus, asked Gaudí's opinion. "My friend," Gaudí replied, "I come here not to learn music but to learn architecture!" He was studying the interior of the church as a space for large choirs, whose voices he wanted to bathe the entire enclosure.

An authoritarian, Gaudí would not tolerate any criticism; he would subdue and impress. According to him, "Men are divided into two categories: men of words and men of action. I belong to the second category, for I lack ways of expressing myself. I cannot tell you about my concepts of art. The hours fly by as I work . . . Are you going to ask me for a picture? . . . I am sorry, I won't give you one. I am nothing, I am only a poor little lamb of the Lord." [10] In fact, Gaudí's conversation was a joy for the mind. Nourished by a rare inner flame, his words struck one with an energy that enlivened the simplest things. "His luminous half-laugh," said Francesc Pujols, "which was brighter than an out-and-out laugh and which demonstrated the naturalness and the ease with which he did and said the strangest things, far removed from ordinary ways of thinking."

His political enthusiasm and his polemical ability were such that his friends wanted him to run for election as a deputy or councilor. But Gaudí refused, stating that "a politician must possess two essential qualities: great passion for public affairs and the will to direct them effectively. I satisfy the first condition very well, but the second I cannot claim." He was, however, aroused by anything concerning Catalonia. Following the visit of Enric Prat de la Riba, President of the Mancomunidad of Catalonia, he exclaimed: "Here is a Catalan who in no time has burned his life out in the service of Catalonia and has made it evident that Catalonia is capable of governing the country, of managing its affairs, despite the lack of means available, and the constant obstacles and pressures of the larger state. Here is a man who has once again emphasized the fundamental differences between Catalans and Castilians: the former have an administrative cast of mind; the latter are squanderers . . . The Castilians are to the Catalans what the Cyclopens were to the Greeks. The Cyclopes had only one eye, and, like them, the Castilians do not see things realistically and in the proper balance: they do not have the perceptive equilibrium or the plastic sensibility of the Catalans, whom reality does not deceive." Gaudí was such a confirmed Catalan that he would not use the Castilian dialect and spoke Catalan only, even in the presence of King Alfonso XIII. A typical instance of Gaudí's antipathy for Castilian concerns his meeting with Miguel de Unamuno, then Rector of the University of Salamanca, who visited him at the site of the church. Gaudí made no bones about his hostility for the Basque writer, and since the feeling was

The sketch by Opisso, at the left, documents Gaudí's visit with the Castilian writer Miguel de Unamuno, Rector of the University of Salamanca. The meeting was stormy, and Gaudí, being stubborn, refused to speak a word of Castilian. From left to right: Gaudí, Unamuno, and the collector Alfredo Riera.

The poet Juan Maragall, shown at the right, was one of Gaudí's intimate friends. The art critic Eugenio d'Ors considered Maragall's *Enlla* "the most pointed and most strident example of Latin romanticism—indeed, of romanticism in general." It appeared to him just as "otherworldly" as Gaudí's works.

THE ARTISANS OF THE CATALAN RENAIXENSA

The painter Alejo Clapés was Gaudí's class friend. Small, with hard features and staring eyes that were meant to startle people, as shown in this drawing by Opisso, he had a violent, boorish personality that was the opposite of Gaudí's, but the architect thought this painter's palette was extremely rich. Gaudí commissioned several works from Clapés. Among the most notable are four large paintings for the salon of the *Palacio Güell*, and the colorful decor of the entrances and patios of the *Casa Milá*.

Count Güell's administrator, Ramón Pico y Campamar, was a poet. He and the Count, along with Gaudí and Clapés, formed an inseparable group which would pursue long and passionate discussions on art, science, and politics, late into the night on the Ramblas.

Santiago Rusiñol, a painter and writer highly esteemed by Gaudí and shown here in a drawing by Opisso. He divided his time between Barcelona, Madrid, Palma. Aranjuez, Florence, and Paris, where he shared a studio on the île Saint-Louis with Ramón Casas, Maurice Utrillo and later, the sculptor Carlos Mani.

Count Güell was Gaudí's principal patron and Maecenas. By depicting him striding by the entrance to the *Park Güell* with baskets full of "rovellones"—the popular and succulent Catalonian mushroom—this caricature was intended to ridicule the "eatable" naturalistic ornament of Gaudí's architecture.

OFFICIAL VISITS AND CEREMONIES AT THE SAGRADA FAMILIA

The two highest religious and political dignitaries of Catalonia paid homage to the highest dignitary of architecture when, in the autumn of 1914, the Bishop of Barcelona, Monsignor Reig, and Enric Prat de la Riba (at the left), President of the "Mancommunidad" of Catalonia, visited the building site of the church.

On the occasion, in July 1915, of the visit of His Excellency the Cardinal Ragonesi, Papal Nuncio in Spain, accompanied by Bishop Reig, Gaudí explained his project and the progress of the structure to his illustrious visitors. They are surrounded by members of the Church Junta and various dignitaries of the city.

"... you are the Dante of architecture ..."
(Cardinal Ragonesi to Gaudí)

The originality as well as the huge size of the *Sagrada Familia* attracted many important people. Here the Infanta Isabella of Spain during a visit to Barcelona is shown making her way toward the building site, accompanied by the curate of the church, the Bishop of Barcelona, and Gaudí, who is walking, bare-headed, just behind.

mutual, the meeting quickly became Homeric. Those who were present remember Unamuno walking around the construction site, taking long strides, punctuating each step with the Castilian words, *"No me gusta! No me gusta! No me gusta!"* ("I don't like it!"). Gaudí, behind him, imitated each of his gestures and repeated each of his words in clearly enunciated Catalan: *"No li agrada! No li agrada! No li agrada!"* ("He doesn't like it!"). Unamuno's judgment is astonishing when one considers that it is the same man who is well-known for the remark, "Only he who attempts the ridiculous can attain the impossible."

Gaudí's choice of friends was often surprising to his close associates. For example, he felt unlimited admiration for an individual who on the surface was not very appealing, the painter Alejo Clapés, a little man with hard features, staring eyes, a pointed beard, and a curled-up mustache sharply poised toward the sky. He wore high-heeled shoes and a little brown hat, and walked on tiptoe, sticking out his neck so that he would look taller, according to Opisso, who had small patience with him. His outfit was completed by a brown overcoat and checked trousers. He was violent, fiery, quite detestable company, and furthermore totally opposed to the political ideas of Gaudí's *milieu*. As Opisso writes, "It was a perfect mystery how two such different and intransigent beings could get along with each other." Actually, Alejo Clapés considered Gaudí to be the greatest architect since Michelangelo, and Gaudí thought the palette of this painter the richest in color he had ever known. He commissioned Alejo Clapés to paint the frescoes at the *Palacio Güell* and in the entrance walls of the *Casa Milá*.

Early in his career Gaudí was beset by financial difficulties. In 1905 Juan Maragall wrote in the *Diario de Barcelona*: "Quite often I have felt proud to be from Barcelona, as proud as an ancient Roman of his status as citizen; but at times I am ashamed of it; and today once again. This man who made the *Church of the Sagrada Familia* told me that the resources for the continuation of the work had been exhausted and that donations had diminished. This means that our ideals are diminishing....

This animated procession is passing in front of the apse during a ceremony at the *Sagrada Familia*. In the lead, Gaudí is guide to the Princess Doña Luz de Bourbon.

If a people in poverty and bloody anarchy is still a people with the right to hope, then a people without ideals is nothing, and has no rights to anything at all. The *Church of the Sagrada Familia* is the monument to Catalan ideals in Barcelona, the monument to eternally ascending piety, the petrified concretion of the desire to rise, the image of the people's soul . . . From the obscure depths of a little shop in the old city (the Bocabella bookshop) came forth a most humble man with a great idea: to build a new cathedral . . . and, with little funds, he began the glorious creation, out there, underground, in a suburb that was still mostly open country . . . Years went by, the small funds grew larger, the stones piled up underground to support the glorious mole of the future; nothing was yet visible, and the city advanced majestically toward it, but knew nothing of it yet . . . And at the moment when the seed germinated and uplifted the mold, when the plant appeared on the surface of the earth to open out in the light, another man, a visionary, loomed up, like an envoy from God . . . Since he was a visionary, nobody bothered with him, nor he with them; but he began to weave his vision, and the church blossomed little by little like a great flowering of the centuries . . . palpitating with Catalan life . . . The city grew and the Church grew, both of them formless . . . And for something so great, I have only heard tell of little alms, what is called the beggar's mite, the most precious, that preferred by God, the most glorious for the work . . . Oh ! why doesn't Antonio Gaudí go out into the street at high noon, with his hat in his hand, begging aloud for alms from everyone for his temple ? I would like to see the well-behaved crowd fall down in holy madness for such a sublime act, and pull their tainted jewels from their arms and their money from its hiding place, the poor giving their poverty and children their toys, in a delirious explosion . . . and then the temple will rise alone in the distance, stones will flower from stones, arches will grow like branches of the columns, the vault will curve softly, the vision will exist, because the people will be present. Thenceforth Catalonia will enter into the coming centuries with the majesty of a people who have erected a new temple. Oh vision ! vision ! I want to believe in you ! I want to provoke you, repeating what Gaudí cried at the top of his voice at high noon in the streets: '*Una graciá de caritat per l'amor de Déu . . . !*' ['Alms, please, for the love of God !']"

This is just about what Gaudí set out to do: a work as important as his, he thought, should not lack support. Giving alms in this case was a religious as well as a national duty. He gave as an example the construction of the Hagia Sophia in Constantinople, which was erected thanks to an extraordinary resolve, and pressing the analogy, he asked everyone's cooperation. Needless to say, when friends saw him in the street, they would cross over to the other side for fear he would ask them for money. And indeed, he went so far as to disturb them and intimidate them when he took up a collection for the church. One day, for example, he asked for alms, saying: "Please sir, do make the sacrifice," and he was answered: "With pleasure, but it is not a sacrifice !" to which Gaudí commented: "In that case, make a sacrifice, give even more." Among the arguments elaborated to support his frequent and insistent pleas, the architect stressed the rapid population growth of Barcelona, which had quadrupled in fifty years. To him this vigorous expansion could not better be symbolized than by the uninterrupted erection of his church, the only type of structure "worthy of the thought of a people, because religion is supreme." In support, Francesc Pujols suggested that for the sum of 250,000 pesetas (of 1905) wealthy Catalans be allowed the right to be buried on the grounds of the *Sagrada Familia*, and claimed that it was a minimal price to pay for the honor of being buried in this sacred place and for the exceptional privilege of having one's name thus acquire immortality for a few centuries. In 1914, however, the Church Junta declared a deficit of 30,000 pesetas, and the serious economic troubles in Spain caused by the First World War endangered the continuation of the project. The number of workers, sculptors, and collaborators

Interior of the Façade of the Nativity in 1904. The geometrical elements of the supporting brackets are in place, as are the apsidal spires to the left in the background. In the foreground one can see the snail-gargoyles made by the sculptor Lorenzo Matamala from natural casts scrupulously enlarged by rule and compass. These are part of a series of gargoyles made in the forms of amphibians and reptiles, which replace the fantastic creatures of medieval Gothic architecture. They have still not been attached to the building today.

Gaudí worked over the watercolor wash, reproduced on the opposite page, so many times that the paper blistered. His fantastic vision of a *Sagrada Familia* bathed in the humid and misty heat of Barcelona emerges as a monumental and other-wordly mirage.

The drawing on the right represents the Façade of the Passion or Death, with the monument to the Bishop Torras y Bages on the left. Gaudí was so enthusiastic about his drawing that he decided to go over the shadowed areas with wash and the light parts with gouache. When the architect Juan Bergós arrived one day at his studio, Gaudí said to him: "You know what I did today? Ironing!" and showed Bergós this design, which he had just flattened out with an iron because the dampness of the wash and the ink had so wrinkled the paper. This final drawing disappeared during the Civil War.

was reduced to six or seven people, and because Gaudí was already sixty-two years old, the administrative council took the precaution of asking the architect to prepare a precise model of the building's structure for the generations to come, since the plans and sketches were insufficient. Lorenzo Matamala and Gaudí both concentrated on the new models. The towers on the Façade of the Nativity and the models were for a while under simultaneous construction, both artists combining their ideas freely, Gaudí pondering every detail and Lorenzo Matamala making endless improvements in order to work out the satisfactory form they were seeking. When the sculptor came down with a terminal illness, the big model was already quite advanced: it consisted of the apse, the Façade of the Nativity, the east nave and its vault, the sacristies, and the upper part of the principal façade, called the Façade of the Glory. Following the Civil War only a few disparate traces of this work were left, but a number of drawings and photographs, preserved over the years by Matamala's son and various of Gaudí's friends and assistants, have made it possible to reconstruct his original structure and vision for the *Sagrada Familia.*

GAUDÍ'S CONCEPT OF THE SAGRADA FAMILIA

When Gaudí undertook the construction of the *Sagrada Familia,* his major preoccupation was the improvement of the initial project as conceived by del Villar in the purest neo-Gothic style, which was then virtually required for all religious buildings. Gaudí quickly pointed out the weaknesses of this system of construction. His opinion was that the Gothic was an art of formulas that cannot in any way solve the problem of very high naves. His aim was to give it the life that calculations with a compass cannot achieve. To overcome three centuries of

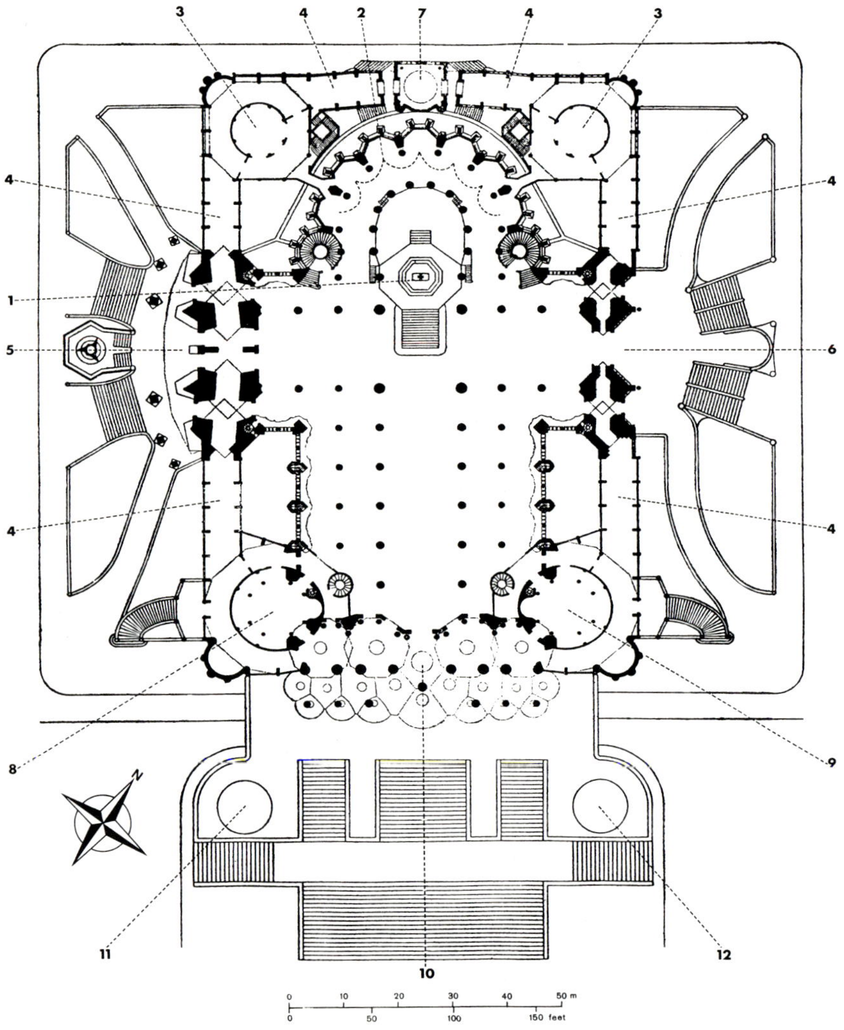

General plan of the Sagrada Familia

1 – High altar, placed beneath the central cupola, in front of the choir.

2 – Seven apsidal chapels dedicated to the sufferings and joys of St. Joseph.

3 – Sacristy and extensions for ritual objects.

4 – Cloister surrounding the church.

5 – Façade of the Passion or Death.

6 – Façade of the Nativity and Childhood of Christ.

7 – Chapel of the Assumption.

8 – Baptistery.

9 – Chapel of the Penitence and the confessional.

10 – Façade of the Glory.

11 – Purification by water; a fountain with a jet of more than 65 feet.

12 – Purification by fire; a giant triple *torchère*.

architecture was a gigantic challenge for a single man, but this doesn't mean that he was not equal to the task.

Giving life to the Gothic consisted in transforming it radically. Gaudí thought it necessary first of all to make structures dynamic, and that the traditional Gothic plan was a dead system, which might be compared with a human being whose skeleton, instead of harmoniously supporting the various parts of the body, was crushed by the weight of the body's flesh and needed crutches in every direction. [1] In effect, up until that time, the traditional methods of stonework made it impossible to build a Gothic cathedral without using a great many abutments and flying buttresses, to prevent the nave from splitting open and collapsing. It was Gaudí's notion that a Gothic building becomes expressive only in a state of ruin, half-covered with weeds and ivy, and contemplated in moonlight or at dusk—in other words, when we are barely able to see it. [5] Further, he wrote that the drama is a result of the ages long past, when faith itself and religious fervor built innumerable cathedrals. Nowadays religious character is indecisive. [4]

A natural law that Gaudí thought was no longer understood is that a force is never exerted altogether vertically. The thrusts of a Gothic vault are dispersed on the outside of the structure. Gaudí sought to concentrate their "vital energy" within the very body of the cathedral, without increasing either the size of the piers or the thickness of the walls. He conceived of the vault and pier as inseparable entities, forming a dynamic unity: he abandoned the vertical Gothic order and adopted the oblique parabolic order. The columns themselves will channel and balance the forces and thrusts; they will be inclined like a cane and will lengthen the vault by constituting a continuous parabolic line. Therein is the basic element of his research over more than thirty years. His genius would have been fully manifest had he applied to the letter what was imagined in theory by certain English and Italian mathematicians of the eighteenth century. In 1748 Giovanni Poleni had defined the ideal form of a construction of compression as being a funicular curve. This curve can be obtained by hanging little weights on a cord, attached to a horizontal support at its extremities. The cord then takes on a form in which all the internal forces are the result of pure traction. If the whole system is inverted, the forces of tension are transformed into pure compression.

The nave and aisles of the *Sagrada Familia* were studied in this manner, on the basis of a principle whose simplicity later confounded the greatest architects, and with the help of a totally empirical method, without any plan ever being definitively established or even drawn directly on paper. Showing César Martinell a sketch that he had made of the *Sagrada Familia*, Gaudí told him that "being very intellectually lazy, I have rejected the procedures outlined in books. You have asked me about certain details of this drawing. I can't tell you anything more at the moment, as I don't know any more myself..." Gaudí seemed not to study his buildings before undertaking them, but would improvise as construction proceeded. Eugenio d'Ors, who was astonished at Gaudí's methods and disconcerted by his disproportionate mysticism, claimed that Gaudí tried to put into effect each day what the Virgin Mary had revealed to him the night before. Actually, Gaudí always sought to perfect his studies through research and cautious experimentation which could continue for years. The façade of the *Palacio Güell* was reworked twenty-five times; the piers of the crypt, which were half-built when he took over the construction of the church, required four years of intensive work; and after fourteen years of analysis, the lanterns of the apsidal chapels were still not completed.

Juan Bergós informs us that it took some ten years to resolve the problem of the nave. In studying its structure Gaudí worked with models when he was not improvising on the site. He used suspended models, inverted, thus verifying in the most concrete way the famous law of Hermes, that everything which is above is also below. It is unlikely that Gaudí was familiar with the funicular theories of Marchese Giovanni Poleni, the eighteenth-century Italian mathematician and architect, who is not mentioned in any documents of the period. Thus it would seem that Gaudí had rediscovered this system and had transposed it into practice. It has been pointed out that such a method was something that only a Catalan could have imagined, that nobody else would have dared, and that no one after Gaudí would probably ever dare do again. In this manner the model for the church of the *Colonia Güell* was fabricated with the help of string, weights, glue, and pieces of stiff fabric that gave the model the rigidity necessary for envisaging also the exterior of the whole assemblage. This church, planned for the workers' community created by Eusebio Güell 7.5 miles west of Barcelona, was Gaudí's architectural laboratory. Work was begun on it in 1898, interrupted by the First World War, and finally given up altogether in 1918, when Count Güell died. Only the crypt was completed: it may be considered Gaudí's living testimony. The model for the project, of which several photographs remain, reflects not only the organization of the architectural volumes but also the skeleton and the mechanical structure of the edifice. Thin string is woven into the form of the vaults and the cupolas, the network of the lines of force, and the inclination of the indefinitely repeated supporting piers that establish the parabolic rhythm of the whole. Little bags of lead shot, representing the active forces that must be sustained, fix the curve of the arches attached to the piers. The model took ten years to make under the direction of his assistant, Francisco Berenguer. It served as a guide for the construction of the crypt from 1908 to 1914, and allowed Gaudí to resolve experimentally the mechanical problem of parabolic vaults supported by inclined piers, and in a single continuous material, which he intended to use in the interior of the *Church of the Sagrada Familia*.

Gaudí accords supreme importance to the framework, just as Dali attributes the highest aesthetic quality to the skeleton, in comparison to the rest of the human body. "The silhouette of a monument is born out of its structure," said Gaudí in his youthful Journal; "everything has a positive reason, and if a line is repugnant to our intuitions it is not right; in tracing a line we do not work solely by the power of rationality . . ." [4]

The parabolic structure of the naves of the *Sagrada Familia* was for Gaudí the ideal constructional solution, because it could outline and re-create an infinite space open to God. It avoided the cadaverous rigidity of the neo-Gothic, and incorporated into sacred architecture the movement and life of the ever-growing vegetal curve.

The parabolic curve, furthermore, guides the spirit in its development toward a culmination in God. Gaudí discovered the key to a universal mystical symbolism in the geometrical properties of the parabolic curve, and in so doing, satisfied his desire and his passion for the total concept, and mastered his vision with troubling coherence. For Gaudí the tetrahedron is the synthesis of space! In the hyperboloid he could see a synthesis of light diffused in all directions. [2] The helicoid [spiral solid] to him meant movement, life, spiritual energy. The hyperbolic paraboloid was the perfect representation of the Holy Trinity—because it was born of two infinite straight lines, the Father and the Son, and united by the placing of a third, just as the Father and the Son are united by the Holy Spirit . . . [5] Actually, all of Gaudí's projects were conceived simultaneously in the three dimensions. It is likely that the plans drawn on paper of classical architecture, however complex and elaborate, and established according to precise calculations, never satisfied or even interested him. For this reason the few drawings from his hand that we know about are always very fuzzy, with only the general lines indicated. All that was valued was the extremely clear inner vision of the total work in question. On one occasion Gaudí told Canon Mas that the architect must be a visionary, that knowing how to organize space means using the most important of the senses, the sense of sight, the only one that has real scope, that allows us access to light, space, life, and infinity, that allows us to comprehend the divine omnipotence and imagine the eternal Glory that heaven promises us. The Canon remarked that he had just uttered a great truth; but Gaudí replied modestly, that he already knew it!

This instinctive notion of unity and totality, such as one can find throughout Catalonia, made it possible for Gaudí to transform the Gothic style and make it dynamic. He insisted that "continuous forms are perfect forms. The formal elements of a work must be welded together, integrated, and fused into an ensemble: they must also lose their individuality and thus contribute more to the unity of the whole. The discontinuity in Gothic is flagrant. They attempted to hide it with ornaments and thus turn the attention away from those points not mechanically resolved. They masked a conceptual deficiency with a visual element." Gaudí's first improvement, in accordance with his famous theory of parabolic curves, was to incline the piers in the direction of the downward thrust exerted by the vault. A vertical column may be considered, from the point of view of statics, perfectly passive, hence useless in the context of the general dynamics of the building. On the other hand, an oblique column becomes part of the movement of the whole. His second solution was to reduce the inert masses and increase the number of active elements, not by using several supporting elements and large vaults, but by multiplying those which carry the weight of individual parts of the vaults. Every column must be conceived as a tree with a trunk that divides and branches out into foliage, with each ramification playing, as it were, the role of an arm terminated with an open-palmed hand that is directly in contact with the vault. This explains why there are such an impressive number of keystones within the cathedral. For thus the pressure of the vaults is diverted into each branch and becomes reduced.

The trunk, the column itself, was for Gaudí the object of several years' study. We know that the architect loved to look at all sorts of wrappings, whether they were rolled and twisted dry leaves, apple parings, or even spiral snail shells and sea mollusks. Gaudí was one of the first to make the column play an active role, on the basis of an extremely simple principle inspired both by the growth of trees and the rotation of planets. Planets, in effect, move in the fixed trajectory of their orbits, while they themselves rotate. A tree develops according to an axis of forces that is the trajectory of its equilibrium, and the growth of its branches follows a helical line. "The tree is my master!" Gaudí would say, pointing to the eucalyptus trees in front of his studio. [1] The horizontal section of the columns of the *Sagrada Familia* is not cylindrical, but is a star-shaped polygon corresponding to many of the grooves on the surface. The column shoots, expands, tapers, inclines, and is fluted with a movement originating in its star-shaped section. "Therein lies all the difference between Doménech y Montaner and Gaudí," explains Martinell. "Doménech decorates his columns with spiral forms, Gaudí conceives his columns as spirals. They are the fruit of a synthesis and are self-sufficient. They need no foundations or capitals or ornament." Indeed, Gaudí had realized a synthesis of all the different styles of column that had previously been invented. Treelike and monumental, they taper toward the top as

The plaster model of the Passion or Death façade, a detail of which is shown here, is today one of the precious and rare documents that allows architects to continue construction of the church.

The plaster model for the Passion or Death façade shows how much it was meant to contrast with the Nativity or the Life façade. The concision of the lines, their sharp severities, and their vertical progression express all the grief and pathos of the climb to Calvary.

their striae multiply, terminating in a knot from which the branches originate. For Gaudí, they play a major role, bringing the column to life, forcing it to stand ever more erect, wake up to itself, and truly live its own life.

At the column's knot the decomposition of the forces begins. The branching-out form of the columns and their great number should give the impression of a forest. The windows themselves were arranged precisely so that the light would be diffused through the spaces between the columns, without revealing the light source. Gaudí likened the effect to that of a forest. At the bottom of the walls of the vaults, he planned to have representations of running water with fish, some swimming toward the altar and some down, away from it, in a form like a seal of office. Puig y Boada said that "the architect became transfigured when he himself described his church and its symbolical meaning. His eyes, a very transparent blue, like glass marbles, would shine with a mysterious fire, vivid and far-away, in flashes. His voice would rise, full of warmth and strange nuances." Seeming to be transported, he would sketch out his ideas, as if he were in contact with some mysterious sacred source. "This man is a poet," said Maragall, "for on his lips all is truth; all is new; it seems that for him each of his words is a revelation, all that he utters seems to him to be unprecedented, and he delights in it with a joyful surprise, igniting himself in the inspiration of his ardent words. Is this

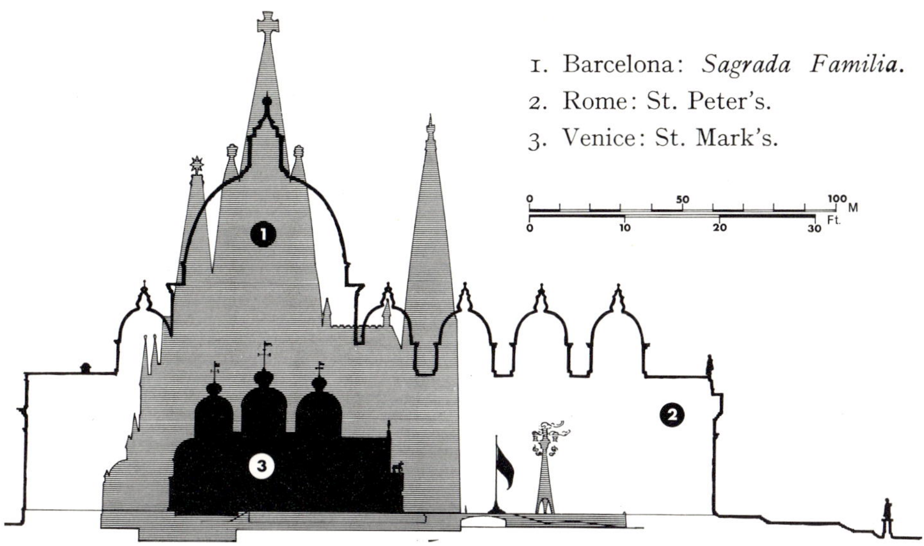

This comparative section indicates the dimensions of the *Sagrada Familia.* The choir would be large enough to accommodate St. Mark's Basilica; and although St. Peter's in Rome is twice as long, the *Sagrada Familia* would still be the highest church in the world.

This panoramic view of the Catalan metropolis was taken from the high point of the *Park Güell.* The picture has been superimposed to show how the completed, looming, huge *Sagrada Familia* would have towered over the buildings of Barcelona.

The Nativity façade in its actual state. Its construction was begun in 1891 and was not finished until 1930, after Gaudí's death. It faces toward the East, and the four bell towers are dedicated, respectively, from left to right, to the Holy Apostles Barnabas, Simon, Thaddeus, and Matthias.

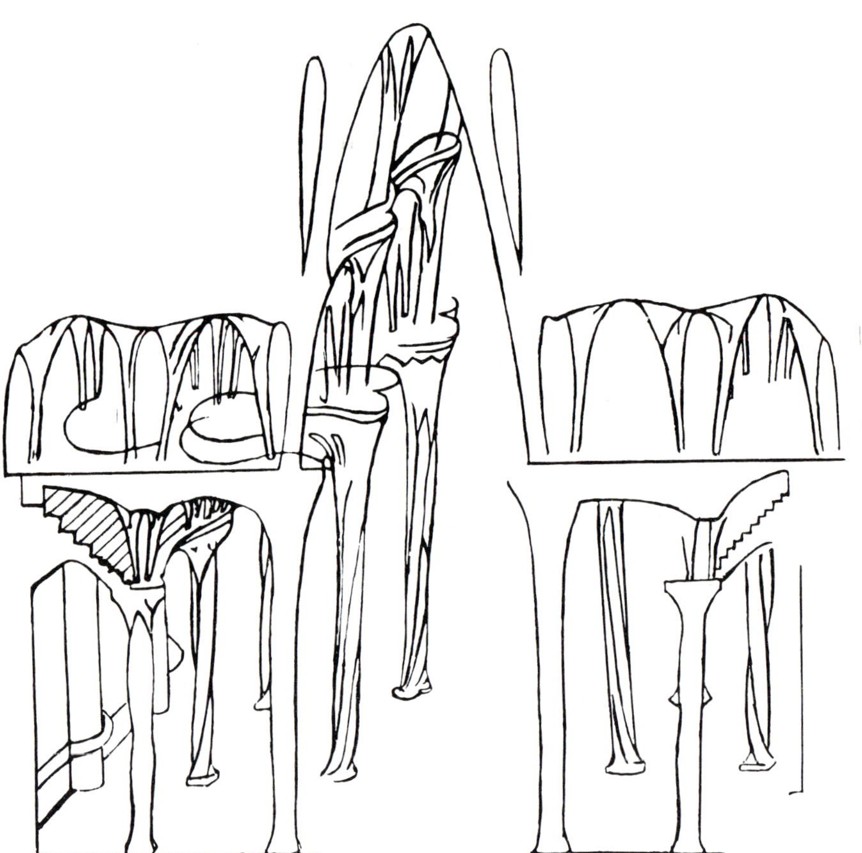

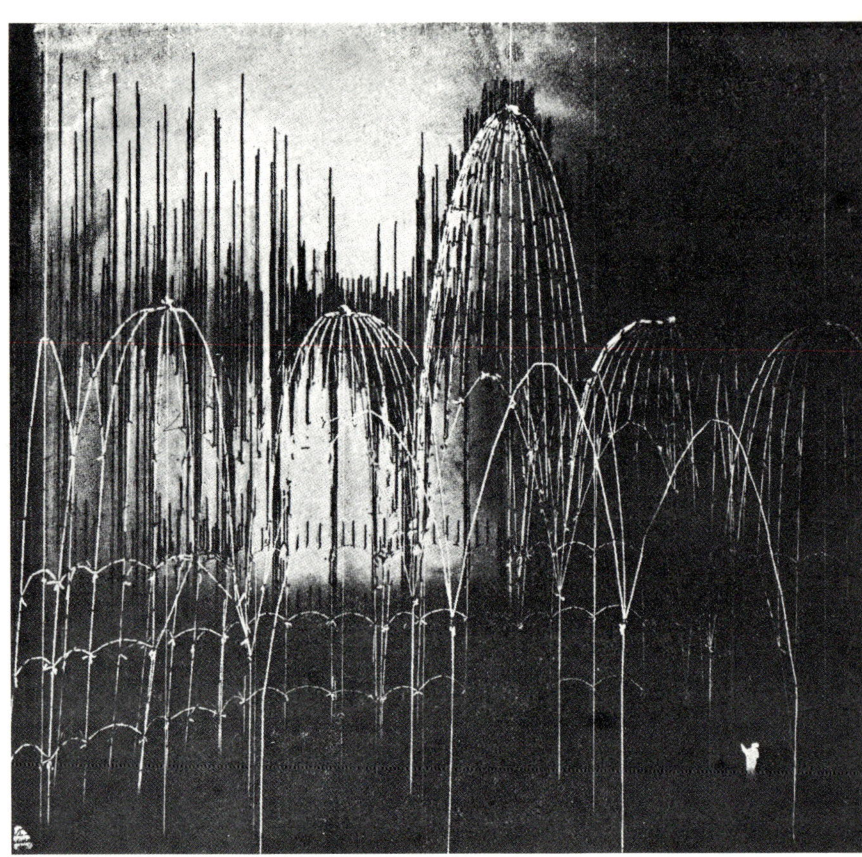

The studies on this page show, on the left, the nave and aisle of the *Sagrada Familia* in a section after a drawing by Gaudí; and, on the right, the church of the *Colonia Güell*, in a model of the interior executed with thin, suspended wires to indicate the rhythm of the vaults and columns. The juxtaposition of these documents shows how the architect based the skeleton of his church (see also page 128 and 129) on the experiments made with wood and bonelike frameworks derived from animal and plant forms in his "architectural laboratory" the *Colonia Güell.*

not a poet?" When, on the other hand, Gaudí was concerned with matters of doctrine, his words were the fruit of long meditation. Often silent, sometimes taciturn and self-absorbed, his attention turned inward, his face would express resolution, a secret determination. As Opisso observed, "It was as if he possessed certain keys, which he could not convey, since he existed in his private world with essentially nothing in common with those who surrounded him, or even with his most intimate friends."

One of the results of Gaudí's being absolutely convinced of his ideas was his rare gift of persuasion. Around 1915 the site of the *Sagrada Familia* was visited regularly by students from most of the Barcelona schools. Gaudí would receive them as a group and explain in detail the techniques of construction and the symbolic meaning of the church. Young architects frequently visited his workshops, where they would even ask him to explain the geometrical concepts they had not understood at their lectures. In 1900 Maragall, following the progress of the *Sagrada Familia* with a lyrical passion, wrote: "The church seems to grow by itself like a tree being born with a gradual majesty. . . The new-born church has a portal. This portal is marvelous. It is not architecture but pure poetry. It seems to be of the earth itself rather than a construction of man, with the stone striving to lose its inertia, and following its own will, and already beginning to take on meaning, and creating images in a vague way—representations of sky and earth—as if the stone were murmuring. The murmuring stone is trying to say Noël!"

The plan of the church follows the outline of the Latin cross of Gothic cathedrals. It has five longitudinal naves and three transverse naves, a lobe-shaped apse, nine chapels, seven of which are on the apse, and two winding staircases at opposite ends. With a length of 354 feet and a height of 557 feet, the *Sagrada Familia* is huge: more than double the size of San Marco in Venice.

Although its length is a little less than half that of St. Peter's in Rome, its projected height, once completed, was to surpass the latter's dome by 65 feet.

The central cupola was to have been dedicated to Jesus Christ, and the four surrounding cupolas, to the four Evangelists, St. Mark, St. Luke, St. John, and St. Matthew. The spired towers were to carry their symbols—the lion, the ox, the eagle, and the angel. It was planned that two beams of light would shine in the night: one toward the ground, symbolizing the Gospel's light falling on mankind; the other toward the central cross, in homage to the divinity of Christ.

The dome of the apse, which was slightly lower, was to be dedicated to the Virgin Mary, according to the Byzantine tradition, and crowned with a luminous star. The twelve bell towers surmounting the three façades were to represent symbolically the first twelve bishops—that is, the twelve Apostles—sculpted in the stone seated in pulpits. "They will be the voice of the Church which teaches and exhorts," said Gaudí. Of the twelve towers, each to be about 300 feet high, only four were actually built on the Façade of the Nativity—those of the Apostles Matthias, Thaddeus (still called Judes), Simon, and Barnabas. Richly decorated with mosaics and large pearl shapes their pinnacles represent the cross, the miter, the crook, and the ring—the episcopal attributes. As Gaudí explained, "The bell towers will contain a great many chimes, tuned by tones and half-tones. Some will be tubular and will ring by percussion. The others, also tubular, will sound by air, like an organ pipe. They will be set in motion by electric keyboards, which will make it possible to play musical compositions as one would on a piano or harmonium. Thus they will be able to accompany the hymns when offices are celebrated outside the church. . . In addition, there will be a third group of ordinary bells."

The bell towers themselves were to be built so that their openings would direct the sound toward the ground rather than disperse it in the air. On the other hand, Gaudí most likely made careful studies of these openings in order to obtain sonorous effects by using the wind. For the architect's constant preoccupation was to sustain the unity of his church. Conceived to give glory to the all-mighty Lord, the *Sagrada Familia* is made up of a series of rigorous convergences. The space was organized very precisely: nothing would be without specific meaning. Everything was designed to help guide the spirit, exalt faith, "make hearts wake from their slumber, give life and warmth to love, and induce the powers of Heaven to have pity on Catalonia," as it was specified in the act of foundation drawn up by the original sponsor of the church, José María Bocabella y Verdaguer. Everything was worked out, concretely analyzed, and built in such a way that everyone who entered the church should in some way and, as it were, imperceptibly, be taken by the hand, conducted, channeled, "obliged," and finally, if it had not yet occurred, converted. . . . Each object and each sculpture played a particular role.

At no moment, even unconsciously, must the mind stop questioning, making associations, relating elements, or seeing as alive all that which, in the traditional and cold conception (according to Pujols) of the classical churches and cathedrals built during the nineteenth century, generally remains incomprehensible.

It is very likely that Gaudí, had he had the time, would have also redesigned the missals themselves, re-engraved the covers in his style, redesigned the images of the first communion, and even invented a new type-face so that the texts might be more easily read or read "differently," more correctly. One can imagine just about anything when one considers that he had gone so far as to make a life-size plaster model for a pew that would be perfectly comfortable when one sat correctly, but which would actually inhibit one from crossing one's legs. This pew was to be made of stone. As Gaudí would say with satisfaction, "In this way its occupants would have to maintain a certain reserve, which is necessary when one is in the house of God—a reserve that men unfortunately do not possess in their natural state."

To imagine the intended density and convergence of the *Sagrada Familia*, it is sufficient to know, for example, that the cloister was planned so that the most monumental processions could take place without a detour into the neighboring streets. Since the cloister was to surround the entire edifice in order to cut off all street noises, its layout was to be completely different from that of the customary cloister. A garden was planned to separate the cathedral itself from the cloister so that outside sounds would be muffled, and the two entrances onto the garden were to be on either side of the main portal.

Gaudí dreamed of building two monuments on the esplanade which were to be living symbols of the two purifying elements—water and fire. In front of the baptistery, four large jets of water, spurting from a single pipe and representing the four mythical rivers of the Terrestrial Paradise, were to rise to a height of more than 65 feet. The water would collect in basins and then descend in spiral torrents and cascades. Flowing permanently, the water would pour from a stone lamb resembling the river of spring water that gushed forth from the throne of the mystical Lamb of the Apocalypse. Symmetrically placed on the other side, an enormous triple *torchère*, like those which burned at the entrances of ancient harbors, was to symbolize the column of fire that guided the Israelites in the desert. It was to burn day and night, facing the Chapel of Penitence, where the confessionals would be located. Finally, four obelisks, placed at the four corners of the church and corresponding to the four cardinal points, were to be the first signposts "to sing in advance the praises of the Holy Family and proclaim the virtues of penitence," as Gaudí explained. He said further: "Covered with inscriptions and allegorical figures, they will symbolize the Ember days—in other words, the four periods of fasting prescribed four times a year by our most holy Catholic liturgy as occasions when we might give thanks for the fruits of the earth and pray to Heaven that the ordination of new priests, which occurs at the same time, will give birth to very faithful and diligent servants of God. This is why the obelisks will be the harvest of the Church." In this way the four elements of the Creation—water and earth, air and fire—would be reunited around the church. As Gaudí said, "The history of architecture is the history of the church." Man created the church, but he never lived in it. This was Gaudí's aim: to make the newly "living" church inhabited, except that, of course, in this case it was not a matter of an "inner" church within each person, but actually a *Sagrada Familia* in stone, destined to be the largest church in the world, the church of universal faith, built after the sacred model of the mythical Jerusalem of the Apocalypse—shining, spiritual, and glorious beyond all expression. One more point is worth emphasizing: in Catalonia nothing can exist in the realm of the spirit that cannot readily be apprehended, seen and felt in the most concrete way. For this reason Gaudí could hope to have not only every man pass through the portals of his church, but all humanity, and to present the message of the Old and the New Testament, sculpted with a realism and common sense that would disarm the observer within and outside the church. For, as at the time of the Gothic cathedrals, the *Sagrada Familia* would be the Pauper's Bible.

The *Sagrada Familia* was to have three façades: that of the Nativity, that of the Glory, and that of the Passion. Of these three façades planned by Gaudí, only that of the Nativity, started in 1891, was erected. Oriented toward the northeast, it is lit by the rising sun and symbolizes the mystery of the Incarnation. It depicts the birth of Christ and certain scenes from his childhood, and it is divided into three doorways dedicated, respectively, to Faith, Hope, and Charity. Illuminated by the noonday sun, the main façade, to be known as the Façade of the Glory or of the Life, was to be a commentary on the evangelizing of Christ. It was to evoke the creation of the world, the evolution and development of man, his genesis, life, and death, hell, purgatory, the Last Judgment, and finally man's Redemption, a synonym for complete glorification. The Façade of the Passion, facing toward the setting sun, was to be consecrated to the Passion of Christ, His death, and His Resurrection. In commenting on the sketch for it (see page 53), Gaudí said: "Its contours will be sober and angular, and the concision of the lines, their vertical progression, will express the pain of the calvary and the harshness of the sacrifice."

The interior disposition of the church was arranged in accord with religious ritual, rigorously following liturgical prescriptions. Attention was to be directed mainly to the altar, which Gaudí had designed without a retable in order to emphasize the importance of the Holy Table, which would be ornamented only with a Christ on the

Interior of Gaudí's 1925 model for the *Sagrada Familia*. This photograph of a nave and aisles gives the impression of a gigantic forest, such as Gaudí envisaged. The monumental columns become narrower toward the top, as their flutings multiply, ending in a knot (the capital), out of which branches spring. The windows were arranged with precision to produce the effect of early morning light in a forest.

The actual state of the Façade of the Nativity with its three doorways: on the right, the Doorway of Faith; on the left, that of Hope; centre, that of Charity.

cross above it, placed under a sort of baldachin-candelabrum. At the base of the cross there was to be a winding vine, its branches intertwined in the candelabrum, in reference to these words of Christ: "I am the vine-stock and you are the vine-shoots." To which Gaudí added: "What could be more beautiful and more moving than a table placed beneath a trellis?" A monumental chandelier with fifty candles, to hang above the baldachin, was to symbolize the Holy Spirit, while God the Father would be represented in the mosaic of the dome above. Then the altar was to occupy the very front of the Sanctuary, framed by the columns of the apsidal nave, the level of which would be six feet higher than the level of the rest of the church. Seven lesser altars would be scattered in the apsidal chapels, with a simple mosaic on the back wall functioning as a retable. The crypt was also to have altars, as was the Chapel of the Blessed Sacrament near the Portal of Penitence on the main façade, and the Chapel of the Assumption of the Virgin behind the apse. Gaudí had worked out the interior plan of the *Sagrada Familia* in such a way that one would see the saints ascending to Heaven and the angels descending. Each column would bear the name and the signs of a saint or an Apostle, in accordance with a precise hierarchy, or the names of the bishops continuing the mission of the Apostles, in which case the column would bear the name of the patron saint of each diocese: those of Catalonia in the transept, and in the central nave those of Valencia, Saragossa, Grenada, Burgos, Seville, Valladolid, Toledo, and Santiago de Compostela. Considered a city without a great cathedral, and not one of the ancient ecclesiastical centers of Spain, Madrid was not mentioned.

We have been told by César Martinell that "for the priests in the Sanctuary, Gaudí had planned to have two hundred seats, which would constitute the choir of the church, a position more liturgical than traditional, since the choirs of medieval churches and most cathedrals were generally situated in the middle, in the part of the nave that extends beyond the transept." Following the same reasoning, an important place, very close to the altar, was reserved for the pulpit. As Gaudí pointed out, "Wanting to be far from it would be nonsense and incongruous. The altar is the central focus whence the divine light shines forth, and high rank must be given the sermons that pierce the weak breasts of the faithful with all their vigor." Facing and in full view of each other, the choirs were placed in the high tribunes and were composed of men, women, and children who would sing the praises of the Lord. Nevertheless, in order to obey as closely as possible the lessons of the liturgy, a gynacaeum was to be provided so that, as Gaudí said, "men would be separated from women when they sing, following the holy scriptures." Designed to hold more than 13,000 seated people, the *Sagrada Familia* was to have two more sacristies, covered by a cupola, and a baptistery. This latter, located to the left of the principal façade and placed symmetrically with relation to the Chapel of the Blessed Sacrament, was to have two entrances, according to Gaudí. The first would open to the outside, to welcome the newly born; the second would communicate with the interior of the church, thus opening symbolically the doors to the Christian life.

Thus the *Sagrada Familia,* "whose portal," Gaudí said, "will be large enough for all humanity to pass through," was to contain and summarize the history of man and his evolution, just as in the Brahman's universe the temple itself is the epitome of the world. It was not a matter of making a work of art, but one of putting art into the service of religion, of sanctifying the paths of the Lord. Here, more than in any other building, it was a matter of being vigilant. It was not important to represent faithfully an object or an animal in all its details, but to re-create its simplified form, the exact and revealing outline which ultimately could alone be translated into the deep imprint of the molding. In this way the *Sagrada Familia* will expand into the sky of Barcelona with stone spikes, flowering buds, and the hieratic stalks of the poppy—a mere enlargement of casts made from the grass and red poppies that grow at the foot of the cathedral. We must see the excess of relief sculpture of the portal as of more than mere aesthetic interest: it shows an absolute necessity for being complete. Gaudí's preoccupation was that everything should have a reason and a just reason. Being complete and "alive," his cathedral would thus fulfill his mission: first in respect to Catalonia, and then in respect to the rest of the world. What the Middle Ages had created in too much haste, with feverish excitement, Gaudí was to complete, giving it a new life. And when he was asked who would finish his work after his death, he replied: "St. Joseph will attend to it."

The East Façade Dedicated to the Infant Jesus

Portal of the Nativity

Doorway of Hope

Anagram of St. Joseph
Jesus in the workshop in Nazareth
Betrothal of the Virgin and St. Joseph
The Flight into Egypt
The Massacre of the Innocents
The Roman soldier

The baby and the flora of Palestine
The dead baby

Central Doorway of Charity

The Nativity
The crèche: "El Pessebre"
Curves of the large parabolic arch
Chaos; mineral and plant

pp. 59/62/63
pp. 69/72/73

The star of Bethlehem p. 73

Doorway of Faith

Anagram of Mary
Presentation of Jesus in the Temple
Jesus and the Doctors in the Temple
Jesus as a carpenter
Vegetation of Palestine

The herald angels pp. 74/75

The crèche pp. 74/75

Angel pp. 78/79

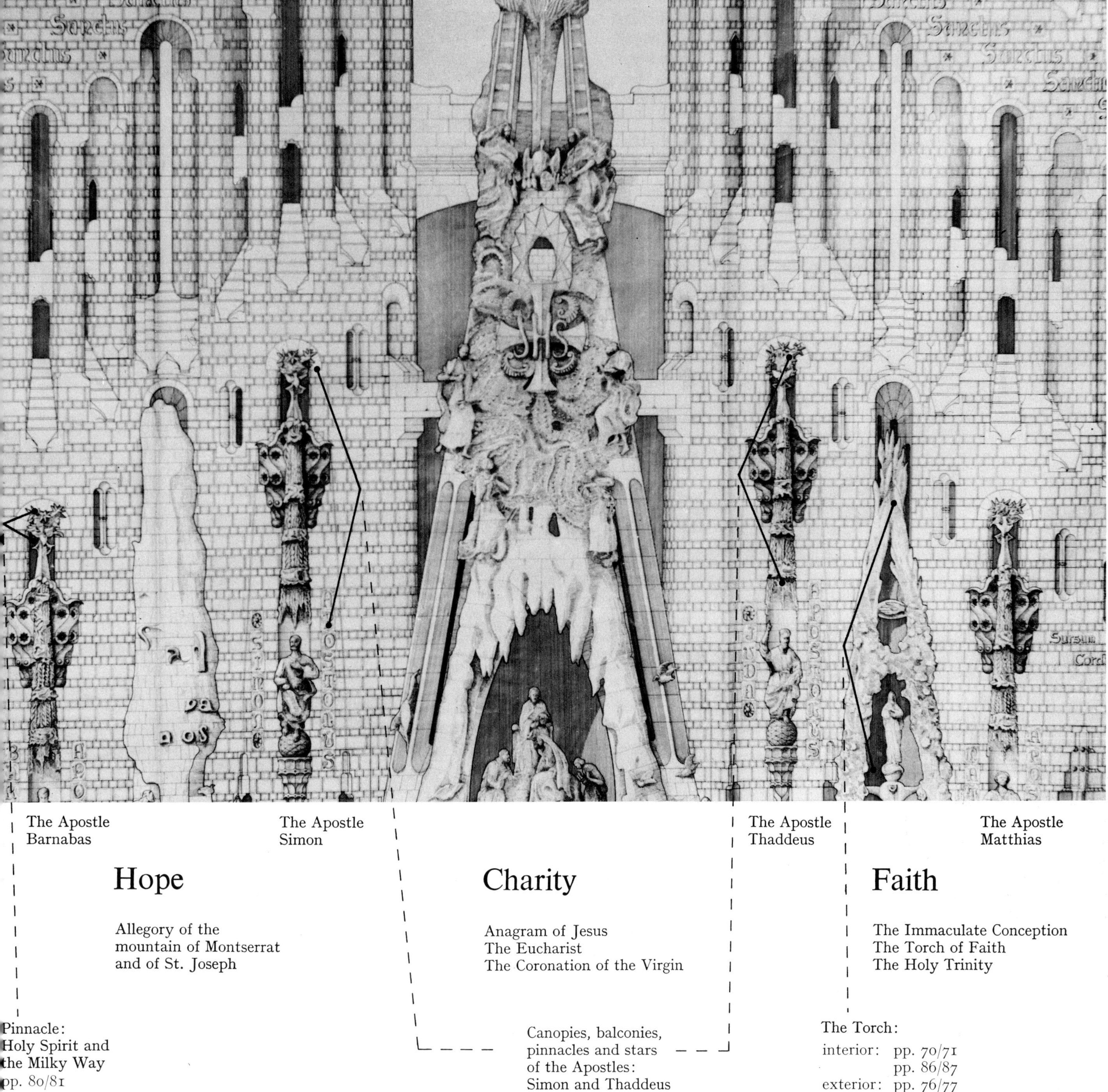

The Apostle Barnabas

The Apostle Simon

The Apostle Thaddeus

The Apostle Matthias

Hope

Allegory of the
mountain of Montserrat
and of St. Joseph

Charity

Anagram of Jesus
The Eucharist
The Coronation of the Virgin

Faith

The Immaculate Conception
The Torch of Faith
The Holy Trinity

Pinnacle:
Holy Spirit and
the Milky Way
pp. 80/81

Canopies, balconies,
pinnacles and stars
of the Apostles:
Simon and Thaddeus
pp. 84/85

The Torch:
interior: pp. 70/71
pp. 86/87
exterior: pp. 76/77

The Church of the Sagrada Familia *is today nothing but an immense façade behind which there is nothing. It rises in all its splendor as a grandiose ruin and a monumental sculpture, with its figurative elements, its assemblages of geometrical forms, and a multitude of religious symbols.*

This drawing of the Portal of the Nativity, *which locates the various groups and sculptured motifs and shows the angle from which several of them were photographed, will make the photographs on the following pages more comprehensible.*

Photographing shows a will to see. It means rendering metamorphoses visible and penetrating to the heart of appearances; transforming vision into a form of violence.

The juxtaposition of two images reveals to those who see them a feeling which is foreign to each of them. The order and mounting of photographs establishes a network of connections and contrasts with their multiple and successive aspects: these are synchronous when the same motif is seen from different angles, rhythmical and pin-pointed when the image is isolated or symmetrical, and syncopated when the page unites images that are disparate in space and time. Sometimes the image is torn from its setting and opens out ideally into symmetry; thus the shadows and light of morning and evening are brought together by this means alone.

The blackness in which each photograph floats, far from being the color of emptiness and nothingness, is the active shade out of which dreams are born.

These illustrations are the landscapes of personal reverie, the decisive moments of an encounter. Each captured form forces one to look at it closely and offers the imagination a resting place.

CLOVIS PRÉVOST

Captions to the photographs of the Sagrada Familia from pages 69 to 93

Page 69	Facing east, the Façade of the Nativity. Genesis of a world and its flowering in stone.
Pages 70-71	The interior of the Torch of Faith. Vertigo experienced while looking toward the light.
Pages 72-73	Looking under the curve of the Doorway of Charity. The starry night of Bethlehem.
Pages 74-75	Above the portals. Birds about to leap into space, the angels of Good Tidings with their celestial trumpets.
Pages 76-77	Metamorphosis of granular rock into crystalline vegetation.
Pages 78-79	The Holy Family.
Pages 80-81	Solidified Milky Way out of which the Holy Spirit soars.
Pages 82-83	Angels laden with flowers.
Pages 84-85	On the sides of the towers. Canopies of the Apostles Simon and Thaddeus. A series of mineral flowers. The light of August.
Pages 86-87	The interior arches of the Torch of Faith.
Pages 88-89	Gradations of shadow and light on the interior structure of the unfinished façade.
Page 90	Corbels for the triforium and for the high galleries of the future nave.
Page 91	Half-archivolt of the central ogival arch.
Page 92	Corbeled brackets of geometrical form. Porches and loggias of the triforium in the void; the large pilaster covered with drops of water.
Page 93	Brackets in the form of cubic pendentives, for the high gallery.

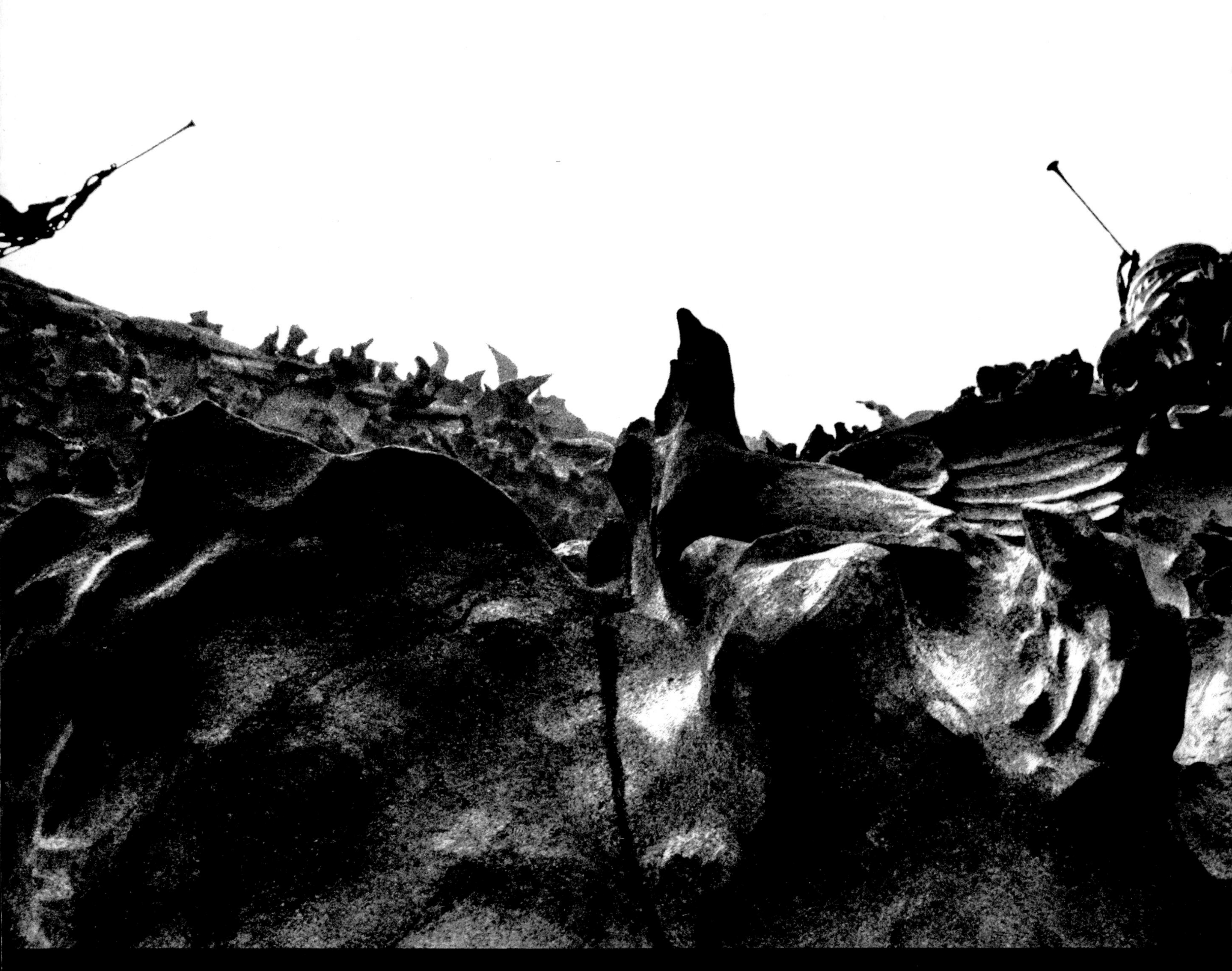

CHAPTER IV

Gaudí, the Master Ornamentalist

". . . order follows disorder. . ."
(Protagoras)

The noise of hammers picking gently away at stone; shouts, calls, excitement. The fascinated crowd could not believe what they saw happening at the building site, but watched, interpreted, and mingled with the workers, as the incredible gradually arose before their eyes. For Gaudí, organizing space did not simply mean constructing buildings; it also meant covering them, bringing them to life, filling them, adjusting all the elements into a clear relation to each other so that they would be revealed, intelligible, and displayed in their true dimensions. Above all, said Gaudí, "it is necessary to dematerialize them," spiritualize them, not through the expediency of cold abstractions, but rather by means of ornament that is "living," realistic, inimitable—the kind of ornament that has been labeled "*superpompier*," or superacademic, but which actually has no specific stylistic identification, despite the impression it gives of being Art Nouveau, Baroque, or Gothic.

Early in his development Gaudí could discern the signs of a materialism that was growing even then. He was anxiously aware of the danger that it represented. In the general excitement stirred up by *Modernismo*, which denied him both clarity and calm, Gaudí had no alternative in his militant search for a truly organic ornament other than to push his anxiety and his obscurantism to the point of deliverance. This attitude of Gaudí's would seem paradoxical if it were not the attitude of a Mediterranean and, particularly, of a Catalan: it was straightforward, strict, and hyper-realistic. The architect thus took sides. For his ornamental language he chose a clear method, derived from the observation of nature: he created a natural grammar.

In a neighborhood that at the time was still a field in the nebulous periphery of Barcelona, the inhabitants of Barrio del Poblet saw, day after day, the most humble elements of their daily life blossoming forth on the Façade of the Nativity. Taken from turkeys on the farm, wild grasses that grew on the site, or the neighborhood ragman, the images were photographed, modeled from life, and reproduced in stone to become the King Solomon of the cloister door; and in this way the ornamentation of the *Sagrada Familia* differed completely from the decorative excesses of the period or the superimposed outer skins designed by architects of *Modernismo*, even by the best of them, such as Doménech y Montaner.

Only the truth of life had meaning for Gaudí, because it alone, as he said, is the reflection of eternal life. "It is mad to try to represent a fictional object," he wrote sometime between 1878 and 1879 in the diary in which he was beginning to note the relations between architecture, ornamental sculpture, and statuary. "One can imagine how coldly the public would react to a statue of an unknown person whose antecedents and individual mythology were unfamiliar, of whom only the artist and a small number of sculptors would be aware ! Everything today is characterized by indecision, and it is for this reason that we must reconsider the criteria for ornamentation applicable to our age, our society, and the geographical region of its origin. The ornamentation must be natural and based on the purpose of our life. There is no question of our imitating any particular style; we must rather work out a system of lines and curves in harmony with the given topographical condition, the climate, and the meteorology of the locale. The result will constitute a style. The next step is to try to increase the importance of surfaces without weighing them down. In this respect there is no more glaring failure or worse example than the Opera House of Paris, which is monstrously and falsely built with marbles from all over the world, but applied in *trompe-l'œil* effects, with overflowing casts, exotic furnishings, and plaster sculptures that imitate everything and satisfy no one; the bronze roof-crests hide miserable terra-cotta bricks; nothing has any meaning; and Napoleon III's entire treasury could have done nothing to remedy the catastrophe once it had been begun." [4]

To enhance his surfaces properly, Gaudí utilized brilliant ceramics (as at the *Casa Batlló*, the *Park Güell*, or on the pinnacles of the *Sagrada Familia*), as well as transparent effects, by placing a hollow glass cloud at the foot of the cypress tree of the *Sagrada Familia*. He accepted the principle of the Catalan sculptor José Llimona, who said that "objects dipped into paste give the impression of being suspended in the air or in clouds." At the *Sagrada Familia* the branches of the trees, the birds that fly, the stars, and the bursting buds are presented in this way. No aesthetic criterion, no particular reference is obvious: only a keen sense of the natural, of timeliness, and of the rightness of a sculpture in relation to its architectural space can help us to understand the ornamentation of the *Sagrada Familia*.

Speaking about the Middle Ages, Gaudí thought it was not at all capricious to put garden vegetables in churches, as a way of giving thanks to God for all His gifts; this, he thought, was the only language that architecture can speak. By comparison, to express the idea of nature, the idea of the countryside, the Greek style used a ribbon of palmettes, and one finds the lotus flower in the Egyptian capital, with the corolla and the capsule, and the acanthus in the Corinthian capital. The finials of the ogival style are in the form of celery, cabbage, and pine cones, and one discovers celery and cabbage, along with parsley, greens, and cauliflower in the many varieties of Gothic capitals. Flowering buds terminate the spires of the chapels of the Cathedral of Barcelona.

At once ornamental and symbolic, the human and animal worlds occupy a prominent place in Gaudí's works, a place as large as those occupied by other worlds—plant, mineral, marine, and aerial. Discussing ways of representing the living world, Gaudí described in his diary of 1878 the ideal naturalistic ornamentation for ceilings: "The elements and their decorative motifs must contrast. If one wants to represent an expanse of climbing ivy, one can integrate into it figurative themes direct from nature: scenes of the wild life of animal and man. Quadrupeds have some decorative value, but they are too heavy and

Gaudí established his general headquarters within the confines of the *Sagrada Familia* building site. As a measure of economy he had not built new premises, but was satisfied with those that had until then served as the administrative and employment center for the construction of the church. At the very end of his life he set up his bed in a corner of his studio and lived entirely within this building.

The sculptor Juan Matamala tells us that "nothing is left now of Gaudí's studio: the studio, the castings, the archives, everything was burnt during the 1936 Civil War . . ." Matamala made this sketch after the master's death, and the drawing evokes memories of activity there before 1915: Gaudí would work with his assistants, Juan Rubió and Francisco Berenguer, at the two tables lit by gas lamps. They always had a pot of eucalyptus leaves on the stove to ward off mosquitoes in the summer and dampness in the winter. Moreover, Gaudí had suspended the casts and models of the swarming gargoyles for the apse from the ceiling of the studio, as a kind of insulation ! Two paintings were hung on the wall—one a picture of the first private house Gaudí had built, the *Casa Vicens* of 1883, in the Gracia district; and the other, a painting of the church. At the back of the studio, there was also a picture of "Don Antonio's" plan of 1893 for the Franciscan Mission in Tangiers, which he was unable to construct. The small library consisted of several books given him by his friends, the writer Maragall and Bishop Torras y Bages, and by other visitors. Gaudí himself bought few books, but he did read and reread Viollet-le-Duc's *Lectures on Architecture*.

Lorenzo Matamala (above) and his sonJuan (below), the faithful sculptors of the *Sagrada Familia*.

In the *Propagador de la devoción a San José* of 1916 one reads that "When we went down to the place where models for the church were made, we encountered in the studios an old man with a flowing white beard, with the face of an ancient patrician, hands covered with white plaster. He was the head of the sculptors." This man was Lorenzo Matamala y Pinyol, known as "Don Llorenç." He is shown here in a picture taken according to the analytic photographic method devised by Gaudí in the preparation of casts. He died at the age of seventy-one, one year after Gaudí. His son, Juan Matamala y Flotats, was born in 1893 and worked in the church workshops from his early youth, assisting various architects. After his father's death in 1927, he was in charge of completing the sculptures on the towers of the Façade of the Nativity.

Ricardo Opisso y Sala was an early friend of Picasso, who sketched this portrait of him. Although Opisso worked for Gaudí as a photographer from 1898 on, he was better known in Europe for his caricatures in the manner of Toulouse-Lautrec.

Ramón Bonet y Save, whom Gaudí liked to call "Ramonet." He subsequently became one of Auguste Rodin's collaborators in Paris, then traveled to England, and finally went to the United States, where he acquired a certain renown. He died in 1952.

THE SCULPTORS OF THE SAGRADA FAMILIA

This portrait of the Tarragonian sculptor Carlos Mani y Roig has been attributed to Picasso. This strange, introverted and almost inaccessible man strongly attracted Gaudí. His sculpture group, "The Degenerates," had already made him famous by 1907, when Gaudí called him to the church project. Mani worked on the figurines of the model sent to the Gaudí Exhibition of 1910 in Paris. He also made the oratory crucifix for the *Casa Battló* and the model for the sculptural group of the *Casa Milá*. He died in 1911.

voluminous. Only the squirrel and the ferret are appropriate. However, birds have the most ornamental qualities, although a material like stone is hardly suitable to represent them. The shiny claws of birds of prey, their hooked beaks, and their pointed wings could be interpreted magnificently in materials like wrought and polished iron, enameled, or lacquered, so long as the subjects do not have to be depicted in life size. . . . The most appealing qualities of little birds are neither their force nor their power, but rather, like insects, bees, and butterflies, they are as appropriate in material and shape for central ornamental motifs; for surrounding motifs, reptiles, dragons, lizards, and snakes are good, with praying mantises, dragon flies, or locusts for the middle . . . To emphasize the contrast between inert lines and interlacings, one would choose a rare flower or a strange, wild fruit, like berries, morello cherries, and mulberries, oak, cork oak, laurel, or olive trees. . . . Praying mantises, bees, and dragon flies will flit in the fresh and abundant foliage. One also could develop the theme of a bird fascinated by a grass-snake in thick vegetation, that of a wading bird killing a water snake, or a scene representing a man crushing reptiles under his foot and overpowering them." [4]

Gaudí involved his faithful assistants in the pursuit of nature. Lorenzo Matamala had to hunt for snails and cut grasses, particularly wheat, to serve as models for the gargoyles of the buttresses and for the finials of the apsidal spires. But it was Juan Bertrán, a sculptural aide, who possessed the most extensive knowledge of botany. As a vegetarian he could distinguish weeds from the rest. He would converse for hours with Gaudí about the

In 1902 when these photographs were taken, the *picapedres* or stonecutters had their studio on the cathedral site behind the Calle Mallorca. They chipped the surface of the stone, quarried at Montjuich, in order to make it vibrate in the light. The *picapedres* considered it a great honor to be commissioned to carry out the sculptural work above the herald angels on the Nativity façade, while the sculptors worked on the sections directly below them. In the casting studio, below on the right, the Virgin of the "Flight into Egypt" is being completed; in the background are two finished angels. The model-maker at the left is studying a staircase for one of the bell towers.

curative powers of certain plants, and he ended by converting Gaudí to vegetarianism, with its slogans, "War on pharmacies! War on meat! Long live wheat and starch!" For him beer, a northern drink, represented the spiritual ruin of Catalonia. However, Lorenzo Matamala sculpted its grain in stone and had it hoisted to the pinnacle of the spires, 152 feet from the ground. One day Gaudí went to verify the placement of these terminal pieces. He led the sculptor as far as the final section of one of the spires, but, overwhelmed by the height, Gaudí became dizzy. Lorenzo Matamala caught him in time, dazed and wavering, and helped him to climb down. Once at the bottom, Gaudí cried out, "Lorenzo, the Saint has warned us. Henceforth we will consider the effect of the sun . . ." And so they continued. Full-scale plaster models of the statues were hoisted to their arranged locations over the Portal of the Nativity. Gaudí would cross over to the Calle Marina, from which point he could harmonize the decoration of the archivolts in the early-morning light. The sculptors, balanced on their wooden scaffolds, placed and replaced each element, remodeling the façade according to his remarks.

Gaudí would often say something like: "The architect is a man who synthesizes, but he does not yet possess the wisdom and infinite intuition of the angels, who alone are capable of building a cathedral without planning ahead. To resolve spatial problems, he must work constantly, as if he had to climb the highest mountain, gauging his energy and devoting himself to the effort, discipline, and ultimate sacrifice, which is indispensable in reaching such an elevated goal." [5] This effort every instant of every day of his life, combined with his astonishing ability, made

One can still visit the workshop in the church basement and observe the evolution of the project in the various models. On the left is the model for the Nativity façade as it was in the course of assemblage in 1904; visible at the base, to the right, is the doorway dedicated to Our Lady of the Rosary, which leads to the cloister. The polychrome model on the right, included in the 1910 Paris Exhibition, shows the first projected solution, with towers and their foliated Gothic pinnacles. The center model shows the roofing of the central nave; and the model in the background shows the final solution for the Façade of the Nativity: the cloister is joined to it, and the towers were lengthened and made geometrical.

THE CATHEDRAL OF THE POOR

During the construction of the church Ricardo Opisso made a great many pencil sketches from life, accompanied by brief commentaries. This one, dated 1897, is a "sketch of a poor young idiot begging for charity at the door of the *Sagrada Familia*."

At the beginning of the century the *Sagrada Familia* stood in a still unbuilt-up part of the city, dotted with little gardens and fields of weeds, halfway between the mountains and the sea, the "people's" *(Poblet)* quarter and the Gracia quarter. Crowds would gather there, and the crypt, at the extreme left of the apse, was opened to the public in 1885. Today everyone is allowed to visit the building site, at the junction of the Calle de Cerdeña (where the goats are wandering) and the Calle de Mallorca, where the sculpture workshops are located.

Grup de mendicants que dema-
naven almoina al portal d'entra-
da à la cripta els quals serviren
de model al pintor Mir pera el
seu cuadro "La catedral dels Po-
bres"

The beggars who served as models for the painter Joaquim Mir i Trinxet in 1897 were a familiar sight around the church. While the artist was at work in front of his easel at the foot of the *Sagrada Familia,* his "sidewalk critics" would speculate about what he was painting. "It's the birth of Jesus with the Virgin Mary and Joseph!" "No, it's not, it's a couple of rogues." The photograph at the left, cross-ruled at Gaudí's request, was one more in Opisso's collection of potential subjects for the Façade of the Passion. His hand-written caption reads: "A group of beggars pleading for alms at the door to the crypt and who serve as models for the painter Mir in his picture 'The Church of the Poor.'"

it possible for Gaudí to improvise on the spot and to participate in every detail of the ornamentation of his works. Opisso recalls how the architect, toward the end of the last century, would spend the most enjoyable hours of his life at the back of a forge in the Calle Roger de Flor. From this shop came the beautiful ironwork of the *Palacio Güell,* the door latches of the *Casa Calvet,* and the grille of the Façade of the Nativity, all of which were forged almost entirely by his own hands. Opisso also remembers how Gaudí interrupted a clumsy workman, and to the astonishment of the others in the forge, rolled up his sleeves quickly, took up the hammer, and, surrounded by a halo of light, proceeded to deliver, according to Opisso, "apocalyptic blows upon the anvil, beginning, with terrible fury and colossal power, to re-form and model the incandescent iron according to his will, while a rain of sparks fell upon his shoulders."

Gaudí sought to practice this kind of permanent improvisation with the total aid of his collaborators. Furthermore, apart from the Alsatian engineer Goetz, who was responsible for technical matters and who always kept to his own discipline, everyone became involved in the diverse activities of the builder and decorator. The most brilliant among them was the architect José María Jujol, who became a designer in ironwork so that he could create the amazing balconies of the *Casa Milá* as well as a colorist in order to work out the mosaics on the façade of the *Casa Batlló.*

Following are the names of those who made it possible for him to create that admirable a body of architecture: his collaborating architects and disciples Francisco Berenguer, José María Jujol, and Juan Rubió; his studio designers José Canaleta, Francisco de Paula Quintana, and Domingo Sugrañes; his sculptors Emilio Fontbona, Carlos Mani, Lorenzo Matamala (known as "Don Llorenç"), his son Juan, and Vicente Villarubias; and finally, his artist-of-all-trades, the designer and chronicler Ricardo Opisso.

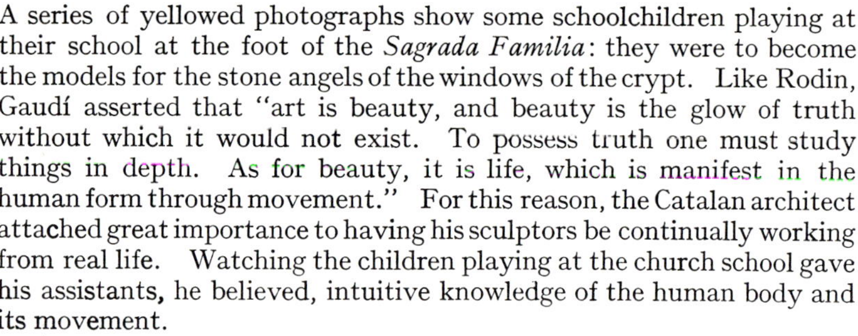

A series of yellowed photographs show some schoolchildren playing at their school at the foot of the *Sagrada Familia*: they were to become the models for the stone angels of the windows of the crypt. Like Rodin, Gaudí asserted that "art is beauty, and beauty is the glow of truth without which it would not exist. To possess truth one must study things in depth. As for beauty, it is life, which is manifest in the human form through movement." For this reason, the Catalan architect attached great importance to having his sculptors be continually working from real life. Watching the children playing at the church school gave his assistants, he believed, intuitive knowledge of the human body and its movement.

The fire that ravaged Gaudí's studio at the *Sagrada Familia* in 1936 also gutted the little parish school. It had been located in the vicinity of the church since 1904, near the sculptors' workshops on the site of the Glory façade. The school was designed to accommodate a child's world of imagination and was specifically built to the scale of children. In these pictures one can see the thatch-roofed hutches in the courtyard and the curves of the roof and walls of the school building. For its construction Gaudí selected tile and put it to use in the most economical and most traditional fashion: the thin Catalan vault.

CHAPTER V

Gaudí: Interior Architect

Once, while attending a lecture on Gregorian music, Gaudí was asked his opinion on the subject. Without hesitating, he replied, "I did not come here to learn music, but architecture." Gaudí never strayed from his vocation; rather, he called upon everything in his experience to nourish it. On frequent occasions throughout his colourful career he would plunge with characteristic enthusiasm into painting, sculpture, interior decoration, even cabinet making. He was an architect as Michaelangelo was a sculptor.

Several of Gaudí's major projects entailed designing interiors and, in particular, furniture. For an artist with such a holistic view of his work, to leave the conception of his constructions' interiors to others would have constituted a gross inconsistency. In every case objects created for interiors were integrally linked to their physical contexts; they literally grew out of them. Unfortunately, many of these contexts have since disappeared or are so totally transformed that they no longer constitute coherent environments. The majority of the pieces pictured here are now displayed in the Friends of Gaudí Museum in Barcelona, where they have been carefully brought together and restored, in so far as possible, according to their original conception.

At the base of that conception was an acute awareness of natural unity. It would have been unthinkable for Gaudí to create an independent object suitable for any environment. Interior — as well as exterior — space was dictated by organic relations. Thus, a piece of furniture was constructed according to almost human characteristics: at the base, a skeleton — its structural plan; then the vital organs — its volume; finally, the skin — its surface decoration.

We can examine these elements one by one. First, the structure. An anecdote indicates how deeply Gaudi understood its significance. One of his closest co-workers, Juan Bergo, recounted how, during the Spanish Civil War, a bomb blast shattered all the windows of the *Casa Calvet.* A chair had been placed just beside one of the windows. So carefully was it conceived and constructed that under the shock of the blast, instead of breaking up in a haphazard way, its members flew apart exactly at their assembly points. It was subsequently a simple matter to restore the chair to its original state. Gaudí the architect, with his profound understanding of structural requirements, was ever vigilant.

The next essential component was volume. If the outer plan was rigourous, no details of the inner structure were neglected. For the *Casa Milá* — his last civic work — Gaudí had planned to run a picture moulding along the walls, from one apartment to the next. This element would serve to transform the walls into a sort of organic membrane, designed to facilitate rapid and dramatic modifications both of the wall coverings themselves and of other decorative features relating to them, such as paintings and tapestries. A building, and its interior, must be made to grow, to change, to evolve.

The final essential element was the surface decoration. Gaudí concerned himself with even the most minute details. If he created floor-tiles, lamps, even door handles, it was not for the pleasure of playing with forms but because of his unshakable conviction that all these elements were essential to complete a whole, fully integrated and self-complimentary environment. Again, like the human body, in which each vital organ is indispensable to the whole in order to sustain life, in a building each object, every detail, visible or not, must contribute to the harmonious functioning of the whole.

How did that harmony relate to human needs ? Gaudí firmly believed that it should address itself as much to the human sensibility as to physical requirements. It had to nourish the spirit; to elevate the senses. This conviction intensified as the artist matured. The marked evolution in his personal and spiritual existence — from the young, exuberant man-about-town to the mature, religiously devout near-ascetic in pursuit of loftier goals — is distinctly paralleled by a clear developmental progression in his furniture design, where an early, highly ornamental extravagance gives way step by step to a clean-lined, distilled and exquisitely expressive purity.

These oak chairs were designed and built in around 1906 for one of the *Casa Batlló* apartments and exemplify the clean lines of the Art Deco style. The splayed legs create a graceful, animal-like stance.

Early pieces, exemplified by the furniture designed for the *Comillas chapel,* were often rigorously symmetrical and highly ornamented; many had decorations rigidly contained within borders, particularly on upper sections of chair-backs and projecting ends of arm-rests.

A certain evolution towards a more symbolic and distilled form can already be noticed in the dressing table and chair of the *Palacio Güell.* Here, surface decoration is replaced by structural re-organization; form becomes decoration. Planes and surfaces inter-relate vigourously, yet all symmetry has been banished. The structure does not contain one right angle; even the mirror defies verticality. The piece creates its own logic. With it, Gaudí the architect achieves his closest synthesis with Gaudí the sculptor.

Most characteristic of Gaudí's mature style of conception and design are the chairs of the *Casa Calvet* and, slightly later, the *Casa Batlló.* These pieces provide the most marked examples of organic symbolism in this period of his work. Legs often resemble either extensions of the human body or animal-like members. Feet may be splayed and paw-shaped or clenched like fists. The rear feet of certain of the *Casa Calvet* pieces, for example, bring to mind with astonishing vividness the paws of a leaping animal. These features are integrated into the form with absolute structural simplicity. Furthermore, the same sense of the practical which is paramount in all of Gaudí's design — the foot-rest of the *Palacio Güell* dressing table was designed especially to accommodate the high-laced boots of the day's fashion — was most successfully synthesized with aesthetic considerations during this particular period. The smooth, generous depressions gracing the upper backs of the *Casa Batlló* chairs, for example, while constituting essential formal elements, act at the same time as practical aids for grasping or picking up the chairs. Similarly, the handles protruding from the arm-rests of a chair for a desk should facilitate changing the chair's position while seated in it.

Though Gaudí was always concerned with function, comfort was not necessarily a priority. First and fore-

This three-seat bench was created in neo-medieval style for the *Casa Calvet*. Celtic motifs inspired the vegetal-like decoration on the seat and back. The slender, slightly splayed legs are indicative of Gaudi's naturalist style, especially pronounced during this period.

most, an object had an intrinsic reason for being, and each of its features had to corroborate that purpose. We are reminded of one of his designs (executed in the form of a plaster model but subsequently destroyed) for a church pew whose very conception rendered leg-crossing not merely awkward but actually painful. The artist could thus rest assured that worshippers would maintain the strictest of postures in the house of God.

Gaudí's naturalism was further expressed in the materials he used; they were often incongruous or even startling. His unique sensibility gave rise to such innovations as waves sculpted from stone, ears of wheat forged in iron, stone roses and brilliantly glazed ceramic trees. He sought to explore the possibilities of every medium to the fullest and to push the material to the limits of its strength. Rather than let a material's natural limitations dictate his use of it, he manipulated and forced it with his implacable will to dominate. He refused every physical and technical constraint; no financial or commercial imperatives could be imposed. His was an unerring vision, and to those who were less convinced, his reply was unqualified: "He who doubts is ignorant".

The surrealists would soon find a source of spiritual as well as formal inspiration in Gaudí's work, extolling in it "the immaculate purity of dream-like interlacings". That purity was the logical result of the artist's driving vision; it characterized every example of his work, from the most monumental construction to the smallest decorative object.

In this detail of the dressing table pictured on page 112, the vitality and grace of the animal-like legs and feet are particularly remarkable. Also of note are the neo-baroque surface decorations.

Below and right: An armchair in oak designed for the *Casa Calvet.* Its lyric form clearly suggests the lines of the seated body which will occupy it. The armrests end in a graceful curve reminiscent of the neck of a violin.

Above: The waiting room of the main floor, with fireplace and entrance to the main salon.

Left: *Casa Batlló,* Paseo de Gracia 43, Barcelona. Built between 1904-1906. Entrance hall and staircase to the main floor. Note the "spinal column" effect of the guard and bannister. The ceiling is painted to resemble a mosaic. The small window at lower left is illuminated artificially.

Left: *Casa Batlló*. A door-wall separation between the main salon and a small adjacent salon.

Above: *Casa Calvet*. Oak armchair. True to Baroque spirit, it contains the essential "organic" elements quintessential to Gaudí's mature style. Note that the rear legs are asymmetrical.

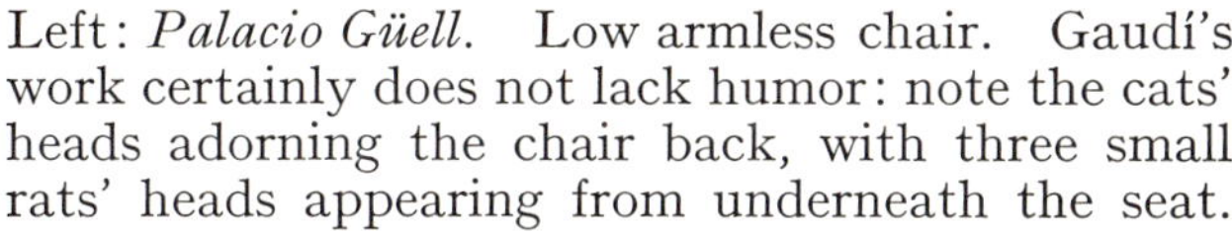

Left: *Palacio Güell.* Low armless chair. Gaudí's work certainly does not lack humor: note the cats' heads adorning the chair back, with three small rats' heads appearing from underneath the seat.

Above left and right: *Casa Calvet.* These oak chairs complete a living room set to which the bench pictured on page 103 also belongs.

Right: *Casa Batlló.* Paired chairs.

Following page: *Palacio Güell.* Dressing table in neo-Baroque style, now in the Gaudí Museum of the *Parque Güell.*

CHAPTER VI

The Realism of the Sagrada Familia Sculpture

"*. . . ornament should be figurative. . .*"
(*Gaudí*)

Church sculpture is the transposition of the imagery from the Bible. Faithful to this principle, Gaudí rejected formal abstraction and the monstrous in order that his sculpture would be clear and comprehensible to everyone, for he intented the *Sagrada Familia* to be a "Pauper's Bible." The more closely his sculpture could conform to God's handiwork, the better it would be. Can one improve upon God's creations? Gaudí's willful realism, his careful exactitude, his respect for nature, all were pre-eminently an act of fervor and adoration. Photography, the new discovery of the century, was a particularly effective tool for this architect's purpose, for he used it in conjunction with plaster casts, a process which in a sense could be called three-dimensional photography.

In an essay of 1878 Gaudí outlined his plans for his statuary, for which he would use an apparently quite efficient technique: the making of casts from living people—a method which, according to him, Pliny said the Greeks had used. Yet, this kind of modeling was condemned by those who defended art for art's sake. Rodin had recently exhibited his "Age of Bronze" at the Paris Salon, provoking a scandal in artistic circles, and Rodin was accused of having cast from his model, a soldier in the Belgian Army. Today pop artists readily use this technique, but the movement is still too new to have modified conventional aesthetic criteria. Many people still feel at heart that mechanical methods are incompatible with the criteria of beauty.

Even in Gaudí's day people were startled by the empiricism and ingenuity of his methods of craftmanship, which appeared to be out of proportion with the grand manner that was considered appropriate for a work on the scale of a cathedral. Given their historical context, however, his methods are easily understandable. In those days photography was considered similar to painting, and the two media rivaled one another. Painters like Manet, *le Douanier* Rousseau, and Cézanne often copied from photographs. Delacroix himself practiced photography, and Degas used it to study movement. Gaudí employed the camera and the making of casts because these were both economical and effective in obtaining the imprint and outline of reality in its dynamic truth: that is to say, as both form and movement. Casts and photographic negatives are merely a means of conserving what is transitory in the nature under analysis: the beating of wings, smoke, the fall of a body, or the expression of eyes or of a face. The materials borrowed from nature itself, both animals and moving people, were studied in their "picturesque reality." In this way Gaudí could capture instants of life. What the architect could not achieve with casts, he would demand of photographs, and he would also analyze difficult poses with natural or artificial skeletons. He would also consider the possibilities of stylization or simplification. He sought to find the synthetic form of the object studied. As a pragmatist, he could easily go from one method to another.

Gaudí, constantly in his workshops with those handling photography, casting, and sculpture, was never satisfied just to control and command; he liked to work with his hands. He himself would cross-rule the photographs he had had taken (see pages 121 and 141); he made mannequins and skeletons in order to study the best postures for his subjects and the best grouping for an ensemble. With the same passion that guided his elaborate conception of the edifice, he would work on the slightest details of the sculpture. He exercised his authority continually, originating and verifying everything. He used his own methods to solve most of the problems posed by the creation of his incredibly elaborate sculpture. On the other hand, he gave his ornamental sculpture a formal unity that fused and integrated it into the mass of the building, so that the sculpture seemed to emanate from the architecture and extend it.

In his buildings as in his statues, it was the skeleton that was of prime importance, for it was the variable element. Every form is but the envelope of an inner structure. It was for this reason that Gaudí attached such importance to the study of the skeleton that structures the human body. As he liked to say: "The most intensive expression of a figure is provided by the skeleton, for this is its basic *variable* element. The rest are only details that disappear at a distance . . ." [5] The skeleton is a mobile structure: it must be considered in both its aspects by a direct study of the bony skeleton and a direct study of a man's movement. In addition to practical experiments, his friends remember seeing him refer to large anatomical engravings taken from an Italian work of the eighteenth century, as well as a little book on anatomy and physiology.

By maneuvering the small artificial skeletons of iron or brass just an inch or so, he could observe the mechanism of movement and then develop his observations using actual human skeletons. For him this amounted to a basic syntax. Given his concept of art, knowledge of the musculature and the skeleton was essential: "Art is beauty, and beauty is the glow of truth without which it would not exist. To possess truth one must study things in depth. As for beauty, it is life, which is manifested in the human form through movement." [5]

The real, however, is not identical with the natural. The objective of all the detailed examinations to which Gaudí devoted himself was less a way of achieving naturalistic sculpture through precise observation than it was a way of revealing and intuitively understanding what is hidden—that is, the mystical and profound architecture of reality shot through with a torrent of dynamic and spiritual lines of force. It was not a question of merely suggesting a form or a natural movement, but of bringing vitality to the representation of that inner spiritual energy that gives truth and character to beings and things. Indeed, the skeleton was for Gaudí not only a reference point for bodily expression but also the very principle of its spiritual expression. As he said, "The expression and appearance of an individual derive from his skeleton." In this perspective the slightest inaccurate line or the slightest error in posture becomes not only a mistake and a denial of truth but a sin against religion. In respect to this subordination of the artistic vision to the religious vision which imposes proportions and postures on the invisible skeletons of ornamental figures so as to reflect more clearly the soul that each is supposed to represent, one can perceive how the slightest of Gaudí's investigations in connection with the *Sagrada Familia* was a work of evangelical faith. For such ornamental figures as those that decorate the interior and the exterior of the *Sagrada Familia*, or the angels for the baldachin of the cathedral in Palma, Gaudí made preliminary studies and sometimes definitive models with the help of metal-skeletoned figurines. In the last ten years of his life he made many of these himself. The rough skeletons were articulated and often stuffed with a supple and thin wire-netting that shaped the body and made it possible for Gaudí to simulate natural movements like the distension of muscles. Often Gaudí dressed them by pasting or clipping on fabrics to give a certain life and precise, realistic movement to the form. He made figurines of this kind about 1/25th of their actual size, for the *Sagrada Familia*'s interior, where the statues were to rise from the columns to the vault: the hallowed elect were drawn up to heaven, while the angels descended, as if Gaudí wanted to transform the interior of the church into an illustration of Jacob's spiritual ladder.

These figurines were to be polychromed so they would blend with the mosaics and other colorful decorations of the interior. Gaudí maintained that statuary of moderate size, inserted within the body of a large cathedral, gives an impression of monumentality to the architecture; very large figures, on the other hand, tend to shrink the building considerably and do not integrate well with the architectural whole.

Thus Gaudí created his statues and his churches with such simple materials as fabrics, glue, and bits of string. This relationship was not fortuitous. In the same way, Gaudí effectively balanced the movements of his figures and the angles of the piers in the *Colonia Güell.* In speaking of his funicular models or his metal-skeletoned figurines, he used the same vocabulary: "This skeleton articulates human movement as if it were a system of pulleys guided by the muscles." In his mind the body of a building and that of a man have the same organic unity and are subject to the same internal laws, for the organization of space is a projection of the body's anatomy. One finds the same conceptual stages in his sculpture as in his architecture: a building is at first a strong infrastructure, then an enveloping sculpture, and finally a polychromy, and a statue is first a structure, the skeleton, then a form, the musculature, and finally a color, the skin.

In this treating two media of the fine arts, architecture and sculpture, in the same way, Gaudí revealed not only his enormous perspicacity but that intuition of the hidden unity in all things which is characteristic of genius.

When, with the help of his little artificial skeletons, he found the definitive position of a figure, he would repeat the result for further precision with a real skeleton. He thus avoided the nonchalance of live models (who are naturally apt to assume the most comfortable postures) and could, without hindrance, fix the slightest details of a pose that he intended to translate into a mold. The young Juan Matamala procured the necessary skeletons for Gaudí. His professor of fine arts did not hesitate to provide them since they were for the *Sagrada Familia.* And Juan Matamala also helped Gaudí arrange them in the proper poses and surround them with mirrors in order to photograph them more effectively.

Photography cannot be considered marginal among Gaudí's concerns, for he was continually seeking to reproduce life without distorting reality. Photography made it possible not only to isolate a gesture at its most expressive moment, but to grasp an instant of reality that the eye itself would miss, such as the precision of a form or the play of light and shadow. Photography is the will to see. But it is also a means of rapidly collecting the greatest possible amount of information and preliminary sketches, which are necessary for the sculpture of a cathedral. Drawing with photographs requires less effort than drawing by hand and yields better results. Therefore the economy of this process encouraged Gaudí to use it as a tool in his daily work.

Already in 1855 Delacroix had observed the value of photography and its superiority over other processes, such as tracing on glass or using gauze, for correcting the eye's miscalculations. But for the painter photography was something more; it was, as he wrote in his journal, "the mirror of the object, and certain details, almost always neglected in drawings from nature, take on a great importance for character, thus giving the artist a complete knowledge of construction; shadows and light are revealed in their true nature—that is, with their exact degree of firmness and softness, a very delicate distinction without which there would be no vitality. The imperfections that photography faithfully reproduces do not shock our eyes when we look at the model without this intermediary; the eye corrects without our knowing it. Photography does the work of an intelligent artist."

The print of a photograph is no more than a beginning; it is, above all, the consequences that count, for it wrenches a fragment of quasi-reality out of the mute world and transforms it into the element of a language, different from that of life, and it is then restructured as a symbol. Utilizing a posed model or a snapshop according to his needs, immediately absorbing the information provided or filing it away for future use, Gaudí made free and effective use of photography. The print of a photograph serves as a memorandum. More precise than a sketch, it is also extremely complete documentation. Whether as a reference or as a model to be reproduced, in each case it was a matter of an approach to reality or of a fixed memory. One of his most important uses of the camera was his contribution to the study of movement. Gaudí sought to obtain synthetic vision of movement with the help of a system of mirrors. His empirical procedure may be compared with that, albeit more scientific, of the French doctor Étienne Marey, who in 1882 invented the chronophotographic machine in order to study the physiology of movement. In the workshops of the *Sagrada Familia* the anatomical skeleton or the model

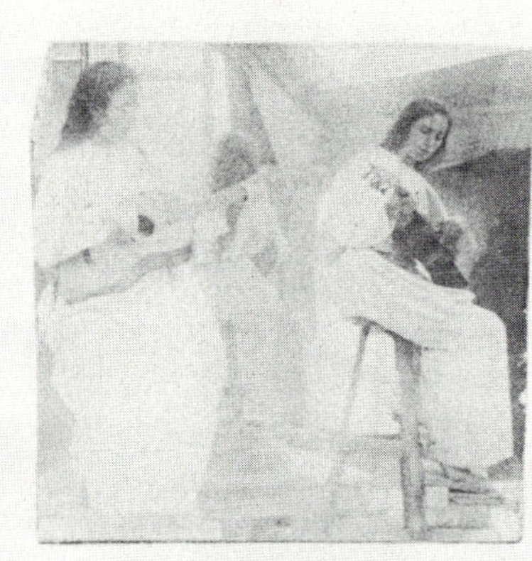

Anys 1892 al 1900. Fotos dels models, els quals un cop fotografiats eran enmotllats directament del natural pera figurar en l'interior del claustre i altres, á la façana del Naixament.

was placed in the center of an arrangement of mirrors, rather similar to that used in fitting rooms, and generally composed as follows: two mirrors placed vertically and another suspended horizontally above the subject. In this way five images are obtained in a single exposure, giving five different perspectives (see pages 134 and 135). The mirrors had simply to be moved in order to analyze all the levels. This method, when used for skeletons, has the advantage of accurately defining and multiplying the visual investigation of the movement of bone structures. A pose, even if it remains fixed and static, is momentary, and Gaudí wanted to catch particular moments. The same arrangement used with living models offered Gaudí the same advantages, but it gave additional valuable information on the way movement affects the intensity of light and the play of light and shadow on the body. Finally, this method made it possible to anticipate the impression that the casts would produce, thus reducing the chances of error and subsequent surprises. This was an important concern, because the making of casts required much care and skill, and there are many drawbacks to repeated sittings.

Gaudí was interested in the visual impressions given by a sculpture from every angle, even though certain parts remain hidden once the statue is *in situ*. To a bishop who asked why he worked so diligently on the tops of his towers, which were so high no one could admire them, he answered: "Your Grace, the angels will see them."

Opisso made an album of the numerous photographs that he and Gaudí took between 1892 and 1900 as preliminary studies for the sculptures of the cloister's Doorway of the Rosary and the Portal of the Nativity. In this album Opisso scrupulously recorded Gaudí's comments. The caption for the page shown opposite says: "Years 1892 to 1900. Photos of the models who, once photographed, were cast directly from nature to figure either within the cloister, or on the Façade of the Nativity." It was possible to make casts of living birds. To do this one had to chloroform the birds and then cover their feathers with grease. Gaudí, however, preferred to capture their movement in photographs. The caption, written in Opisso's clear hand, that accompanies the document shown on the right, reads as follows: "Photos of the fowl which were used in modeling the friezes for the Façade of the Nativity." These friezes were placed on either side of the three doorways.

Certainly, however, the most important and fascinating aspect of photography for Gaudí was the snapshot, the isolation of the instantaneous. In the case of a living subject, difficult or at times impossible to shape, the print of the photograph itself became the model. Turkeys spreading their tails, flocks of fowl, flights of pigeons—indeed, any number of subjects—cannot be modeled from nature but can be caught by a camera, making it possible to reproduce them in stone. The task of the sculptors was to effect this transposition with the use of mechanical aids and precise measurements: squaring, enlargement to scale, and so forth. The snapshot could also serve as a base for composition by presenting an image of mobile elements spontaneously assembled. A photograph of children gathered together in a courtyard was used by Gaudí in that way (see page 104) for his preparation of a stained-glass window in the crypt of the *Church of the Sagrada Familia.*

On other occasions Gaudí used snapshots merely for information, in order to work out particular stylizations. In connection with this, Opisso has recounted the anecdote of how Romeo became a gargoyle in the *Park Güell*: "Gaudí needed some photos of a lion's head, with its mouth open. I thought of Romeo and Juliet, a magnificent pair of beasts in the Barcelona zoo, and went there, Kodak in hand, to wait for Romeo to open his mouth. Hours passed, and it was I who yawned with boredom until it was contagious and Romeo succumbed; he opened

his enormous mouth and I clicked the shutter. I returned to the *Sagrada Familia*, developed the negative, and showed the print to Gaudí. He admired it, looked at it once, twice, and finally, staring at me intensely, he said sharply: 'You took the picture from too far away, Ricardo, I think you'll have to take it again up closer.' I returned to the zoo and jumped over the railing that separates the cage from the visitors, but suddenly the beast, on seeing me, roared, became ferocious, and opened his mouth, while I shot a picture point-blank. . . . In the age of Roman circuses Christians were thrown into the arena to be devoured by the lions: I just managed to escape becoming yet another martyr !"

The Cathedral of Chartres is decorated with more than 10,000 statues ! Such an abundance of figures explains why Gaudí, for the *Sagrada Familia*, amassed considerable

ANATOMICAL STUDIES

Fascinated by his research into structure, Gaudí asked Lorenzo Matamala to secure for him some real skeletons which he wanted for the studio at the *Sagrada Familia*. There he would photograph them in every possible position in order to study and capture the harmony of the human body, from its bony framework and movements to its slightest details.

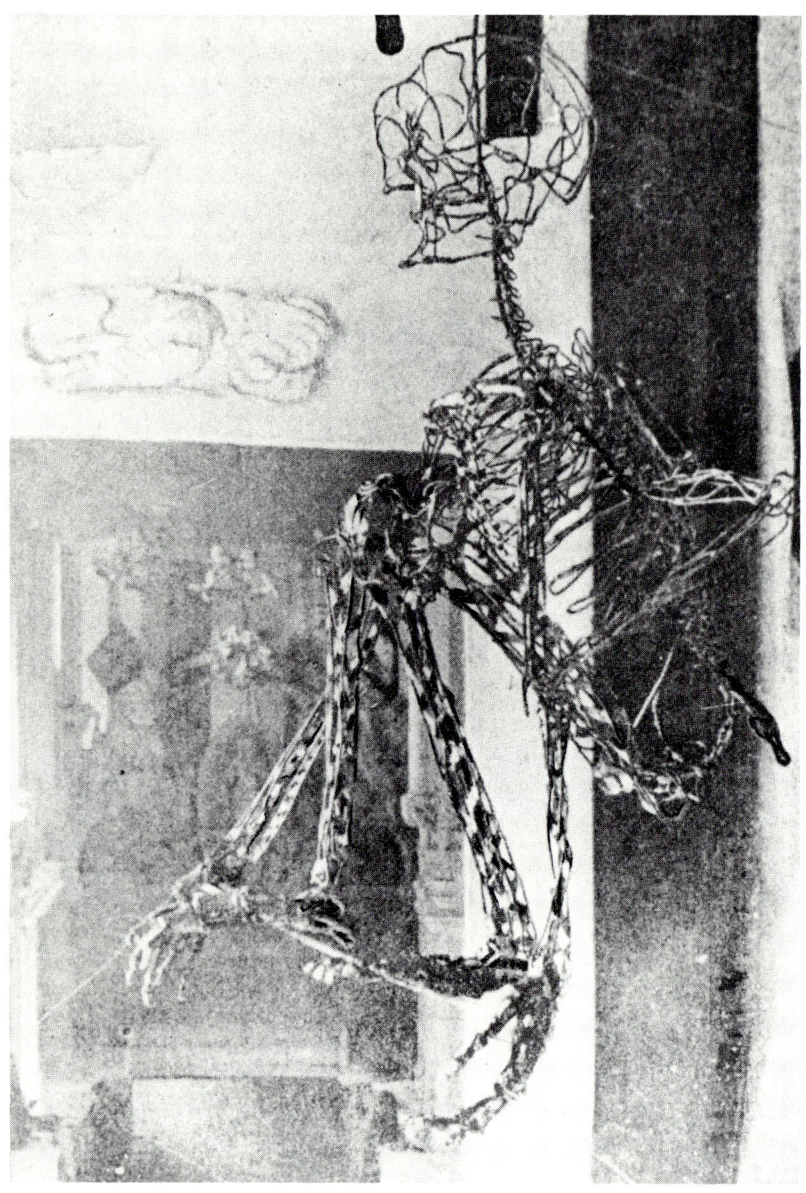

When he was sixty-five Gaudí began to suffer from arthritis and he was advised by his friend Dr. Santaló to do manual exercises every day. He equipped himself with a workbench and a complete set of tools, and set to work making brass figurines and articulated skeletons. The skeleton shown on the right was attached to a cross and for many years hung on his studio wall as a model. This structure served as a basis for further studies, covered with mesh wire. A large number of small metal skeletons (like the one shown on this page), useful because they could be adapted to any desired position, were also used in the studio. They helped Gaudí to discover all the possible nuances of the human body and its plasticity. Today these models have disappeared.

"*. . . if necessary, we will seek unity in variety. . .*"

(Gaudí)

photographic files. Young Opisso was in charge of recruiting models, photographing them, and then filing away the prints. In this way he assembled an archive, thanks to which we know today who the saints and angels and other figures for the Portal of the Nativity were to have been.

Gaudí's workshop was a human Noah's Ark. One would encounter there the most unusual and dissimilar characters of the neighborhood: the bishop and the ragman, a noncommissioned officer and the goatherd, a tavern waiter, a construction worker, a sculptor's daughter, painters and poets who were friends. More than his model's "beauty of form," what interested Gaudí was the truth of their expressions—the inner truth reflected in the features of the face, in gestures, and in the behavior of the being as a whole. The resemblance Gaudí wanted to procure was that of the soul, which for him was beauty itself. The architect José Ráfols wrote: "Gaudí saw the reflection of eternal beauty in life's truth, and a particle of God in each man." In fact, Gaudí's working method may be compared to Dali's, for as Dali has said, "To photograph God is an act of the purest faith, in the most profound medieval spiritual tradition. To do so is to express one's vision by an intensely realistic act!" Unamuno said it once and for all: "realism is the coherence of mysticism."

All those who passed through the Field of the Harp, out of interest, friendship, or habit, and everyone who

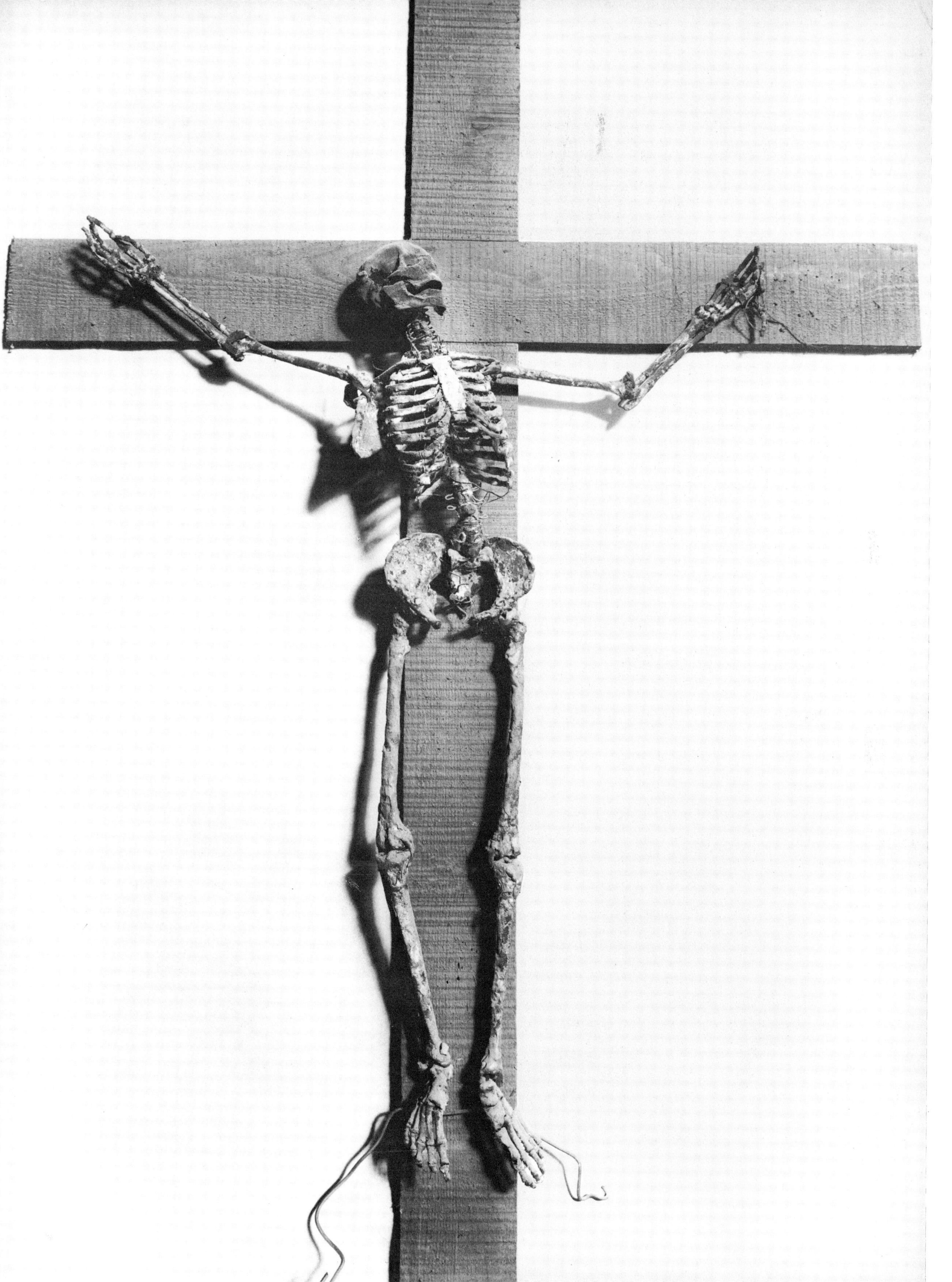

Gaudí made several visits to Majorca in the years between 1904 and 1914 in connection with the restoration of the Cathedral of Palma. There he worked in solitude and extended the scope of his studies, often empirical, of sculpture. He had a number of studies made of the structure of the human body which became models for the execution of this angel; his skeleton-model was covered with a fine and flexible wire mesh which could be shaped.

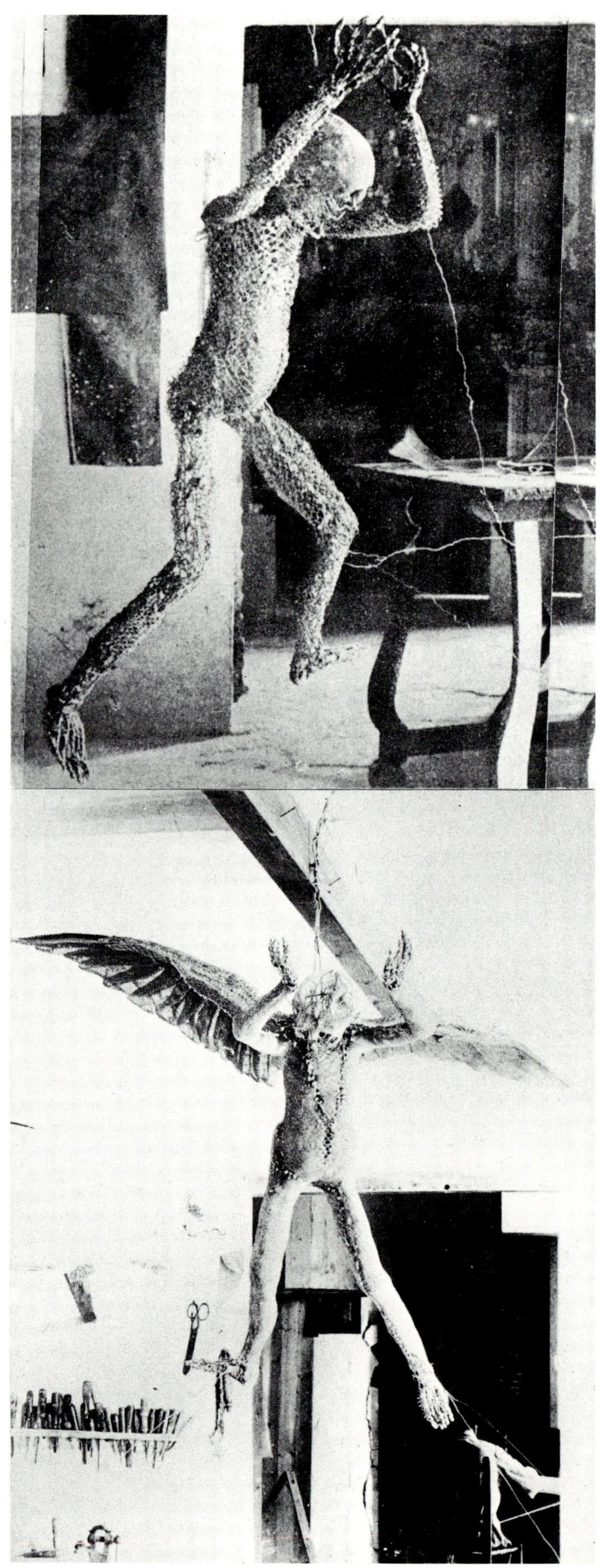

First state

Angels for the baldachin of the Cathedral of Palma in Majorca.

Second state

On this skeleton of the angel that was to support the baldachin of the high altar of the Cathedral of Palma, a metallic netting was inserted where the muscles were located and it swelled like natural muscles, according to the desired movement. The bodily volume thus recreated gave form to the model, and a sense of the inner reality of movement was for Gaudí the breath of life.

Movement was suggested in this model not only by means of the position chosen but also through the addition of extremely realistic symbolic elements, such as the spread wings. The entire model was subsequently covered in plaster (the completed angel weighed more than sixty-five pounds). The statue was then to be painted and gilded to resemble living flesh and assume a nimbus of celestial and angelic light.

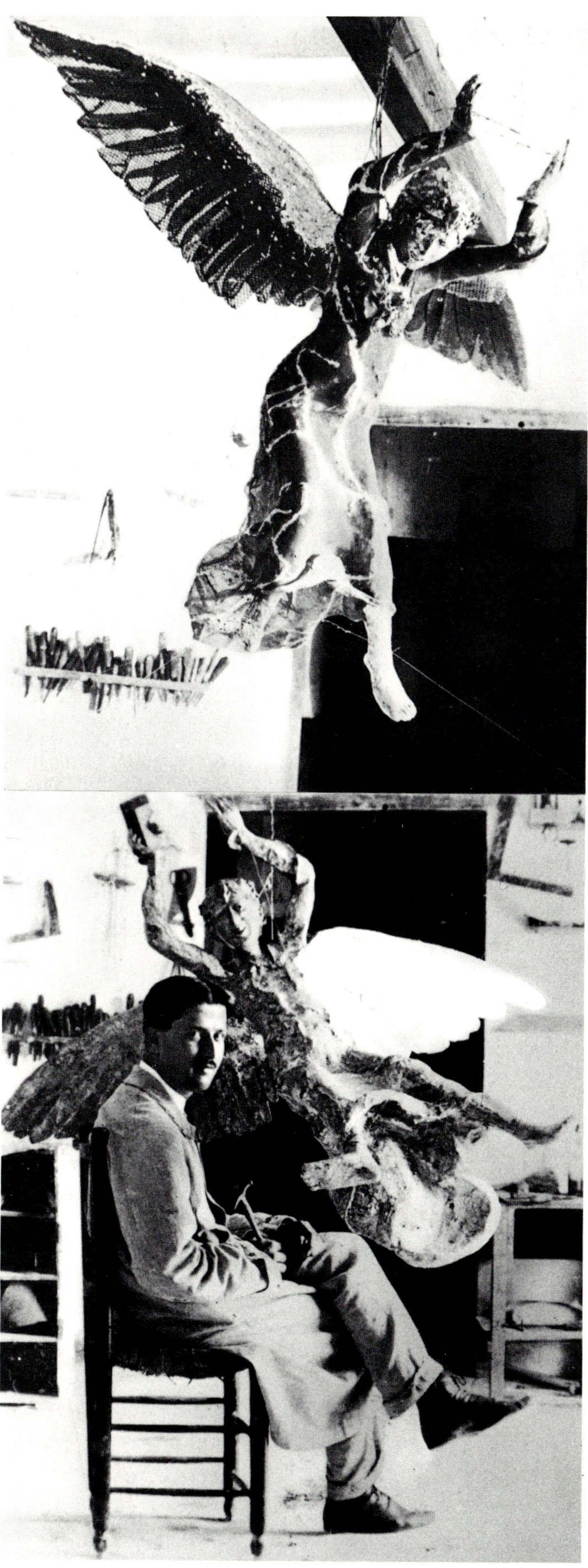

Third state

Angels for the baldachin of the Cathedral of Palma in Majorca.

Fourth state

In 1904 Gaudí entrusted the creation of his angels for the high altar in the Cathedral of Palma to one of his co-workers, Vicente Villarubias (shown in this photograph). The sculptor scrupulously applied the working principles of his master. He also worked with Gaudí on the astonishing model of the *Colonia Güell,* which can be seen in a photograph and a drawing on the following pages.

While he was already working on the portals of the *Sagrada Familia*, Gaudí was put in charge of a projected church for the *Colonia Güell*, a workers' village created by Eusebio Güell, about eight miles to the west of Barcelona, in the midst of the pine woods of Santa Coloma de Cervello. Working from a photograph like the one on the left, Gaudí made the wash drawing reproduced on the opposite page. This sketch of the interior of the church was rediscovered in 1967.

The funicular model for the church of the *Colonia Güell*. It remained intact until 1916, when it began to collapse. Today all that remains are a few photographs taken of the projet. The photograph of the model is reproduced here upside down so that the reader can compare it to Gaudí's drawing. Gaudí's construction of his building models was in this case quite revolutionary. In order to reveal the organization of the architecture, volumes, and the framework of the structure, he assembled his models to hang upside down, working with suspended cords and weights to form a kind of inverted skeleton of the edifice.

Although it was not completed, the *Colonia Güell* may be considered to be Gaudí's true architectural testament, and the Façade of the Nativity of the *Sagrada Familia* his ornamental testament. In making his wash drawing, Gaudí used photographs of suspended models, like the one shown at the bottom of this page. The sketch (above) indicating his vision of the exterior of the *Colonia Güell* contains forms that recur in the *Casa Milá* and in the bell towers of the *Sagrada Familia.*

GAUDÍ
AND THE ARCHITECTURAL SKELETON

Before he made designs on paper, Gaudí would work directly with a model. He used the same methods with architectural models as with studies of skeletons, proceeding with slow and painstaking examination and working with cautious experimentation. Thus, by the time it was possible to take the photograph reproduced here, the experiments undertaken by Gaudí, along with Berenguer on this particular structure, had already gone on for ten years.

This bronze crucifix, inspired by ancient Catalan tradition and intended for the oratory of the *Casa Batlló,* was executed by the sculptor Carlos Mani in 1907 according to the "mirror" method. In the name of bourgeois good taste, contemporary critics, who were particularly fond of pleasant forms, reproached the sculptor for the painful realism of the agonized body.

THE CHRIST AND HIS MODEL

"... as long as I see men dying,
I believe in immortality..."
(Gaudí to Pujols)

Mani chose as his model one of the overseers of the stone-cutters whose features and whose expression the sculptor thought evoked those of Christ, and also, like Christ, the model was thirty-three years of age. Although this crucifix was not made by Gaudí, it bears the stamp of his rigorous working method: the multiplicity of reflections makes it possible for the viewer to embrace the various proportions of the body in a single glance. In accordance with realism, the sculptor has even conserved in the final work the little seat that supported the model while he was being photographed.

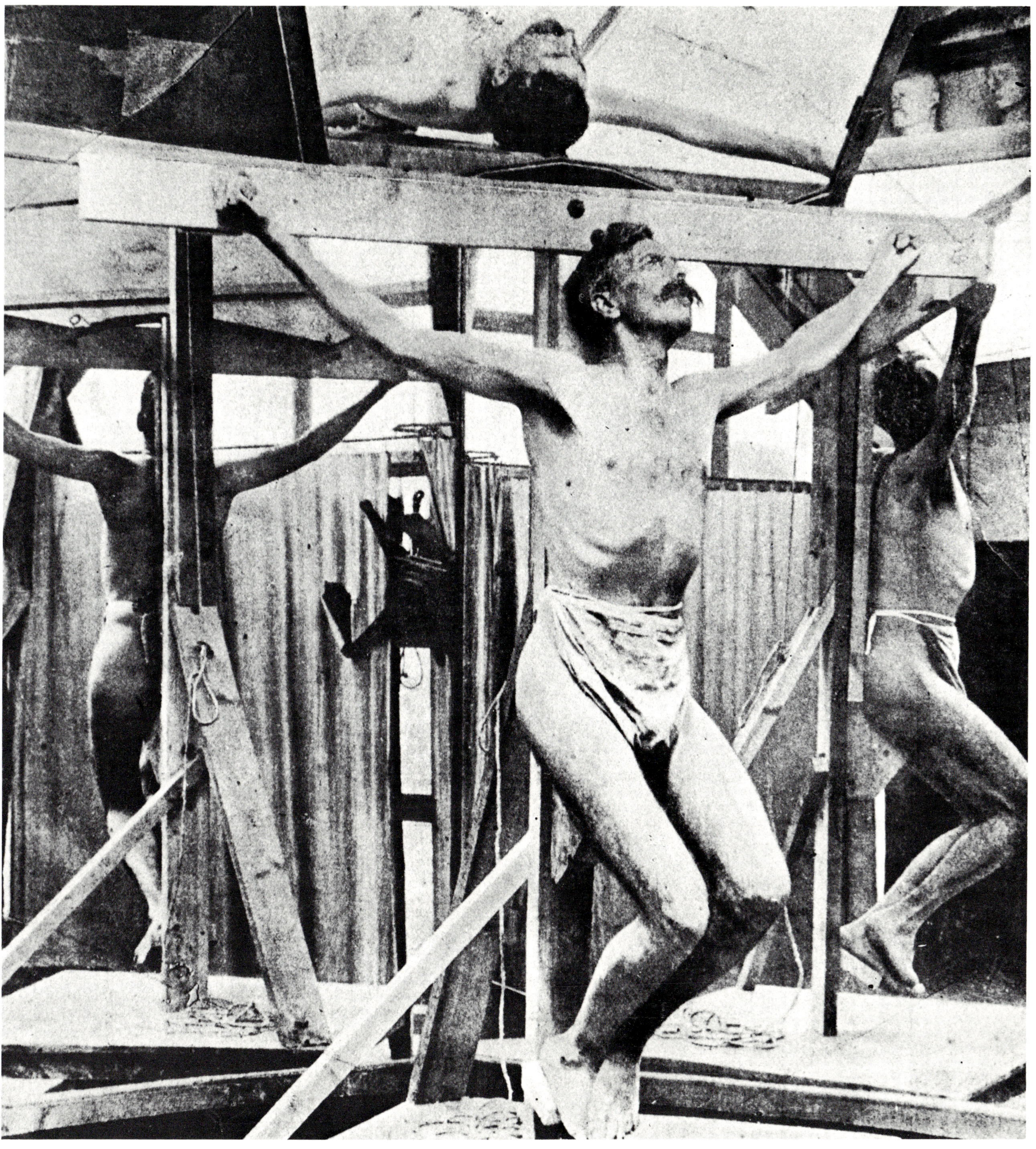

In 1898, Joseph, the caretaker of the *Sagrada Familia* site, was used as a model for Judas despite his given name. Ricardo Opisso has written under this photograph of Joseph and his family that the caretaker died later of delirium tremens.

Gutierrez, a goatherd in the "Poblet" district, known as the "herder with the huge belly." In 1902 he became a model for the Pontius Pilate of the Passion façade. Opisso recounts that he was also called "They're-not-your-onions" — an expression meaning "it's none of your business"—because he repeated the expression incessantly and for no reason, and it was thought to be the equivalent of the words of Pilate before Christ: "I wash my hands of it!"

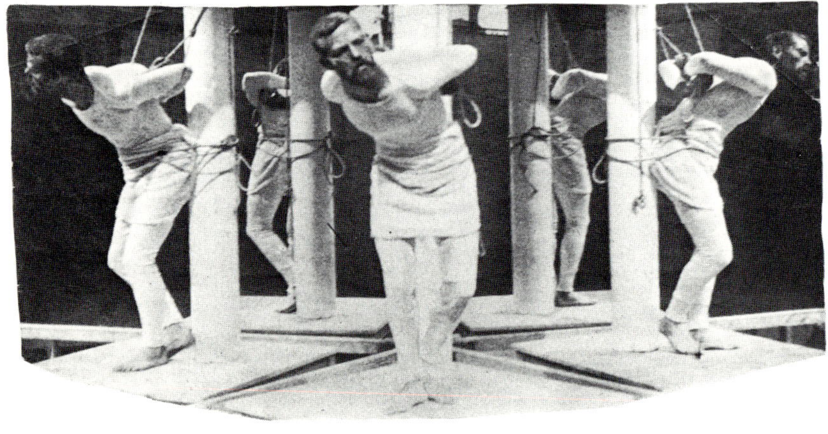

THE MODELS

This "Christ at the Column," studied and photographed with mirrors in 1900, was to become a cast that would be used for sculpting one of the elements of the Passion façade.

This is the model (left) in a 1900 photograph for the musician-angels which were to be placed at the right of the central archivolt of the Façade of the Nativity (the sculptures made from the casts were destroyed in 1936). Gaudí also used photography to create the fall of the angels, who figure in the allegories depicted in Gothic rose windows. The young girl photographed here, the workers at the construction site, their wives, children, and family, the children at the parochial school, newlyweds, in fact the entire *Barrio del Poblet* (People's Quarter), came to be photographed without cost at the *Sagrada Familia* and entered into Gaudí's archives. Ricardo Opisso was in charge of getting the materials together, as well as taking the photographs. The faces of the humble neighborhood people were to become immortal in the sculpture of the church. The architect José Ráfols wrote in 1929 that "Gaudí tries to reproduce life as it is, as if life and art were one and the same thing. It is in this respect that his sculpture is tragic."

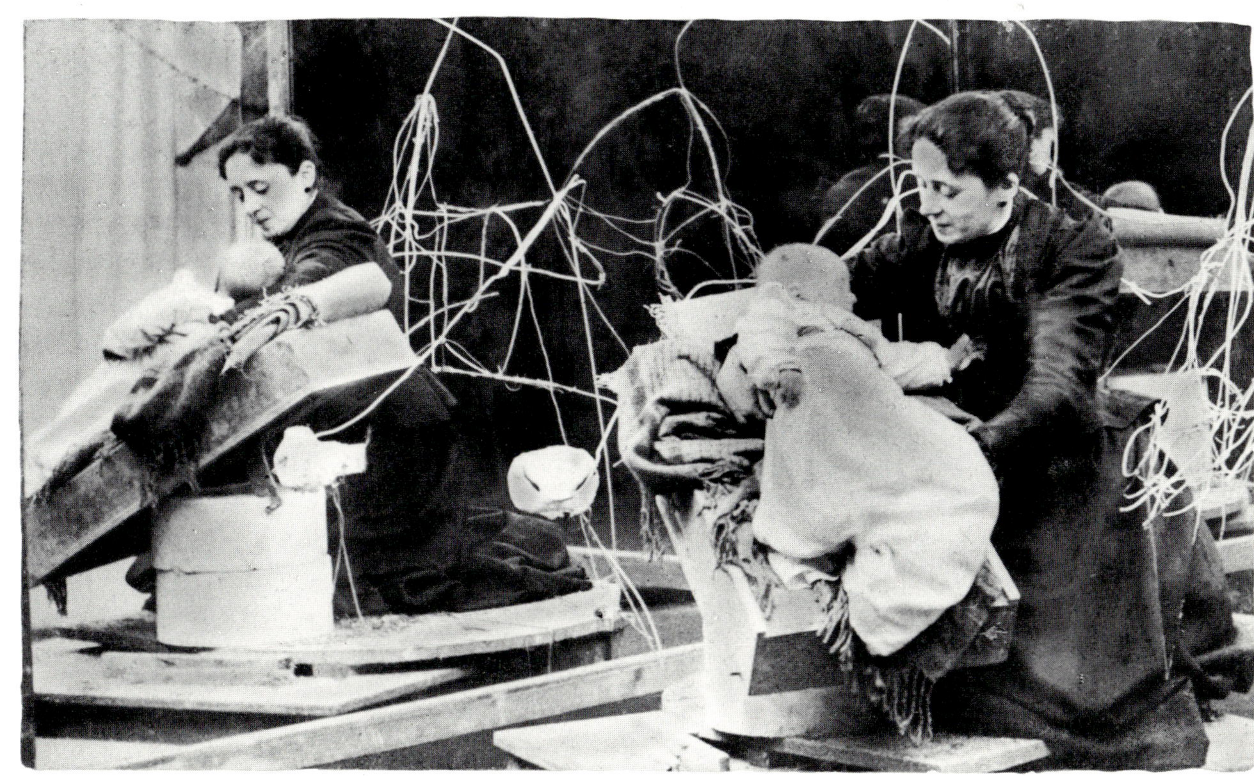

A spinster, a sister of one of the masons at the *Sagrada Familia*, was one of the models for the Virgin. As Ricardo Opisso writes, "This very pious woman wanted to go to the Holy Land when she was young. She left Barcelona and set out on her journey. But after twelve miles, arriving near Premia de Mar, she cried out: 'My God, it's far!' and boarded a train to return home." In this photograph the infant Jesus in the model's arms is the granddaughter of Lorenzo Matamala.

worked there or sought work there, the school children who played in the area, pedestrians and visitors—all were considered possible models for figures on the church façade. Each one could hope to become a stone saint and, while waiting, could get a free photograph of himself. Gaudí did not accept professional models. In choosing his characters he tried to respect the traditional types from Christian iconography and approximate them as nearly as possible. Thus the model for the Christ on the cross was thirty-three years old; the one for the Virgin was a pious spinster; and it happened that "Judas," the caretaker of the site, was to die tragically. A waiter from a tavern was cast as a Roman soldier. He was Tarragonese, and, according to Gaudí, the inhabitants of that ancient Roman colony were similar in type to the Roman emperors and patricians. In the same way, Gaudí thought he could find the Greek type in Ampurdan, and the Phoenician type in the natives of Ibiza.

Often, however, the reasons for Gaudí's choices remain inscrutable, and it is possible to justify some of his decisions only on the basis of the influence of a mystical inspiration. This, for example, is how St. Joseph was

The photographs on these two pages show the collection of casts as it was in 1917: among them are the different elements and individuals destined to decorate the *Sagrada Familia*. They illustrate the extreme realism of Gaudí's works. At the right of the picture below, one can identify the two angels who lean toward the crèche on either side of the Doorway of Charity in the Portal of the Nativity.

chosen. A stonecutter was away from the site for several days, and Gaudí, Juan Matamala, and Opisso went to see him at home. They found him lying on a miserable worn-out mattress full of holes bulging with straw. Several engravings of saints were pinned to the wall. The man's wife knelt by his side and held his hands as they sang a hymn to the Virgin for his recovery. While his assistants were busy comforting the couple, Gaudí murmured to Opisso, "Ricardo, we have found our St. Joseph !"

Often the choice of Gaudí's models depended on chance encounters. According to Opisso, "During a visit from Bishop Torras y Bages, the object of which, apart from his desire to greet the architect, was to examine a project for a bishop's crook (which was never actually made because it was too costly), an infernal racket that managed to reach the roots of the eardrum made it impossible for the two eminent men to carry on their discussion. The strident and discordant din came from two young army recruits who were learning how to play the trumpet, accompanied by drums whose abrupt and terrifying beatings made the studio windows shake. It sounded like the end of the world. Gaudí was beside himself with

This storehouse of casts made from nature is proof of Gaudí's tenacity and the wide range of his means. A series of casts of babies hangs from a beam in the center of the picture; these casts were made by Lorenzo Matamala from stillborn infants at the Santa Cruz Hospital, whose director was one of Gaudí's friends. From the ceiling hang the fruits and flowers of the doorways.

These young soldiers who had once bothered Gaudí by their loud trumpet playing were invited by the architect to pose for the herald angels. They are seen here united in a group, in front of mirrors, for the customary photographs taken by Opisso.

annoyance and cried out in an authoritative and superior tone of voice: 'Ricardo, go down and make those fellows shut up!' As soon as silence was restored, the two sergeant-musicians and their sublieutenant burst into the room and were made even more furious by the fact that Gaudí greeted them tersely in Catalan. The situation took a turn for the worse when Bishop Torres y Bages, throwing his cigarette on the floor, put on his miter, struck the floor with his crook, and strutted majestically up to the sublieutenant to restore peace. Stupefied, the soldiers saluted and stood at attention, petrified before His Excellency. They finally presented their swords and kissed his Bishop's ring. It was an extraordinary scene. When they had calmed down, Gaudí was able to persuade them, with his diabolical cunning, to be models for the trumpeting angels on the large columns of the Façade of the Nativity. They are still there, those three trumpet players whom Gaudí once in anger ordered to be quiet. Their cheeks are puffed out as they blow their trumpets, those noble instruments with souls of air and symbolic of fame, announcing the name of the immortal architect to the entire universe." Ricardo Opisso himself was the fourth trumpeting angel.

One can see that Gaudí's methods of recruitment led him to meet the oddest kind of people. For the King Solomon of the cloister portal he chose a ragman who wandered around the streets of the Ensanche quarter of Barcelona with a wagon of rags and papers. Every once in a while he would stop suddenly and begin to shout in Latin, as he pointed to the sky: "*Ipso facto! Abusus non tolit usum! Amicus Plato sed magis amica veritas!*" ("It is self-explanatory: abuse does not eliminate use!

Even Ricardo Opisso, the photographer, lent his own face and body for a herald angel: today, in the company of the good soldiers, he faces the rising sun, halfway up the two striated columns that support the central archivolt.

To me Plato is dear, but truth is dearer still!") Later, the modeling done, he cried out: "*Consumatum est!*" ("All is consummated!")

At once ornamental and symbolic, and sometimes even in the form of a functional object, the animal world occupies an important place in Gaudí's work. It exists everywhere: in stone, in iron, in ceramic. A "flutter" of birds, their wings spread, makes the *Sagrada Familia* Façade of the Nativity quiver. A bird lightens stone, makes it fly and rise into the air. And Opisso said, "I was, by Gaudí's decree, the executioner of all these birds on the façade. I was the butcher and dissector of animals: I would kill them first and then arrange them with their wings open, once I had removed their viscera, so that the sculptors could use them as models." All these models, from the strangest to the most unexpected, were cast in this way. Following preliminary studies of the skeleton and photographs made with a set of mirrors, plaster casts of them all were made. This was the final step before sculpting the statue in stone. If photography was an avant-garde technique at the time, casting, the second of the preliminary steps, amounted to a sort of "snapshot in relief," well before the invention of the daguerrotype, since Pliny wrote: "The first who effected a man's portrait by casting his face, reproducing the mask with the help of melted wax poured into plaster, was Lysistratus of Sicyon, the brother of Lysippus." And Vasari reports that Andrea del Verrochio made casts of hands, legs, arms, and torsos, in order to copy them when it was convenient. As for Piero della Francesca, it was his custom to make clay mannequins which he would cover with carefully pleated drapery and then copy in his

A tavern waiter, about six feet tall, was discovered by Gaudí and became the Roman soldier for the Massacre of the Innocents on the Doorway of Hope. As it is related by Juan Matamala, "When we asked him to pose, we found that he had six perfectly formed toes on each foot. I still see them. When he was obliged to put a pair of Roman sandals on him, my father wanted to hide one toe on each foot, but Gaudí interfered, exclaiming: 'No, no! On the contrary! It is absolutely necessary to have them the way they are. It is an anomaly, just as it is an anomaly to kill children!' "

This is the plaster model, divided into sections, of the "Roman soldier who grasps hold of a baby as if it were a frog." The alteration of the proportions by enlarging the figure at the level of each joint was necessitated by the distortion due to distance between the viewer and the elevated sculpture. This was the final step before cutting the figure in stone.

paintings. Gaudí used this method in his studies of the clothing for the statues for the *Sagrada Familia*.

The making of casts from nature as it was practiced in Gaudí's day was a delicate operation that demanded great care and was therefore a considerable headache for the architect. This is clear from a manual that was popular at the time: "Unless the caster is certain of his dexterity, he should never try to make a cast of the face or, more especially, of a living person in his entirety, because he runs the risk of seeing his model perish in his hands. The expansion of the plaster requires the greatest speed and skill.... To make a cast of the torso, you make the model sit on a backless seat, having him rest his arms on a support to hold them up; then, with a paintbrush, you cover the skin of his chest with a little olive oil. You take some fine and quick-drying plaster, mix it with lukewarm water, and as soon as it begins to take, you apply it to his entire chest; as quickly as possible you take the long-haired brush that you have been using and place several strands of tow onto the first coat of plaster. This binds the plaster, which you must apply with precision and rapidity. The intense heat given off by the plaster, the humidity, and strong pressure caused by this operation will produce a very dangerous suffocation that could be fatal. Once the plaster has taken and is dry, which should only be a question of a few seconds, you ask the

Fowl were brought to market in Barcelona by train from Salamanca. Upon arrival, flocks of chickens, cocks, and turkeys would cross the field in front of the *Sagrada Familia*. Gaudí could not be indifferent to such a spectacle. Since he could not make casts from life of their feathers in movement, he would photograph them in such a manner that their movements would be captured; then he would study the photographs and cross-rule them, as one can observe in the picture at the right, taken from Opisso's album.

person to get up slowly and move backward as you slowly lift off the cast by its edges, using a strong towel. If you take these precautions, your cast will be intact and similar in front to a cuirass.... It is, above all, in casting the face that the artist needs all his dexterity. First he applies some grease to the roots of the hair, the eyelashes and eyebrows, and the beard, if he doesn't want to lose it, with pomade or some fresh butter. If the model is a man, he must be freshly shaven; then the caster lightly oils the face and wraps it in one or two towels to prevent the plaster from flowing into the hair or the ears. The person must be lying horizontally, with eyes and mouth closed. In order that he may breathe freely, you must place the quill of a feather in his mouth and nostrils. When all is prepared, you mix some very good plaster with lukewarm water and let it take somewhat in order to reduce its effect on the face; then, with a fine paintbrush, you apply the plaster, beginning with the forehead and cheeks and ending with the mouth and the nose. The plaster will take immediately: a minute, at most, is enough. Then you must quickly lift up the model, and

"... the whole Sagrada Familia is nothing but hens and roosters..."
(Gaudí to Pujols)

In his articles Opisso has recorded how the birds had their necks twisted before casts were made. In fact, to avoid the infliction of pain, they were chloroformed, but we must understand how the painful memories of Opisso, who once was himself a model, may have transformed his judgment. In order to verify the realism of the attitudes revealed in the casting, Gaudí had a chicken coop built in the garden outside the sculpture studio, and he scattered life-size plaster casts among the chickens for comparative study. The casts would then be enlarged and the distortions corrected. For the visionary architect, the friezes of fowl corresponded to a symbolic program: they represented the creation of the world. Still, for many observers, these chickens and turkeys were the food of Christmas feasts.

the mask will come loose by itself. In order to prevent bad effects of plaster on the skin, it is necessary to wash the skin with pure spirits, or spirits diluted with a little water. . ." Gaudí and his sculptors proceeded in this very manner—in other words, with many difficulties. Ricardo Opisso, who as we have seen was the fourth herald angel, recalls the biting experience he had at the time (he was then twenty-five years old): "I undressed down to my underpants, and Gaudí imperiously ordered me to assume the pose he had in mind. Then the sculptors Lorenzo Matamala and Ramón Bonet covered my body with plaster. All of a sudden I was overcome by such a bad cramp that I fainted."

In the workshop they made casts not only of people and animals, but of plants, leaves, and fruits and ordinary objects such as the scissors and hammer belonging to Joseph, the carpenter. The ass of the Flight into Egypt was actually cast from life. As Gaudí replied to Juan Bergós when the latter asked about the architect's procedure: "I bought the old donkey from one of the neighborhood laborers. When I saw the animal kicking and pushing against the cast-makers, I had him hoisted into the air in a large girdle. As soon as he felt himself suspended in the void, he remained calm, and it was thus possible to cast him easily."

Photographs of the store of casts (see pages 136 and 137), which no longer exist today, give a good idea of the manifold uses Gaudí made of this process. All the molds were stocked and numbered in the church workshops, as well as in an annex. Some of them were interchangeable and could be assembled as if they were parts of an anatomical erector set. These are the various steps required to make a figure after a living model:

(1) After making studies of ideal structure, expression, and attitude with his small metallic skeletons, Gaudí would apply them to an actual anatomical skeleton. Then he would make rough silhouettes with pieces of wire, approximating the volume of the anticipated sculpture. Following this, the living model, often along with the wire model (see, on page 135, the photograph of the Virgin), was placed in front of a series of hinged mirrors and was photographed. Thus, with the help of the live model, Gaudí would give final shape to his rough model.

(2) The dimensions of the statue were then studied in relation to the location of each element on the façade or within the church and in relation to their liturgical meaning: the statues were enlarged in proportion to their distance from an observer at the foot of the building and according to their relative importance in the symbolic hierarchy, in such a way that each would be visible. Gaudí had written in his journal thirty years earlier: "Art is created by man for man and therefore should be rational, understandable. It is mandatory for sculpture to be positioned in such a way that it will be easily seen; otherwise, it will be superfluous and destroy the ensemble."

(3) A cast of the live model was made, following the pose of the rough model. But casting from nature did not always show the desired movement of drapery or hair.

(4) For this reason, the amount of plaster was reduced by half. Fabrics of varying quality, according to the desired costume, were draped on the preliminary clay study; Gaudí first carefully examined the composition and the pleats that were solidified by coats of plaster. The beard and hair were made of hemp dipped in plaster and sometimes of wire to keep the hair from being blown by the wind.

(5) After the plaster had set, Gaudí made an initial copy out of clay, one-quarter its final size.

(6) A second clay copy was modeled in the desired size.

(7) Because the final model had to be of a substance which could be sawed into sections, the second clay copy had then to be cast in plaster.

(8) The sections were divided according to the future assembling of the stones: at the level of the neck, chest, waist, and knees. The cast model was then hoisted into the appropriate place on the façade.

(9) At this point Gaudí would cross to the far side of the Calle Marina to work out corrections based on the effects of lighting, perspective, and the architectural and ornamental environment.

(10) Like Phidias at the Parthenon, Gaudí would correct the visual distortions by lengthening those elements

1 Frieze of fowl
2 The musician-angels
3 Massacre of the Innocents
4 The Flight into Egypt
5 The herald angels
6 The Nativity: the ass, the ox

The Portal of the Nativity or Portal of Life was in this condition in 1906, with its three doorways, from the left to right, of Hope, Charity and Faith. One can see the six bas-relief friezes of fowl on either side of each doorway halfway up the walls of the foundation, and the brackets waiting to support various sculpted groups such as the Flight into Egypt and the Massacre of the Innocents, on either side of the Doorway of Hope. At that time these groups were no more than plaster casts that were meant to serve as models for the sculptors. However, the scale of the composition is final: in the course of preparations for the last stage, all the plaster casts were put into place on the façade in order to examine any distortions due to perspective, so that changes could then be made on the actual stone sculptures. The musician-angels, located in the archivolt of the Doorway of Charity, and those which surround the crèche were actually in stone and placed on the building, but they were destroyed in 1936 during the Civil War.

Inventory of the church

With the profuse ornamentation of its porches, its vaults of sculpted foliage, the multitude of its outgrowths, the cupolas, towers, and pinnacles, the *Sagrada Familia* is like a forest. Its thousand branches are loaded with fruits and vegetables and innumerable birds, and it is peopled with petrified creatures. Through it resounds the clamor of the streets of Barcelona, the murmur of the fields and surrounding orchards, mixed with the Mediterranean breezes and the bronze song of the bells. The *Sagrada Familia* is the image of the living Creation; the nourishing Catalan earth its flesh and blood, the visible element.

Human

Beggars
A ragman
Women from the "Barrio del Poblet"
Children from the parochial school
Some trumpet-playing soldiers
Stillborn infants
A tavern waiter
The goatherd Gutierrez
An organ builder
An unemployed workman
A carter
A sculptor from the church workshops
A stonecutter
The foreman
The youngest daughter of the chief sculptor
The caretaker of the church construction site.

Bestiary

Shellfish and reptiles
Murex and snails
Salamanders and lizards
Water snakes
Sea urchins
Sea anemones
The web-footed tortoise
The clawed tortoise
The fowls decorating the porches
Roosters, hens, chicks
Turkeys, ducks, geese, and rabbits
Façades alive with wings
Birds in flight
Eagles and doves
Gulls, jays, and nightingales
Nested swallows, pelicans
Signs of the Zodiac
The Ram and the Goat
The Bull and the Lion
The Crab and the Scorpion
The lamb of Abraham's Sacrifice
The ass and the ox
The ass of the Flight into Egypt
Romeo, the lion from the Barcelona zoo.

Flora

Weeds from the site
A dandelion and a thistle
Graminaceae and wild mint
Ears of corn
A cypress from Mont Negre
And its opened fruit
Seaweed and reeds
Moss and ferns
The acanthus and the sacred lotus of the Nile
Mushrooms and buds
Roses
Flowering almond trees
Foliage laden with fruit
Olives, oranges, and pomegranates
Vines with heavy bunches of ripe grapes
Ivy
Palms
Tree trunks
Flexible branches of the nave aisles
The high forest of the aborescent vaults
The trunk-columns of the Sacred Wood.

Mineral

On the wall surfaces:
Living rocks fused together
Flowing lava
The crystalline frost of grottoes
The sands of Egypt and Palestine
The waters of the Nile
And of the Mediterranean
The dew
Drops of blood
The erosion caused by wind and rain
The rocks made jagged by the Tramontane wind
A smooth rock from Montserrat
Hardened snow in stalactites of ice
The constellations of the Zodiac at winter equinox
Their starry concretions
The Star of Bethlehem.

Tools and Instruments

A stick, a sword, a bomb
Saw and T-square
Chisel and scissors
Nails
Mallet and hammer
A hatchet, a workbench
Baskets of braided straw
A boat, an anchor
And the fisherman's lantern
A seat
Trumpets
A guitar and a mandolin
A flute and an oboe
A harp and a violin
Rosaries and crosses.

that appeared too small from below: he would add two to four inches of thickness in stone at the level of the joints, and in this way gradually adjust the proportions until they looked balanced to the eye.

(11) Finally, the plaster cast was taken down, with the corrections noted on blocks that were already roughhewn, and then the definitive figure was sculpted.

Thus the humble parishioners of the Ensanche and the Barrio del Poblet were made immortal in the sculpture of the church, "as if," wrote Ráfols, "life and art were one and the same thing. It is in this respect that his [Gaudí's] sculpture is tragic."

Only the tower dedicated to the Apostle Barnabas was complete a few days before Gaudí died, on June 10, 1926. Gaudí had imagined the four towers of the Nativity as tongues of fire soaring into the Barcelona sky. He had planned to complete the three other towers by giving them forms similar to the first, except for a few modifications in color, which he wanted to be still more brilliant, as was the practice in ancient Greece.

For a few years Gaudí had worked in collaboration with the architects Domingo Sugrañes and Francisco Quintana. Following the master's death these two men took over the management of the site. The Church Junta put Juan Matamala in charge of the sculptural groups for the façade. He was then thirty-three years old. Since his childhood, at his father's side, he lived in Gaudí's world, and from an early age he was studying the sculptor's craft at the studios of the *Sagrada Familia*. Matamala continued working on the sculpture of the church until 1935, the year when all activity at the site was halted. Many years later, in 1950, attempts were made to continue: two new groups were added to the Façade of the Nativity, consisting of, at the center of the portal, St. Joseph and the Virgin bent over the infant Jesus, and above the star of Bethlehem, the Annunciation. These sculptures were not made according to the methods employed earlier; it is easy to detect that they were conceived and executed by someone who had not worked closely with the architect. On the other hand, Matamala, who had not only worked with Gaudí but had lived continuously at his side, knew exactly what he was doing when he had to finish the towers, the lateral lanterns, and the large central cypress, according to the models that had been sent to the Exhibition of 1910 in Paris and which he himself had made, along with Carlos Mani, under Gaudí's direct supervision. "I am the memorialist of the collaboration between Gaudí and Mani!" he said.

Juan Matamala, between 1928 and 1935, made about twenty sculptures that had been planned by Gaudí, and he faithfully followed the principles of his master. These statues included: Jesus as a carpenter; St. Joseph and the Virgin presenting the Christ child at the Temple; the groups of the Visitation, the Marriage, the Coronation of the Virgin, etc., as well as the four Apostles: Barnabas, Simon, Thaddeus, and Matthias.

Inspired by Gaudí's example, the sculptor searched the cathedral site and the streets for models for the apostles and saints, and immediately photographed and made casts of them. In this way he discovered the Apostle Matthias in a pathetic unemployed worker whom he had seen sitting on a bench near the site. As Matamala explained it: After taking a number of snapshots of the man, "I asked him to come and see me about finding a job, but when he reappeared two weeks later with a look of happiness on his face, he was no longer appropriate: he had found work...." The man who posed for the Apostle Simon was a stonecutter from the sculptor's workshop; as for the Apostle Thaddeus, Matamala had met him in the street, perched on a cart. In his own words, Matamala "needed a thin man with fine features, because, according to the Gospel, Thaddeus represents, among the twelve apostles, penitence itself, which one can hardly imagine in the form of a fat man. This carter thought I was about to arrest him for something, but I explained that I was only interested in making a portrait of him so that I might finish a statue I was working on nearby. He followed along with me and would take no payment. Neither would the other models, except for 'Matthias,' who insisted on being remunerated when the time came to make a cast of him." The models for the apostles, photographed, draped, cast, and finally cut in stone, according to Gaudí's techniques, today flank the bell towers that are respectively dedicated to them on the Façade of the Nativity. The position of the sculptures, which were placed half-way up the towers,

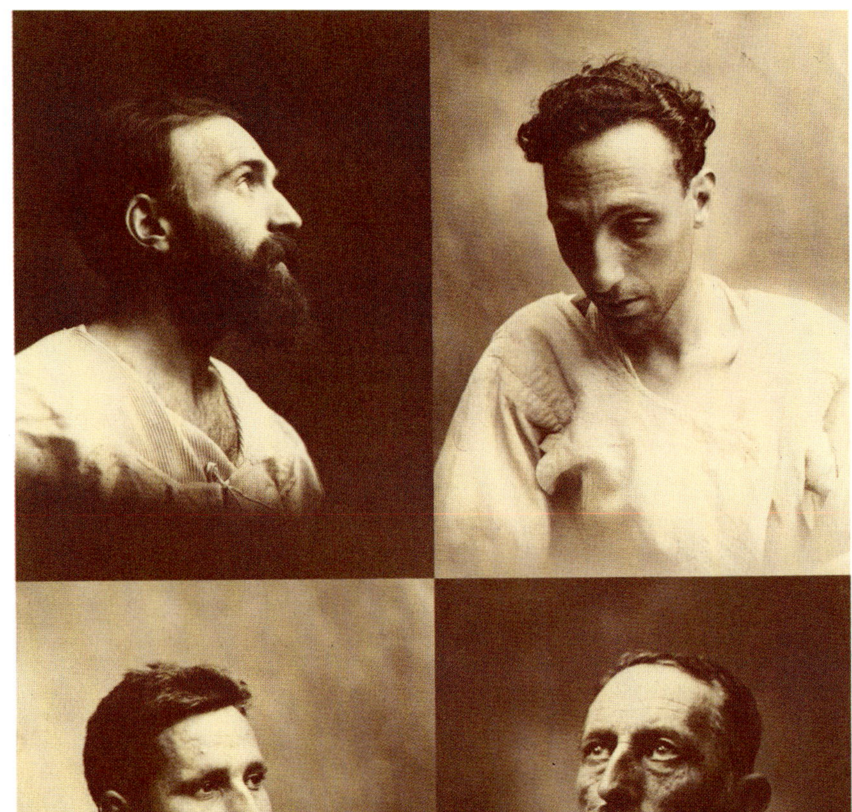

St. Joseph: a stonecutter

The Apostle Thaddeus: a carter

The Apostle Simon: a sculptor

The Apostle Matthias: an unemployed workman

Juan Matamala's photographic file contains this portrait of an organ builder, well known in Catalonia, who was the model for Barnabas. Barnabas, according to legend, received contributions directly from Judeas and represented, both physically and morally, economic and governing authority. Matamala tried to express the spiritual force of this preacher of faith rather than his mysticism.

ENLARGEMENT AND CORRECTIONS

Gaudí never saw this statue of Barnabas, made three years after his death, in 1929, under the direction of Juan Matamala. Here it is seen in its finished form, in the middle of the sculpture studio, where it can be judged for scale alongside the cabinet maker and the stonecutter who are posing at its feet: it measures 10 feet in height. The cutting of the stone was preceded by sketches modeled in clay, then plaster in quarter size, half size, and full size, as they can be seen in the studio (on the right is Thaddeus in the second stage). The face and body of the Apostle Barnabas were elongated to compensate for the optical distortions. In the photograph shown on the far right, the statue is enthroned at the corner of one of the four towers of the Portal of the Nativity, as are Simon, Thaddeus, and Matthias, all of whom are easily identifiable from their names inscribed in Catalan in the stone.

DISTORTIONS OF PERSPECTIVE

"The statue is not a moment of action;
it is the whole act condensed. . ."

(Gaudí)

The model for the Apostle Thaddeus

After the death of both Gaudí and his father, Juan Matamala continued to work on his own with the sculptures for the Façade of the Nativity. He applied the same methods and principles of investigation and execution devised by Gaudí; thus a carter hailed in the street lent his face (above) cast from life, to the statue of the Apostle Thaddeus. Once the preliminary model was finished (at the left), Matamala tried in the darkness of the photographic laboratory to obtain on paper (the pictures are reproduced on the facing page) the necessary distortions for the definitive sculpture.

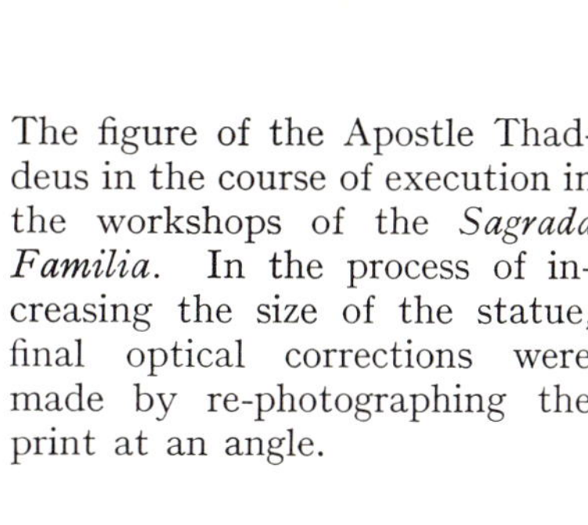

The figure of the Apostle Thaddeus in the course of execution in the workshops of the *Sagrada Familia*. In the process of increasing the size of the statue, final optical corrections were made by re-photographing the print at an angle.

created a visual distortion that had to be corrected. In order to do this, Matamala followed Gaudí's rigorous methods of the Greeks.

The following year the outbreak of the Civil War, and in 1936 the disappearance of Domingo Sugrañes, interrupted all construction work. The workshops of the church were ransacked and burned, all the archives disappeared, the casts were destroyed, and many sculptures on the façade were broken and chipped, especially the musician-angels of the central portal.

Many critics have developed theories about Gaudí's sculpture, in his own day and in ours. None of them has been able to explain it, but they have all written on the state of uneasiness which his sculpture seems to provoke. To realize this, all one has to do is to read the manuscript notes of one of Gaudí's closest collaborators, Ricardo Opisso: "If Goethe has written: 'Nature is a goose which we try to transform into a swan!' it is the contrary with Gaudí! His sculpture is but the slavish copy of living reality: it is exempt from the mystical aroma exhaled by the statues in Gothic cathedrals. . . But it participates in the astonishing and unquestionable unity of the motifs of the Façade of the Nativity."

Explanations and theories about his sculpture are irrelevant, however. Gaudí's only concern was with saints and angels, and both for him and for Dali, saints and angels are "the winged vehicle that leads to God. The mystics see the angels before they find God."

Christ crowning the Virgin, and St. Joseph kneeling at their feet, framed by a Gothic rose window (on the facing page), are located above the central archivolt of the Nativity façade. This group was sculpted in 1934 under the direction of Juan Matamala.

The plaster model for the Coronation of the Virgin was photographed before it was enlarged to its final proportions and was then divided into sections so that corrections in relation to perspective could be made. The group, a pyramidal composition, rests beneath a parabolic arch of stalactites, made, in this photograph, out of wood.

Angels commissioned for a special service (the first mass celebrated by Father Norberto Font y Sague) were for Gaudí a pretext for making a study of the way a body falls through space. In this drawing of 1900 a variety of positions recreate bodily movement. The angels of the Nativity façade, on the opposite page, represent the culmination of Gaudí's research. They surround the rose window and fall toward the Christ and Virgin, singing, with parted lips and eyelids closed, the "Sanctus Deus."

SPACE - COLOR - SCULPTURE

. . . *The* Park Güell, *masterpiece of* modernista *"total art"*. . .

In the *Park Güell,* as Dali wrote about this photograph, which appeared in *Le Minotaure* in 1933, "one can penetrate into the grottoes through doors shaped like calves' livers." This grille opens into the caryatid gallery (below).

Amid the palms and the pines of this fabulous park, the treelike columns of the gallery, covered with stone mosaics, turn into naïve caryatids, and seem to lean with the winds that blow from the sea, as they support long porticoes which are cool and shaded against the full summer heat. The twisted crutchlike columns that support the terrace are mixed in with wild Virginia creepers, and seem to extend them (below, right).

CHAPTER VII

Gaudí and Nature: The Nourishing Catalan Earth

. . . a polychromatic architecture, sonorous, plantlike, and geological. . .

Leaving the grotto of Montesinos, Don Quixote cried out: "This isn't hell, it's a region of marvels. Sit down, my children, listen carefully, and believe what you hear." As Eugenio d'Ors has said: "Sometimes I must confess that I cannot think without terror of the destiny for our poor people, who must manage to sustain, on a delicate balance, the weight, grandeur, and glory of those two sublime anomalies: the poetry of Maragall and the *Sagrada Familia*." As an illustration, think of Maragall's poem in which he tells about the arrival in Catalonia of a Carlist revolutionary soldier from Madrid, who, in Castilian, asks a woman in the fields, "Where are the men?" Because she replies in *catalán*, he cuts out her tongue and repeats, "Where are the men?" but her eyes still answer in *catalán*, so he puts out her eyes, asking once again, "Where are the men?" The vibrations emanating from her body are still intolerably Catalan, which is why he kills her. But what the soldier didn't know, concludes Maragall, is that a child lived in the woman's womb, and that this child's heart would continue to beat in *catalán*. . .

Maragall's *Enlla* appealed to Eugenio d'Ors as the sharpest and most strident example of Latin romanticism—indeed, of romanticism in general—and as "otherworldly" as Gaudí's works. Neither one nor the other can be understood without a feeling for the elemental Catalan excess from which they spring, without knowing the exaggerated steps that led to the creation of the *Sagrada Familia*. Maragall spontaneously remarked, "It is necessary to know just when one can go too far." In Catalonia one must always know just when one can go too far. This is the process of all growth. Vegetables and all living organisms are formed in this way: by dynamic expansion and attraction of similar elements deriving from a single seed. Thus the *Sagrada Familia* was the product of an unbounded vision and a slow, difficult constructive mechanism. One must simply try to imagine how the church would have been had it been completed: its size, its appearance, the enormity of the whole complex, the giant *torchères* burning day and night, the running water, the sound of the wind continuously blowing through the twelve bell towers built for this purpose, the choirs and the music spilling out into the streets, the mobile angels turning slowly in the sky, the incredible mixture of colors—for one always forgets that every last detail of the sculpted elements was to be in polychromy like the Greek temples!

It is often said that there are two types of artists: one type imprints his own vocabulary on the world's page; the other type imprints his own page with the world's vocabulary. Gaudí belongs to neither category, and for this reason it is difficult when discussing him to speak of art in the classical sense of the word. Gaudí's vision, like Maragall's, takes off from Catalonia and ends up in Catalonia; Catalonia itself is the master of his creations. Someone once remarked to Gaudí that this notion was interesting enough, but that everyone knew he had rarely been out of the country, and that Catalonia had never really proved anything at all in any realm whatever; Gaudí exclaimed heatedly, "All the more reason then! We must believe that she can become something. All that remains for us to do is to get to work." He would exhort students and others who came to the site of the church to contribute according to their abilities to the creation of the church in a spirit of sacrifice.

The aim was not to create a work of art. It was at first to make something of Catalonia with Catalonia. It is essential to understand this point. Since it was destined to shine across the entire world in the sacred name of the Catholic religion, the *Sagrada Familia* was to be nothing less than the church of Catalonia, the very expression of Catalonia's spirit, its living manifestation. The only lesson that will mean anything to a Catalan is that which is expressed in the purest realism. The only transcendence that exists in the Catalan's world is that which is contained in substance itself—under the circumstances, his own soil—and he must reveal this transcendence. Thus Gaudí was successful in achieving a double *tour de force:* he gradually introduced to the astonished and troubled eyes of the children of Barcelona, under the pretext of building a large church, the very soul of their country; and he also gave to the Catholic religion, under the pretext of realism, a completely unprecedented and singular dimension, something "uncomfortably provocative, fortunately unpleasant, and for this reason immeasurably useful," as Dali put it; "a generator of remorse of the conscience, a performance not achieved by any other Christian iconography for centuries, except perhaps the Saint-Sulpician iconography of Paris."

Gaudí, who could not bear abstraction, went, with rage, through the 1917 Exhibition of French Art in Barcelona, calling each Fauve or Cubist canvas a scandal, an abomination, a worthless nothing; he did admire Fortuny as a painter because of his passionate veristic exactitude, and possibly because the painter was also born in Reus, yet in sculpture he would tolerate only details that were in strict accord with the sought-after goal of the artist. It was not enough, in his opinion, to give the merest detail of a bird or a leaf the appearance of life by means of skillful casting. Skill was not enough; one must put the parts in proper order into a perfect context.

As an example, the façade of the *Sagrada Familia* opens in three doorways. The middle one represents the deep grotto of Bethlehem, full of flowers and birds in flight. Nebulous and imprecise forms emerge from the archivolt. His use of intense azure evokes the color of a clear winter night, with constellations of white almond flowers and twinkling stars. The constellations of the Zodiac are shown in their exact positions: Taurus and Gemini where they happened to be on the day of Christ's birth, with the great Star of the East above the *Pessebre,* a polychromed Catalan manger.

Ricardo Opisso wrote that "the entire ensemble recalls more the explosion of a spring day than the harsh solitude of winter." To counter this springlike impression, Gaudí thought of placing at the crest of the three portals symbolic icicles and immense stalactites, as an allegory of winter; the icicles would be meant to make observers shiver with cold.

All the beauty of the plant and animal kingdom is there with "the skylarks, the sparrows, and the owls, which fly by the great open doors along with fowl from the farm"—in the words of Francesc Pujols. The fact of having put hens and roosters on the façade of a church caused quite a scandal. To Gaudí they corresponded to a poetic symbol of the Creation of the world, but to many others they were fowl for a Christmas feast.

On the right side of the façade the Doorway of Hope, with the Flight into Egypt, is closest to the sea and is filled with marine imagery. It is dedicated to the kingdom of water, with lotuses, papyrus, palms, ducks, and the web-footed sea tortoise. All the vegetation of the Nile blossomed out in tones of green that graduate to a purplish blue toward the top.

The doorway on the left, that of Faith, with Jesus as an apprentice carpenter, is the most northerly, in the direction of the mountains of Catalonia. Dedicated to the kingdom of the earth, and with its imagery of the flora and fruits of the field, scrub vegetation, and land tortoises with clawed paws, the Doorway of Faith was to be the color of burnt sienna, like the sands of Palestine.

In Gaudí's mind all these sculptural elements could not attain their definitive glory or fulfill their true role without being colored, a primary condition of mimesis. Art as a whole is the world of reflections, and as Gaudí wrote more simply in his journal of 1878: "Art is beauty, beauty is life, which color alone can express." And he added: "Ornamentation has been, is, and will always be polychromatic. . . Coloration may disappear, but time will see that it is replaced by that proper and precious patina of antiquity. Who doesn't recall the golden tonality range of the stones of the Mediterranean regions? Doesn't a recently finished building display a repellent coldness? . . . When the natural coloration of time is not present, painting is indispensable. . . ." [5]

Since ancient times in Catalonia, polychromy has been an essential element of architecture. Gaudí related this tradition to Mediterranean culture and antique art, in which light and colors were inseparable, having mutually engendered each other. As Hittorff has proven, the Greek monuments were painted, and we know from other sources that their colors were even more glowing by the use of beeswax encaustic. According to Gaudí, the Greek temples could be seen from a great distance because their lines were sharply defined and their elements simple, with no flourishes and no disorder. Distance played a great part, and the intensity of the light made it necessary for violent colors to be used. Gaudí claimed that the *Sagrada Familia* derived from the purest Hellenic tradition, and he sought to give it Hellenic aesthetic qualities: a precision and rhythm of lines, a harmony of proportions, and a vigor of forms defined by color. It might be surprising to compare the *Sagrada Familia* with the linear purity of a Greek temple. Yet this is what Gaudí thought should be done, and indeed he claimed to have been influenced essentially by Greek art. The archivolts of the portals and the sculptures were to be entirely painted. "The Greeks," he said, "never hesitated to paint the marble of their temples—a marble as crystalline as sugar and of great beauty—for color is life. . . We must draw inspiration from it directly." He reserved the most intense polychromy for the lower parts of his buildings, those that are least likely to be struck by the rays of the sun. The central archivolt of the actual façade was to be painted a deep blue, like the tympanums of Greek pediments, so that the blue would absorb the shadows of the statues, whose vivid colors would then be more clearly distinguished. To the architectural role of color was added a symbolic and liturgical meaning. Within the cathedral the right aisle was to be white and gold, symbolizing joy, The left aisle, leading from the Portal of the Passion, was to be painted in purple and black tones, colors of mourning and penitence.

Following the popular Catalan tradition of ceramic revetment, Gaudí covered the tops of the spires of the *Sagrada Familia* with Venetian gold mosaics, and dreamed of adding them as a veneer to the undersides of the vaults, cupolas, and domes of the church, as was done in the most luxurious Byzantine basilicas and as he had done in the Cathedral of Majorca. The "Sanctus" motifs that are sculpted on the towers of the Façade of the Nativity stand out in glazed polychrome ceramic from the rough stone and emphasize the spiral bracing of the bell towers. As Martinell lyrically phrases it: "The Sanctus, Sanctus, Sanctus. . . they coil around the towers in triple dedication to the triple Father, Son, and Holy Spirit. The first Sanctus, dedicated to the Father, will be yellow, like the light of the sun. The second, dedicated to the Holy Spirit, will be orange; and the third, dedicated to the Son, will be vermilion, the martyr's liturgical color. The Holy Spirit's orange will unite the Father and the Son, like a blend of yellow and vermilion. And each of the three tones will stand out from its sober complementary color: violet, blue, and green. There will also be some aluminum-painted stars on a white ground to give life to the stone. And all who read this banderole will intone a hymn to the Holy Trinity as they, in discovering them, murmur 'Sanctus, Sanctus, Sanctus' . . . and the song will draw their gaze upward to the sky."

Arousing some thoughts that we may have long forgotten, Gaudí explained that "writings on stone are like dewdrops in the grass. The Arabs have long known how to make majestic use of the process." Thus, mixed in with the sculpture on the church are fragments of psalms, Christ's initials, and various emblems, such as an entire rosary (fifteen decades) strung across the façade. As Gaudí said further, "Each element of the Creation possesses not only its own color but its own particular sound. The air is their common vehicle. This is why it would not be enough to want to reproduce solely the light of our Mediterranean sky." He planned to attribute a different note and different qualities to each of his bell towers. The very material used for the bells was analyzed

The athletic prowess of the "Xiquets," young gymnasts from the little town of Valls, near Tarragona, were famous throughout Catalonia. Gaudí recognized the laws of equilibrium and the form appropriate for the towers of his church in the "castles of the Xiquets," human "castles" six "floors" high, which are still performed today.

in relation to the climate, the hygrometric degree of the air, and the atmosphere at varying times of day. Some of the bells were intended to ring most particularly at dusk, the hour at which Gaudí thought that bronze harmonized most expressively with the surrounding atmosphere. On certain days he would arise at dawn and travel to various parts of the city to observe the direction of the winds in the early hours of the morning; he would look for particular phenomena, such as the quality of vibration produced by one or another apparatus of his invention, and he desperately tried to find ways of reproducing the extreme sounds at the limits of human perception. The helical form itself of the church towers played the double role of transforming sound and light. Francesc Pujols wrote in 1914, in his inimitable style: "So do let Gaudí make a wind tower for the four winds that will show their direction like the rose of the winds and will whistle and howl like the winds themselves . . .

According to Juan Matamala, another perfect form of nature—the egg —inspired Gaudí's project for a lecture hall which was prepared for a professor who was reluctant to raise his voice in order to be heard. The architect is said to have recommended that the walls be curved in, so that everything the professor said would reach even the students farthest from him. The oval form of the egg seemed to him to be the perfect volume. Juan Matamala has drawn this sketch (above) of the unfulfilled project. The same sinuous rhythm is evident in the amazing little parochial school of the *Sagrada Familia* (left).

It would have to be higher than the entire city! its trumpets will be oriented toward the sunset and its flutes toward the sunrise so that the winds from the east and from the west would play them. There will be cornets for the *garbi* (the southwest wind), horns for the *tramontana* (the north wind), and flutes for the *marinade* (the east wind), which will blow over all of Barcelona. The *garbi* will sing 'Gaudí! Gaudí!' and the reddened sky will signal the rains and the winds, and the soundings of the trumpets and all the wind instruments like so many petals of the rose of the winds. The people of Barcelona will have only to listen to the bells to know the direction of the wind; and what the wind knows and the torrent doesn't know, the instrument of the tower of the winds will know. . . and the whirlwinds will sound all the instruments of the tower of winds as if with the winds the rose of the winds will shed its petals which the winds will scatter to the four winds. . ."

The project of 1892–93 for the Franciscan Mission in Tangiers is a good illustration of Gaudí's love for nature: the towers have the form, both light and sturdy, of certain kinds of sea shells. Gaudí studied nature's most intimate structures, and was not afraid to borrow from it elements of decoration and structure.

In the *Sagrada Familia* one comes across the towers originally designed for the Tangiers project; shells like these at the right may have inspired their helical development. Gaudí said that "the form of the church's towers, vertical and parabolic, is a union between gravity and light."

The opened fruit of the cypress lends its form to the cross that one sees on all of Gaudí's buildings, whether religious or secular. Placed on the top of the cypress that surmounts the Nativity portal of the *Sagrada Familia,* this mosaic cross symbolizes the energy and vigor of Catholicism by the blossoming of the ripe fruit.

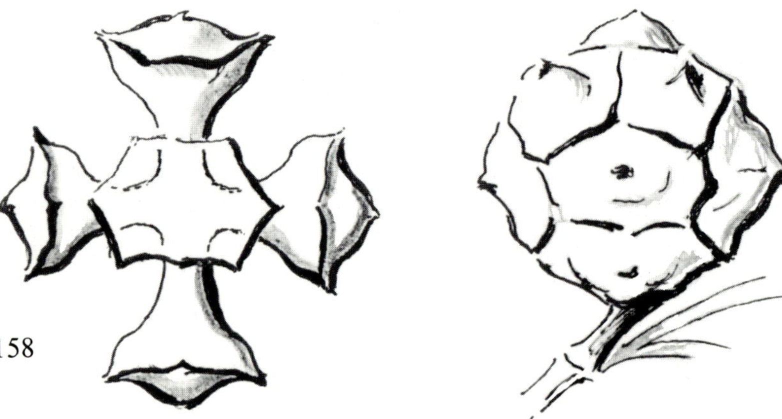

Gaudí's enthusiasm for the naturalism of forms coincided with the publication in Barcelona, in 1903, of the art critic John Ruskin's works, in which the Englishman upholds nature as the unique source of inspiration.

Deeply opposed to the superficial dynamism of the traditional baroque style, Gaudí still managed to incorporate unheard-of elements into his architecture: elements of muscle, bone, fish scales, seeds, flowers (*Casa Batlló*), trees (*Park Güell*), foam, water currents (*Casa Milá*), ice, smoke, and clouds (*Sagrada Familia*). These various elements have no intrinsic value, but they serve to suggest an integration between the building and the landscape. In this relationship lies all the originality and the true *raison d'être* of naturalism, which means, not making a chair with feet in the form of dog-paws, but making a dog-chair. Nor does naturalism consist in ornamenting a façade or a balcony with a bouquet of stone irises, but rather in constructing the whole balcony in the form of an iris. Spreading out his fingers, Gaudí would exclaim, "Look, these are paraboloids," and then demonstrated how one had merely to turn from the waist, arms extended for helical forms to appear. Thus he suggested that one observe the profusion of curved surfaces in nature and the hidden grace of certain forms, however extravagant their appearance. In this fashion apparently elusive elements would be re-created, as were those in the *Casa Batlló*: as Dali wrote in 1933 in the surrealist magazine *Le Minotaure,* "The house built by Gaudí on the Paseo de Gracia is made of the tranquil waters of a lake. This is not a question of deceptive metaphors or fairytales, etc.... this house exists... It is a real building and the true sculpture of the reflections of twilight clouds in the water, which was made possible by recourse to a huge and insane multicolored mosaic, shining with pointillistic iridescence from which the forms of water emerge, water that has spread and is spreading, forms of stagnant water; forms of shimmering water, forms of wind-sprayed water: and all these water forms designed in an asymmetrical and instantaneously dynamic succession of reliefs broken and syncopated by, interlaced and mingled with, 'naturalistic-stylized' water lilies and Nymphaea... This building, therefore, was built to be habitable (and also, for me, edible), and with the reflections of twilight clouds on the waters of a lake, the work should also convey the maximum amount of naturalistic rigor and *trompe-l'œil.* I declare that this

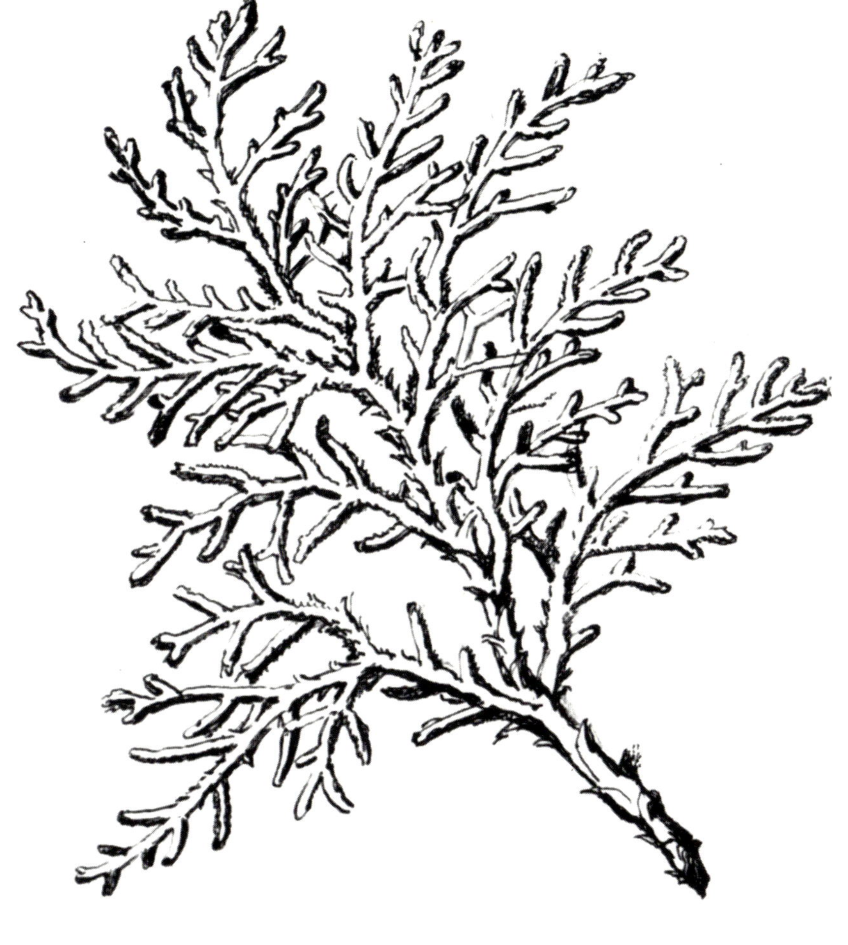

The mythical meaning of the tree was dear to Gaudí. For him it meant, above all, the "tree of life," a symbol of immortality and incorruptibility. In the compact tangle of the ceramic branches of the large cypress (at the right is a detail), alabaster doves are nested. The drawings reproduced on these two pages are by Juan Matamala.

work represents a gigantic step beyond the simple Rimbaudian submersion of a salon at the bottom of a lake."

Mosaic was used extensively by Gaudí, usually in the form of scraps of ceramic and broken bits of colored glass. These materials were chosen not simply as a result of Gaudí's modest finances but as part of his general conception of polychromatic ornament. Catalan tradition dictated his choice of other materials. In his journal he wrote: "These other materials should include unpolished ashlar, brick, and terra cotta for ornament, and sometimes bronze, iron, and lead, but rarely wood." [4] And these are precisely what he used: stone and brick are standard in his works. These are furthermore the materials of the soil, hence the most economical: stone that was excavated on the construction site, and brick that was made on the site out of clay from the surrounding plains. However, Gaudí eventually started using new techniques that came from England and France; he was one of the first in Spain to use reinforced concrete, at the *Park Güell*; and at the end of his life he considered steel and concrete the

CATALAN GEOLOGY

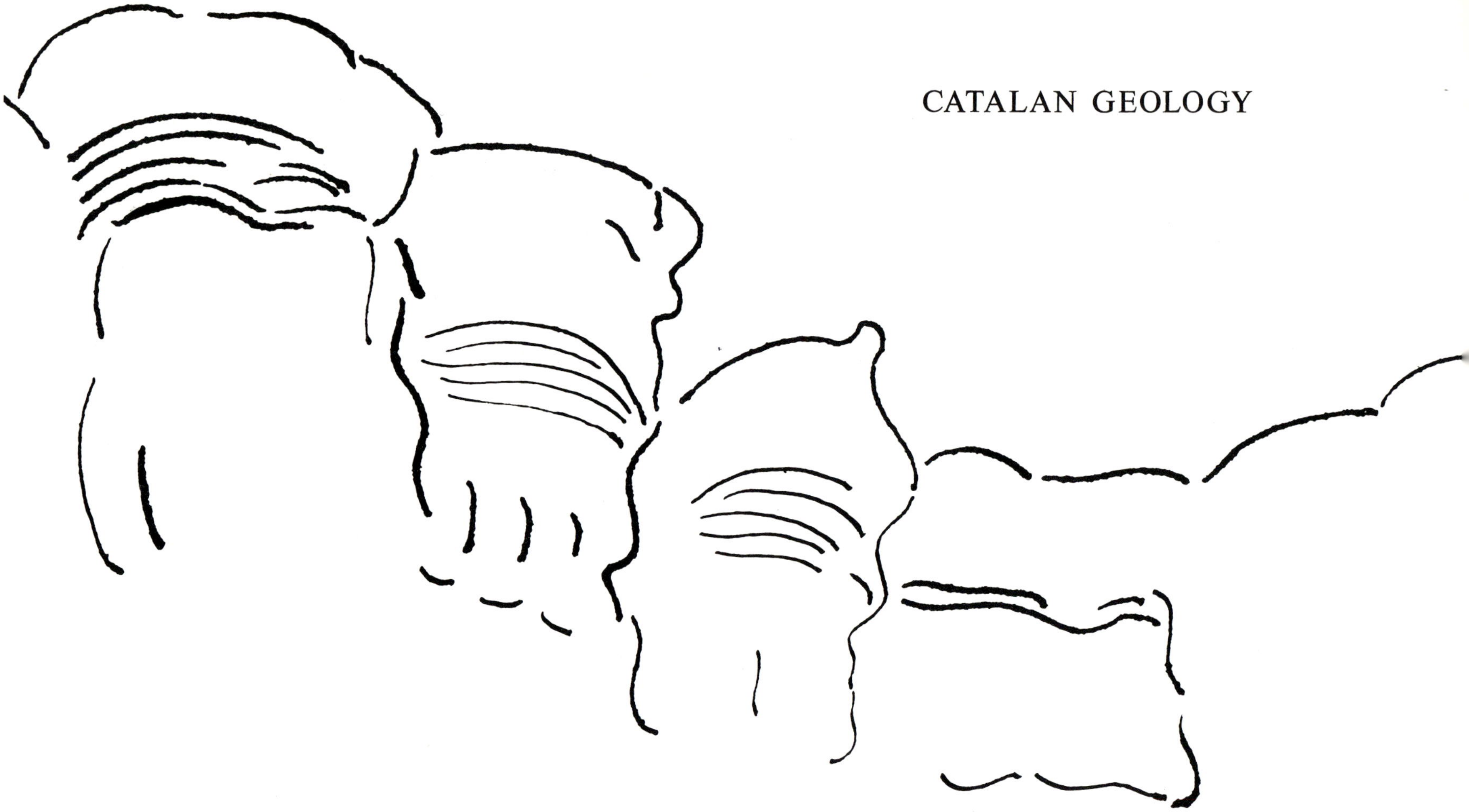

The rocks of San Miguel del Fay, in a drawing by Juan Matamala. Matamala still remembers how Gaudí liked to go on archeological tours of Catalonia: "Gaudí knew every part of the province; he was a most eager excursionist! He was a member of the 'Catalanista Association of Scientific Excursions,' which was founded in 1876 . . . The hikers arrived one day at the hermitage of San Miguel del Fay, about twelve miles north of Barcelona. The sanctuary sits on a high rock-ledge of white limestone which juts out from a bed of red rocks. Partially petrified cascades dominate this strange bluff. There, one can still visit an ancient troglodyte's chapel . . . This extraordinary landscape certainly influenced Gaudí when he designed the project for the *Casa Milá* in 1905."

Gaudí often went to Montserrat, where as a student he assisted in work on the project for a sanctuary. Struck by this sweep of sandstone with its strange polished reliefs, a kind of Wagnerian phantom, whose immeasurable domes and pinnacles rise in the middle of Catalonia, he used their forms and dynamism in some of his constructions.

materials best adapted for his interior structures of the *Sagrada Familia.* Gaudí thus re-evaluated the artistic possibilities for these materials, but he also gave new meaning to traditional Catalan ornamental art. Ornament was to be integrated into the architecture, it was to become constructive: the Catalan tile vault and the stone column were combined with the wrought iron of the grilles and the balconies, as well as with the polychromed veneer of the walls. He used materials and colors to emphasize his volumes: at the *Park Güell* the roughhewn stone of the columns of the viaducts is, in its regularity, in contrast with the unpolished stone that falls in stalactites from the vaults, while a mosaic of little white pebbles outlines the ribs of the groin-vaults. In the crypt of the *Colonia Güell* gray basalt piers and columns of brown and purplish brick support a brick porch incrusted with mosaics that are glazed with vivid colors. For Gaudí, polychromy itself could constitute a landscape. A combination of burnt browns and mortar of slag and ferruginous stones gives the lower levels the exact tone of sandy terrain; up above, the gray is silvery and similar to the color of the trunks of the pine trees that surround the building; even higher up are purplish greens and blues created with materials glazed to harmonize with the nuances of the tops of the trees and the hillsides that nail the horizon to the sky. Textures that are smooth or rough, amorphous or leafy, as well as brilliant or dull colors—all are blended together in the light.

Such is the case at the *Casa Milá,* known also as the *Pedrera* or "Quarry," where the wrought iron of the

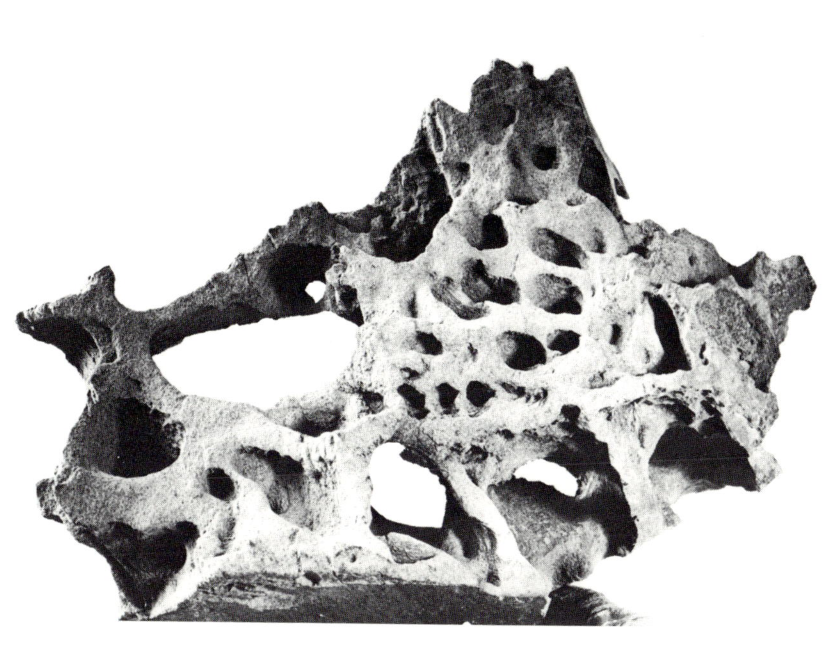

The illustrations on this page show two fragments of weathered rock. They come from Cape Creus, in the extreme north of Catalonia, a peninsula that juts out from the sea, as Dali says, like "a colossal example of geological Art Nouveau." Their forms recur both alive and eroded, in stone, concrete, metal, and ceramic in Gaudí's architectural sculpture, both in the over-all impression of the *Casa Milá* and in the mineral-inspired ornamentation of the *Sagrada Familia.* This geological universe helped Gaudí to go beyond the smooth forms of Art Nouveau and to keep alive the ribs of Gothic architecture.

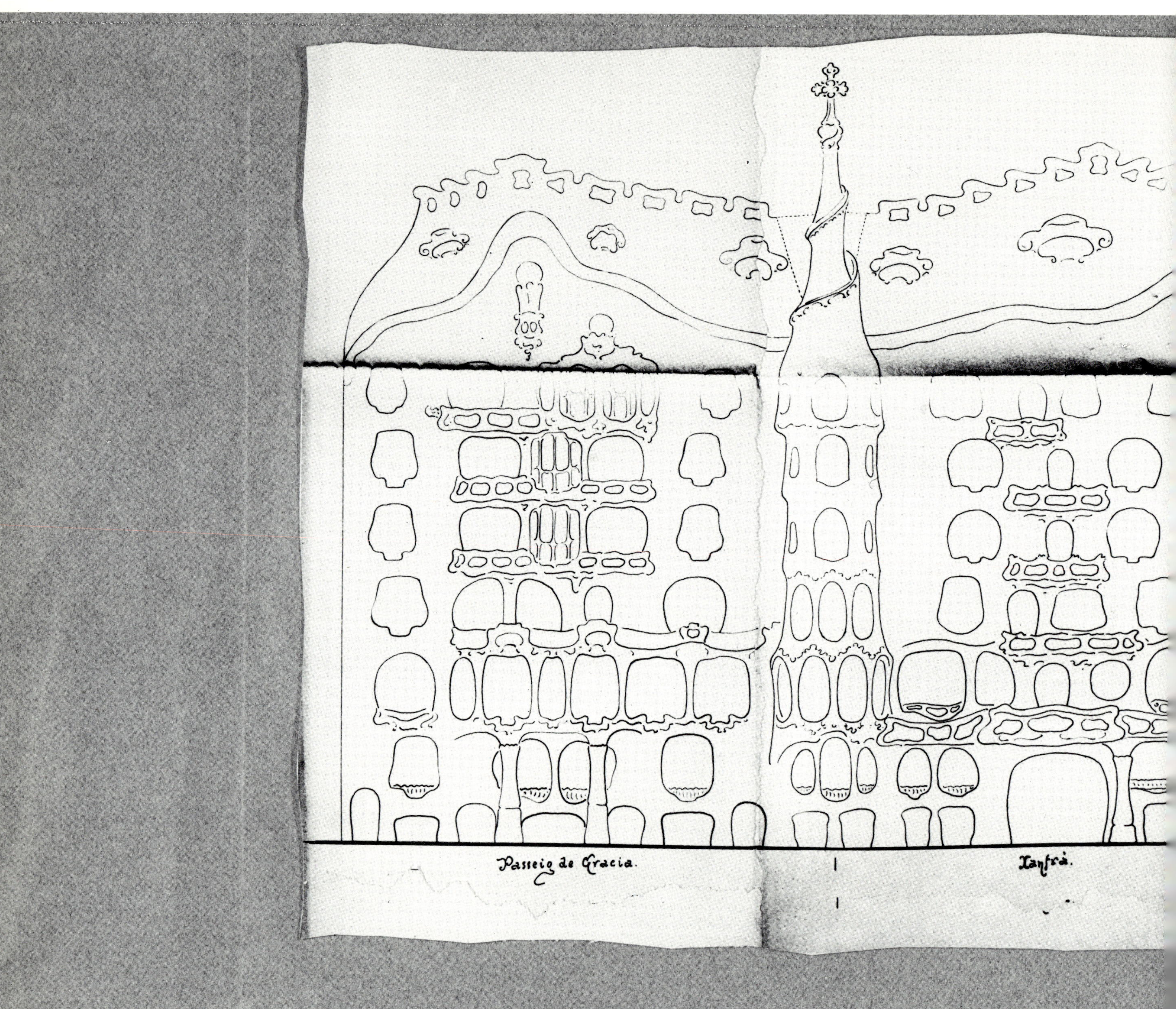

". . . The Casa Milá, *which draws the palpitation of the surface of its façade and walls from the sea of life. . ."*

(Francesc Pujols)

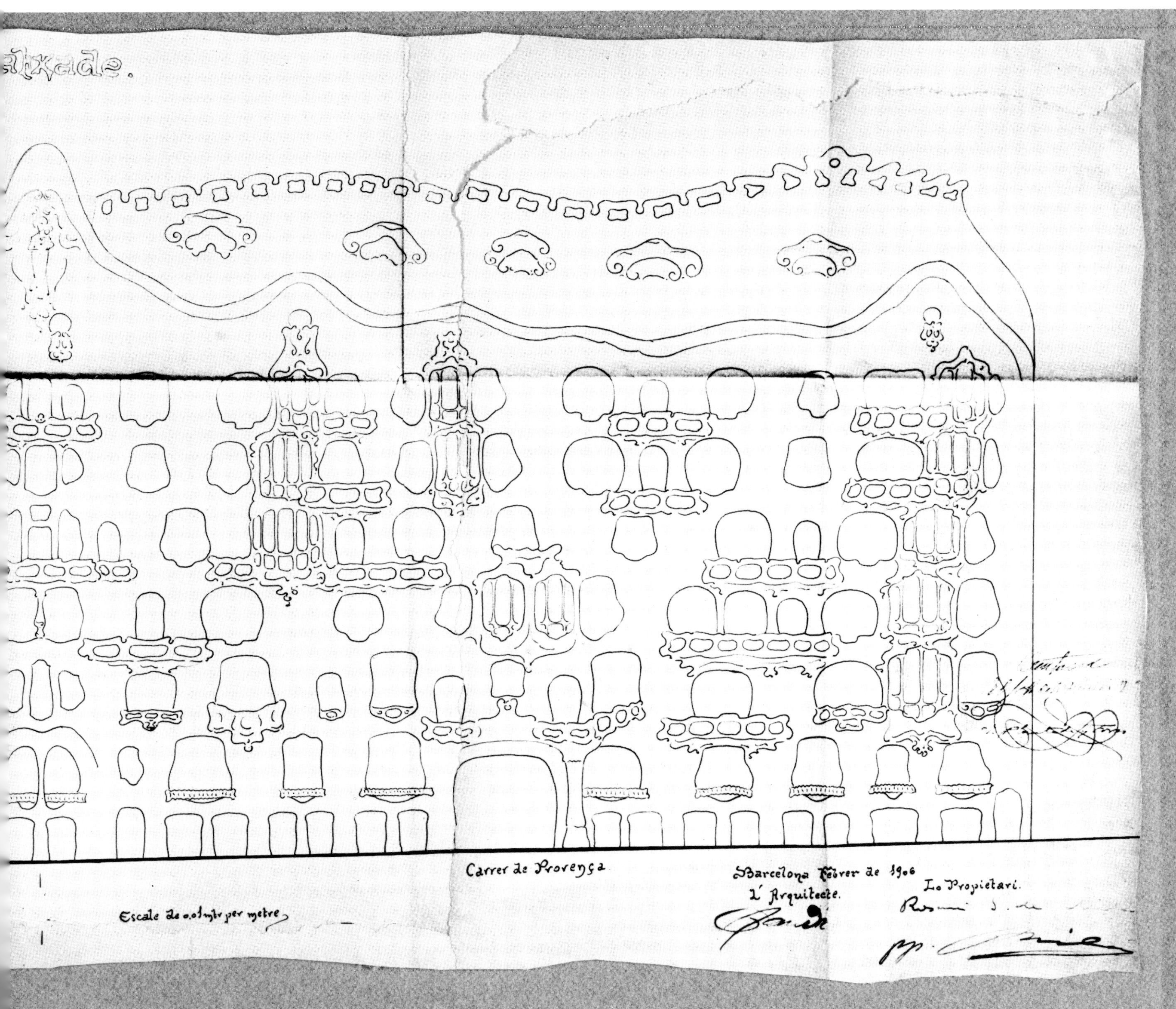

THE CASA MILÁ

The first project for the *Casa Milá,* submitted by Gaudí to the municipal archives of Barcelona in February 1906. It is signed by the architect as well as by his client Roger Segimón de Milá y Camps. This house takes its forms from the swelling tides of the Mediterranean. The waves become ever more gentle as they descend to the area surrounding the feet of the Virgin who crowns the façade. The appearance of the building earned it the name *Pedrera* or quarry.

balconies emphasizes the undulating forms of the façade and stands out against the blocks of coarse-surfaced stone. As the sunlight plays on the pitted stone surface, it gives it an appearance of density and vibration that reinforces the expressive form of the whole. Finally, the tactile effect of these surfaces is often as important as the visual effect. Intended as the immense base for a monument dedicated to the Virgin Mary, as well as an apartment house, it bears the inscription "*Ave Maria, gracia plena*" on the upper part of the façade. The façade seems to imitate ocean waves, less clearly defined as the building rises, and which were meant to appear calm at the feet of the Virgin, surrounded by angels in flight with their wings opened out. The sculptor Carlos Mani made the model for this huge sculptural group, which was to be executed in stone, gilded metal, and crystal. However, following the uprising of the Semana Trágicá of 1909, in the course of which twenty-two churches and thirty-four convents were burned down, the proprietors of the building, fearing reprisals, thought it prudent to give up such a project.

So they rejected the monumental sculpture and a small tower to the Virgin surmounted by a foliated cross, which was to accent the façade as in the *Casa Batlló*. Gaudí was so disappointed that he abandoned the project completely, allowing the architect José María Jujol to finish it. Jujol designed some of the chimney groups and most of the ironwork balconies, as well as decorations for the apartment house where he collaborated with the painter Alejo Clapés. The project that had been accepted by the municipality was rather vague in its presentation, as if it had been merely a preliminary sketch that was to be substantially modified. And this was indeed the case: Gaudí constantly improvised on the site, forever insisting that a project is merely paper and can always be reworked. The truncated building that one sees today stands like "a headless giant" where once stood an altar dedicated to the Virgin of the Rosary, at the junction of the Paseo de Gracia and the Calle de Provenza. "It's a shelter for dinosaurs and dragons !" exclaimed President Clemenceau on seeing the *Casa Milá* as he passed through Barcelona. Built between 1905 and 1910, this imposing dwelling astonishes and provokes heated discussions. According to the March 1911 issue of the journal *Nuevo Mundo*, "This house resembles nothing else in the world ... With its six stories and innumerable windows in the shape of caves, it recalls grottoes cut into the side of a cliff . . . The *Casa Milá* seems to be a cavernous ocean, a habitable Atlantis. Gaudí has found a new rhythm, a rhythm of the sea and of the mountains." The enormous mass of the edifice makes some of the surrounding structures look insignificant. Against the attacks of people of "good taste," the defense of poet-philosopher Francesc Pujols was: "Undoubtedly we will never discover anywhere in Europe modern architecture that is similar to the *Casa Milá*, which draws the palpitation of the surface of its façade and walls from the sea of life: not only will we find nothing that distorts and deploys the general lines of the mass in the way Gaudí does, but we will see in it all the spontaneous movements of ancient architecture. If for the ancients life was the basis of the work of art, our Gaudí seeks this basis vigorously in the heart of the aesthetic soul in order to extract its entrails and make its sap flow . . . This titanic creation was and always will be criticized by the tenacious partisans of the formal perfection that was left to us by the Greeks. But it will always inspire us . . . Our Gaudí had the grace to return the Paseo de Gracia to primitive architecture by keeping his distance from modern architecture."

When Gaudí was about to work on the foundations, he was asked how the *Casa Milá* would look; he took a sheet of paper, crumpled it between his fingers, and set it on a table: "Just like that !" he said, casually. "The house will be just like that." And he added: "I wanted to make an apartment building with a central patio and a double ramp in the form of a spiral that would make it possible for the tenants to reach their apartments by car . . . But there is not enough space on the plot." He divided the building into two volumes, each one centered around a glazed court, with both courts communicating and allowing the cars parked in the basement to circulate. Apart from the mezzanine and the main floor, which were served by a separate staircase, the apartments were to be reached through inside elevators (there was a service stairway as well).

Gaudí conceived the façade as a single mass that he had kneaded into large bare and undulating surfaces, alternately falling into shadow or bursting into light. As he wrote as early as 1878 in his journal: "Large masses are always themselves an ornamental element . . . The best ornamentation emphasizes the purity of grand masses by setting against them subtle yet energetic and delicate projections that reveal the fineness and the richness of the material and the beauty of the whole. Forms expressed with simplicity have more ornamental beauty; those that derive from geometry have clarity and distinction: the more perfect they are, the less they need to be decorated."

The building, as Dali has noted, "leans on grandiose columns and moderate-sized inclined columns that are incapable of standing up by themselves, like the weary neck beneath heavy hydrocephalic heads: they emerge for the first time in the world of the hard undulations of water sculpted with a photographic concern for the instantaneous, unknown until then. They rise in waves of polychromatic reliefs, whose immaterial ornamentation solidifies the convulsive transitions of weak materializations of the most fugitive metaphors of smoke . . ." These columns rise throughout the building and branch out into beams that support the floors. The interior has no walls! They are replaced by movable screens, which alone break the space into changing volumes. The sinuous rhythm of the façade reflects the completely flexible arrangement of the interior, where there are no right-angled forms, and where no room is exactly like any other. It is a Wagnerian house pierced by an ash tree from the "Valkyrie" (then being performed in Barcelona); the tree is the pier, and its branches support the roof and the walls. Sea plants wind around the piers, and the ceilings are like sandy shores with surfaces that seem to tremble with wind-ruffled water, spiraling eddies, and festoons of foam left by the receding waves. On the ceiling of a child's bedroom in an apartment on the second floor, one can still read: *"O Maria no te sapiga greu lo ser petita també ho son les flors y ho son les estrelles"* ("Oh Mary, don't be sad because you are so small, the flowers and the stars are small too").

The flooring is of hexagonal, clear green cement tile, designed by Gaudí, with starfish and curling octopuses set in relief. The grilles of the interior courts look like coral reefs, and the ironwork of the balconies and entranceways resembles seaweed. The people of Barcelona say that snakes slither through the window openings; and the painter Santiago Rusiñol remarked jokingly that the Milá family certainly should not have a dog or a cat in such a house, but rather reptiles or toads. Originally, the balconies and verandas were painted in the colors of luxuriant vegetation; but the sea breezes and smoke from the city have effaced them and have darkened the light limestone. In the entrances to the building the frescoes of Alejo Clapés have disintegrated to the point of being almost invisible. The bare stone, chipped with hammer and chisel, contrasts with the revetment of white marble on the mansards: the latter forms, along with the scraps of white ceramic imbedded in the stairways leading to the terraces, a sky of snow and shining clouds at the feet of a Virgin, from whom some stones are missing, "precisely those," wrote a critic in 1927, "which, by their quantity and size, would have given such a gigantic pedestal its reason for being. This house is a Trojan horse without riders: those happen to be in the belly of the building," waiting on the terrace that resembles a strange battlefield, immobile, desolate. There, groups of helmeted warriors with hidden faces, which function as chimneys and air vents, seem to watch over the city and look out for an invisible enemy that might spring forth from the sea or the mountains in the distance.

The writer José Plá recalls a dialogue between the great architect and the painter Carlès. This conversation, held on the roof terrace of the *Casa Milá*, is a fitting conclusion to the vision of Gaudí, that master ornamentalist:

"How," Carlès asked, "do you justify the curvilinear forms and volumes of this façade?"

"They justify themselves, for they are united to those of the mountains of Collcerola and Tibidabo, which you can see from here."

"But from here, from the top of the *Casa Milá*, one also has a view of the sea, and the horizon line is straight!"

"The straight line does not exist in nature!"

"Nature isn't mathematical, but, a regular form, a style, is pleasing to the mind. Anything that isn't chaotic satisfies man."

"But the idea is that one must not try to satisfy him!"—otherwise, he was saying, man will remain confined to his lower-middle-class and commonplace ideal. The fortunately provocative *élan* which springs from the depths of any soul blissfully contemplating the *Casa Milá* and which forces each one to choose and to act—this is the only true homage which may be paid to Gaudí and which justifies all his experiments.

The juxtaposition between the drawing of the *Casa Milá* (overleaf on the right), executed by Juan Matamala, and the photograph of the terrace (above), emphasizes the formal unity of the building, which is treated like an organic whole. Each part is developed and flows into the other parts: the undulating rhythm of the façade comes to life on the terrace, and it suggests various kinds of movement to the imagination. The strange forms of the chimneys and the staircase exits loom into the sky, following a sinuous labyrinth with the expressive tonalities that suggest a dramatic happening, an articulate language. One discovers this all over the terrace without ever encountering the same silhouettes; they blend with each other and get in each other's way, as on a chessboard.

A general view of the intended *Casa Milá* as drawn by Juan Matamala.

Captions for the photographs of the Casa Milá on pages 169 to 183

Page 169	A Moorish chimney, helmeted, blindly staring.
Pages 170-171	Façade of the *Casa Milá*. Fossilized waves and foam of wrought iron.
Pages 172-173	The loggias are holes of shadow entwined with living plants.
Pages 174-175	On the roof terrace the chimneys and twisted stair heads are covered with white mosaics.
Pages 176-177	A group of chimneys. Depending on the shadow and the light, the helmeted warriors become either aggressive birds or veiled women.
Pages 178-179	Interior. An indiscreet ear to the adjoining room.
Pages 180-181	Sometimes the ceilings give rise to enormous tadpole-like shapes that bear the words *Ave Maria*.
Pages 182-183	The roof of an entrance pavilion in the *Park Güell*. A carousel of broken plaques and variegated debris.

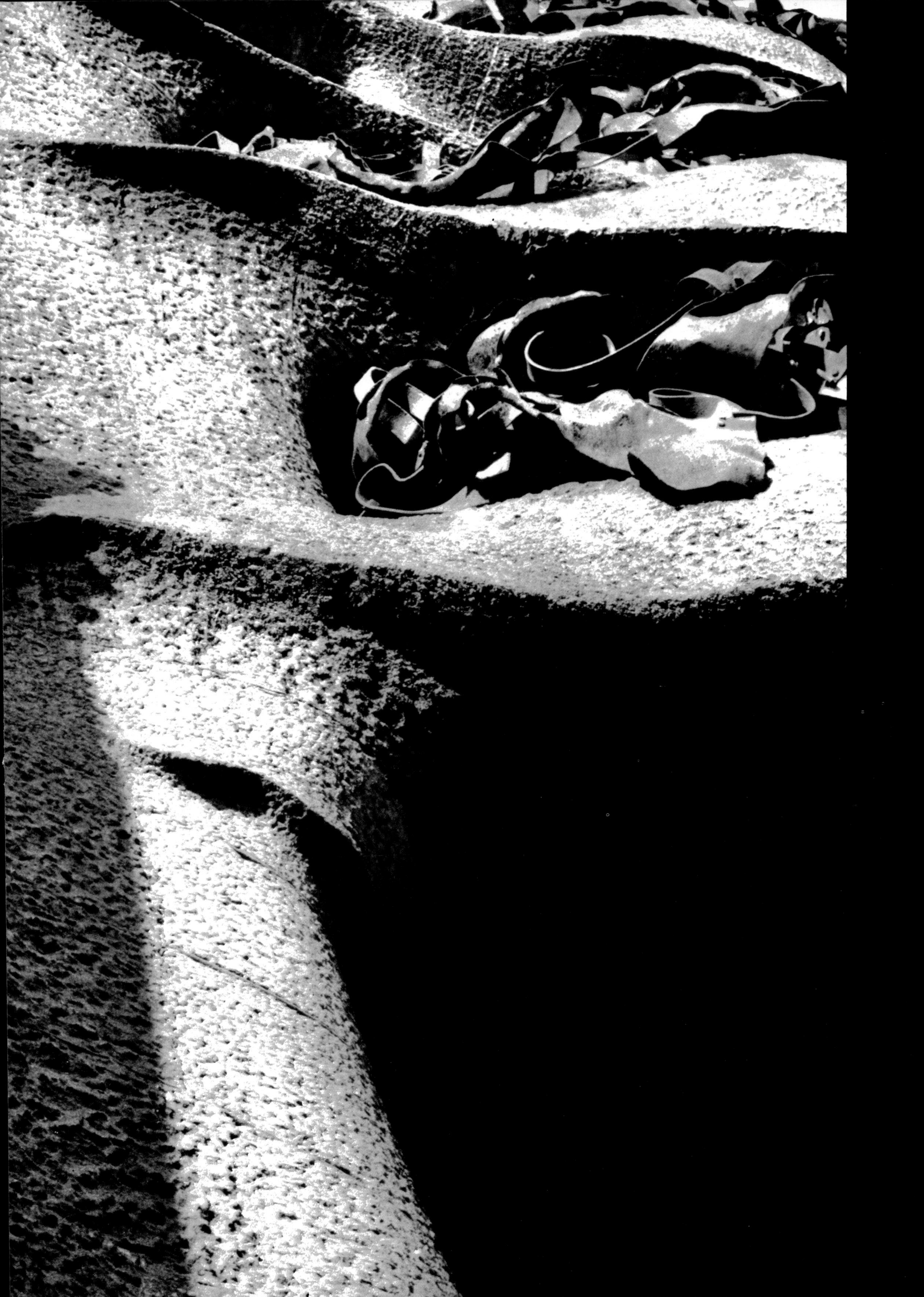

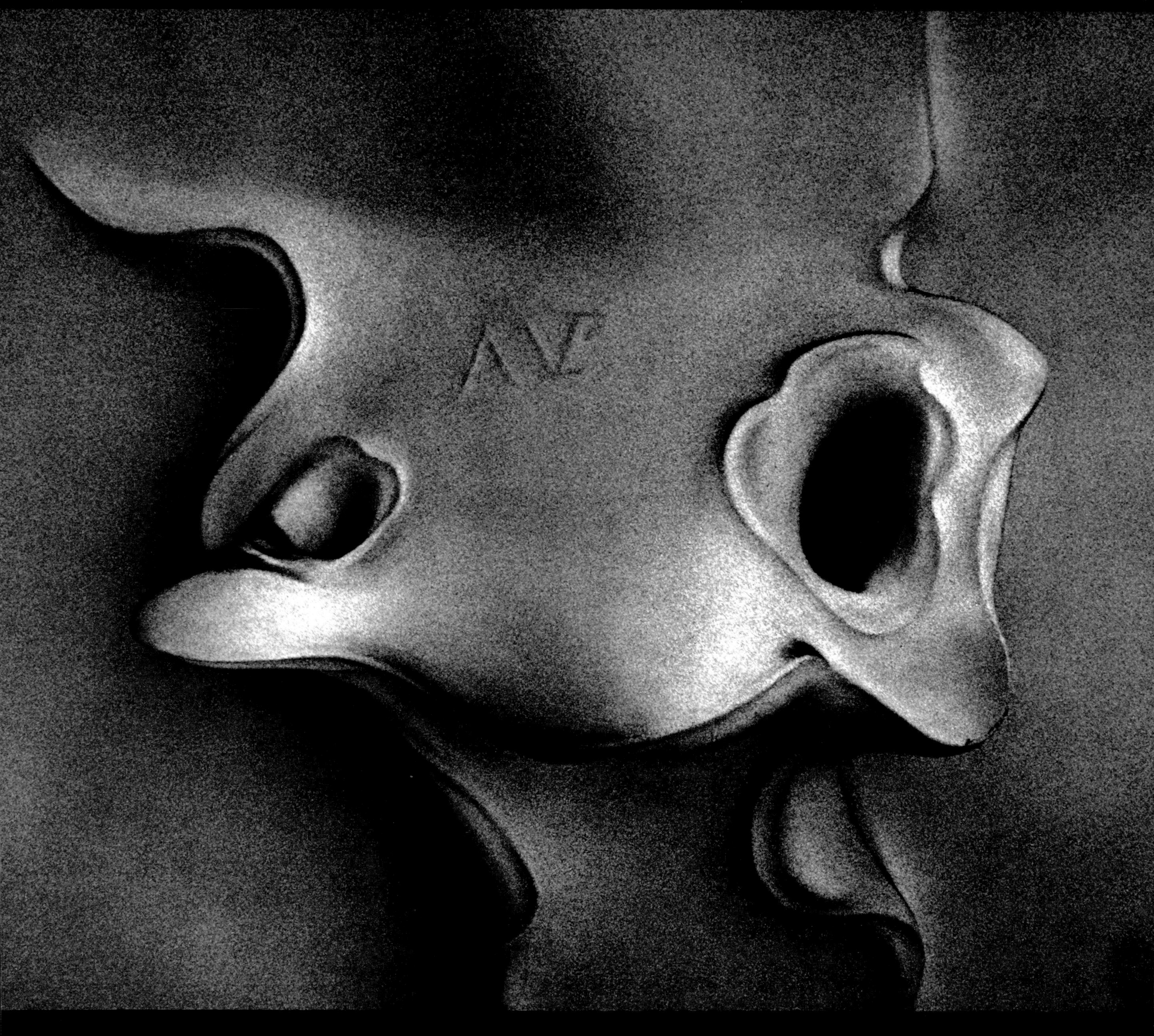

Gaudí said that "color complements form and gives it life." He wanted the archivolts of the portals and their sculpture to be polychromed. With the architect José María Jujol, he experimented on the models that were sent to the 1910 Paris Exhibition. The central archivolt was to be an intense blue suggesting the night at Bethlehem, surrounded by a constellation of almond flowers and stars of the Zodiac. The Doorway of Hope (at the left) was to be green, like Nile vegetation, becoming purplish blue toward the top. The Doorway of Faith was to be burnt sienna, to recall the sands of Palestine. The large cypress surmounting the Portal of Life was covered with brilliant green ceramic tiles; the doves lodged upon it are of pale alabaster, and the cross at the summit is made of red mosaic.

This sumptuous mosaic is a detail of the astonishing *trompe-l'œil* that covers the façade of the *Casa Batlló* with sky, clouds, and water. At No. 43 Paseo de Gracia a quite ordinary house was transformed, decorated, and metamorphosed by Gaudí between 1905 and 1907, for a couple named Batlló, who owned the property. Gaudí covered the basement front with white stone from Montjuich; made window openings with "soft" outlines and slender supporting columns, which suggested the "House of Bones" as a nickname for the residence, and topped the building with a roof of glazed scales, flanked by a turret with a foliated cross. The colors of the façade's ceramics were determined by the architect José María Jujol.

The scintillating spires of the *Sagrada Familia* are visible from a distance: the white, gold, and red Venetian glass bits blend with the dull blacks of the projecting bricks and contrast with the neutral stone of the towers of the Nativity façade. Gaudí himself supervised the coloring of the south tower, which is dedicated to St. Barnabas. The architect Domingo Sugrañes followed this example when he worked on the three other spires. As Gaudí said: "Architecture does not have to renounce color but, on the contrary, should make use of it to bring forms and volumes to life. Color complements form and is the clearest manifestation of life."

Gaudí's collaborator José María Jujol decorated the ceiling of the hypostyle hall of the *Park Güell* with ceramic medallions studded with mosaics of brilliant color. These medallions are further bossed with various little porcelain objects, bottoms of bottles and cups, and large smooth stones, all of which are arranged in stars, spirals, or sun disks.

". . . a huge and insane
multicolored mosaic,
shining with pointillistic iridescence
from which the forms of water emerge . . ."
(Salvador Dali)

LIGHT - ARCHITECTURE - LANDSCAPE

On the undulating terrace of the open-air theater, which follows the contours of the hill like an immense multicolored serpent, the cement benches are incrusted with bits of ceramic, glass, and porcelain, and sprinkled with the bottoms of angel-decorated plates and bottles that came from one of the local potteries. These humble scraps were at the time both extremely economical, and also the starting point for the spontaneous invention of a thousand arrangements made up of unexpected and always different materials and colors. This type of "collage" blends admirably with the fluid lines of the benches.

Right: *Casa Batlló.* Mosaic decorated ventilation pipes on the terrace-roof.

Parque Güell. Ceramic/mosaic disc which serves as a light reflector on the ceiling of a large hall of Doric colonnades which supports the grand plaza. Designed by Jujol Gibert, one of Gaudí's collaborators.

Below left and right: Square ceramic motifs from the side wall of the entrance stairway.

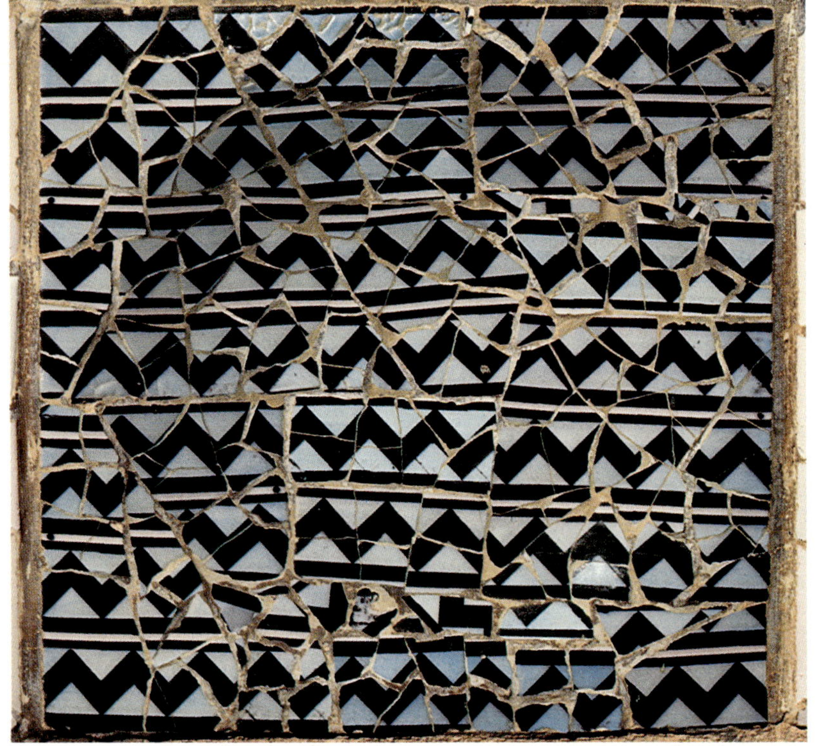

Right: *Finca Güell.* 1884-1887. Now contains offices of *Catedra Gaudí* and *Amigos de Gaudi*. This is a detail of the iron-worked "Dragon Gate" at the property's entrance, inspired by the "guard dragon" of the Garden of Hesperides.

Left: *Casa Vicens,* Calle de las Carolinas 24, Barcelona, constructed between 1883-1888. A detail of the entrance hall's grilled windows on the building's street side.

Below: *Finca Miralles,* Paseo Manuel Girona, 53. 1901-1902. Entrance gate.

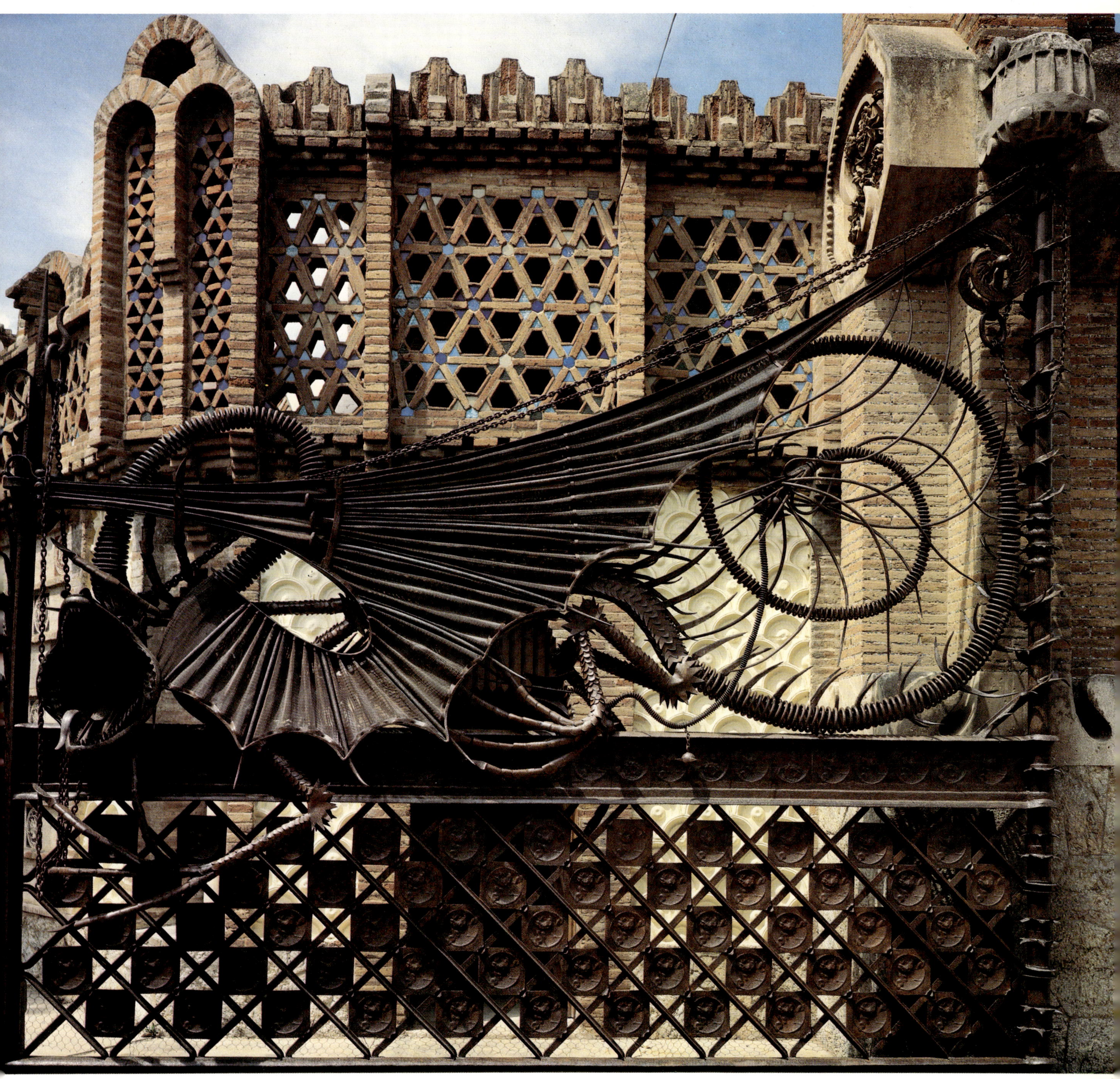

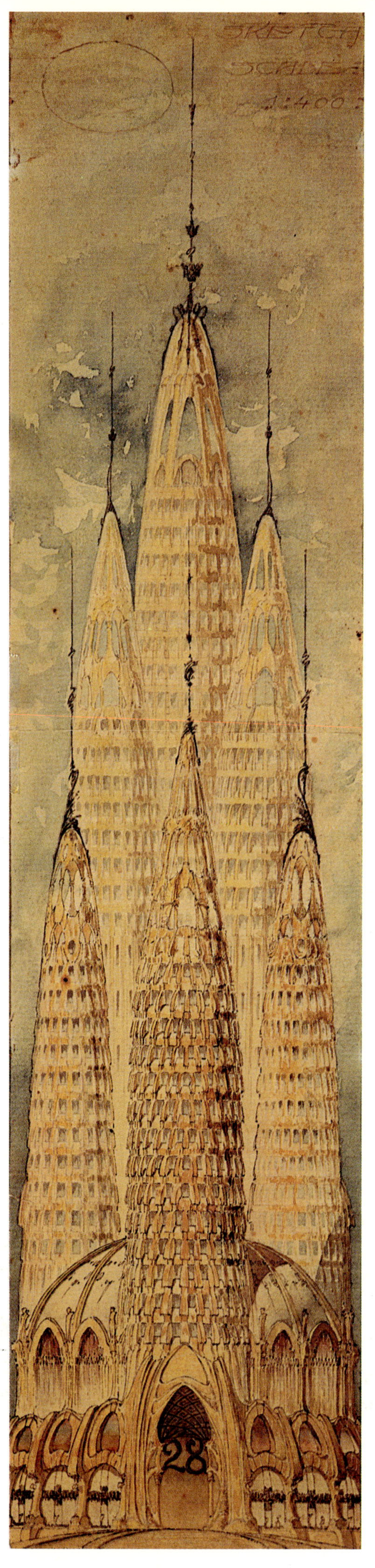

Early sketch for an American Hotel, attributed to Gaudí. City Library, Réus, Catalonia.

Erratum

Robert Descharnes, not George R. Collins, is the author of Chapter VIII, "The American Hotel." Professor Collins was incorrectly cited on page 193 of this edition.

CHAPTER VIII

The American Hotel

by George R. Collins

Design for a grand hotel in New York. A sketch by Gaudí, drawn in 1908, shows the building in cross section.

One thousand and sixteen feet high, multiple towers and balconies, huge halls and fantastic decorations: that was the most fantastic, the most gigantesque of Gaudí's projects, and the only one the architect designed to be built outside Europe. It is also the least known.

It could be considered the synthesis of the towers of the *Sagrada Familia*, the undulating forms of the *Casa Milá*, and the culmination of the experimental researches of the *Colonia Güell*. Destined for New York in 1908, it enables Gaudí to be seen outside the limits of Catalonia, it demonstrates his vision of the American contemporary scene of the time, and shows, once again, the point to which his conceptions far outstripped all the architectural ambitions of his time.

The would-be proprietor of the hotel, a rich American financier, having arrived to confide the architectural design to Gaudí, started by visiting the *Parc Güell*, the *Casa Milá*, then under construction, and the *Palacio Güell*. Thunderstruck, he immediately changed his concept... He had thought of a luxury hotel, decorative, in the traditional spirit, but much more monumental, much more exotic than strictly functional... Sited outside New York, it would be surrounded by gardens, joined by rapid transport to the centre of the city, and visible for miles.

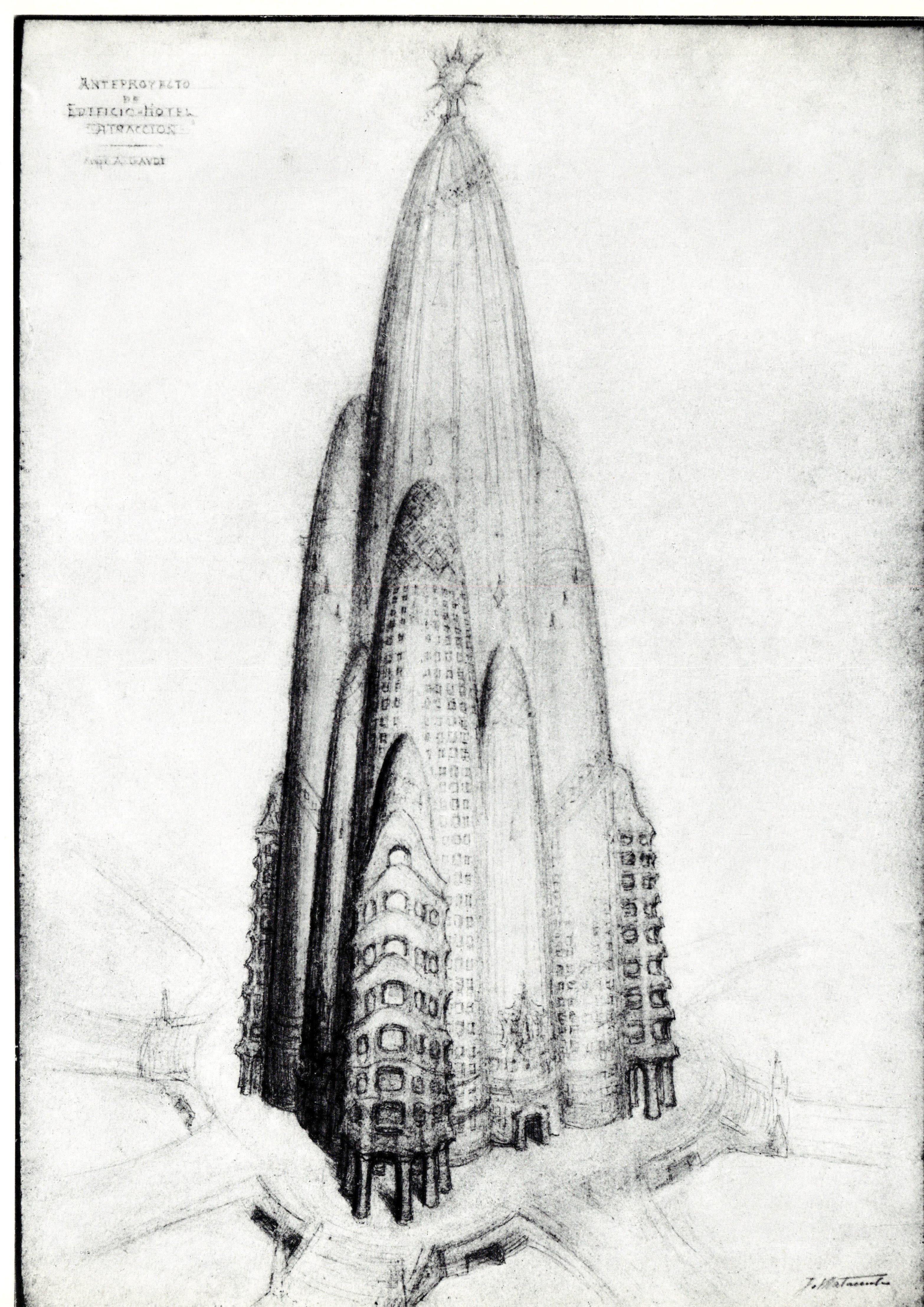
ANTEPROYECTO
DE
EDIFICIO-HOTEL
ATRACCION
A. GAUDI

A general view of the preliminary project worked out by Gaudí and his collaborators during the year 1908, for a large New York hotel with rooms for entertainments. This drawing is by Juan Matamala.

The age was an age of giganticism. Vertical giganticism with the Eiffel Tower was preceded by the horizontal giganticism of the London Crystal Palace and the *Galerie des Machines* in Paris. America, seized by the turn of the century fever, gave itself up to a highest skyscraper race. That Gaudí, himself an enthusiast, saw the possibility to enter the competition and to win it, there can be no doubt, especially if it is remembered that he had already postulated that the hotel in question should have the height of the Empire State Building, built some twenty-two years later, and which reaches 1250 ft!

Gaudí's enthusiasm can be better imagined in reading the description made by Jules Huret of the greatest New York hotel of the period, the Waldorf Astoria, which was demolished to make way for the Empire State Building. 'The building is situated between 33rd and 34th Streets. It contains 17 floors and 1500 rooms, 1200 with baths. The ground floor of the hotel includes several lofty and immense dining rooms, each decorated in a different style and containing small tables. The walls are of carved stone or of stucco. Stucco in the vast corridors, stucco on the stairways, stucco everywhere; elaborate, gilded, as in a Byzantine cathedral. In all the corridors that run right round the gigantic caravansarai, two rows of guests, or visitors sit, chatting and smoking—for anyone who wishes may come in, everything is public. There is an orchestra there, on the mezzanine floor, between two corridors, that plays from morning to night. There are large and numerous offices rented to a bank which deal with stock exchange matters: market prices are posted telegraphically, at the same time as they appear on the floor of the Exchange. Next to the bank, there is a florist's window, a photographer's display unit for the studio on the 17th floor, a telephone office to communicate with town and country, a telegraph office, a doctor's consulting room (the hotel has three doctors, one always on call); there is the hotel reception, the cash desk, huge safes. On the first floor there are no private rooms: on one side there are two huge ballrooms, concert halls or theatres, with boxes, stage, and cloakrooms. These rooms are of unparalleled luxury, with marble walls, heavy Oriental carpets, enormous mirrors, ceilings painted by the best artists of America. The other side, there is a multiplicity of lounges and of dining rooms in every style and size, which may be hired for club dinners or by guests who do not wish to eat in the public dining rooms. Near these rooms, there are vestibules filled with plants and marble statues. After a meal, they may be used to meet guests, smoke, sing and dance. The 16 floors above contain the bedrooms, suites, and the services for them. The 17th floor is the roof of the hotel. In summer, awnings are spread, and amidst flowers, plants and ventilators, an open-air restaurant looks over the Hudson.'

Gaudí gathered together his closest collaborators, the architect Francisco Berenguer, the sculptor Lorenzo Matamala with his son Juan, to decide on the general outline of the whole building, to establish the proportions, and to plan out the basic decoration. It is easy to imagine that in a very short time the American financier's dreams were largely overtaken: on the ground floor, the usual size of a New York block (circa 360 ft by 360 ft), a gigantic hall was planned for reception, surrounded by huge saloons. Above, in the principal tower, five outsize dining rooms, symbolic of the five continents. Their decoration should represent the characteristics of the five parts of the world: stone elephants for Asia, rhinoceros and giraffe for Africa, fishes, flowers and birds for Oceania, mythological subjects, galaxies, naiads and atlantas for Europe. Constant in his realism, Gaudí intended to wait until his arrival in New York before deciding on the elements for the America room. On the 6th floor was to be another dining room in which the structural elements should remain visible. Thus the decoration could be changed according to circumstances and the seasons. Above was to be an exhibition hall, showing with models the course of construction and the techniques used in the building of the hotel. Higher still, a vast theatre or conference room, nearly 150 feet high, was destined to be used for congresses and conventions. Finally, for the sake of appearances, the apotheosis of giganticism, a hall 375 feet high, as high as the towers of the *Sagrada Familia*, symbol of the young America. Surrounded by interior and exterior galleries, lit by immense triangular bays made of assemblies of coloured glass reminiscent of cathedral windows, the hall

Juan Matamala's rendering of one of the six dining rooms: this one is dedicated to Europe. It was to accommodate four hundred people, who would dine to music played by a large symphony orchestra. The polychrome decoration was to have had a mythological theme. The ceiling was to have been supported by Atlantas and naiads, representing the galaxies.

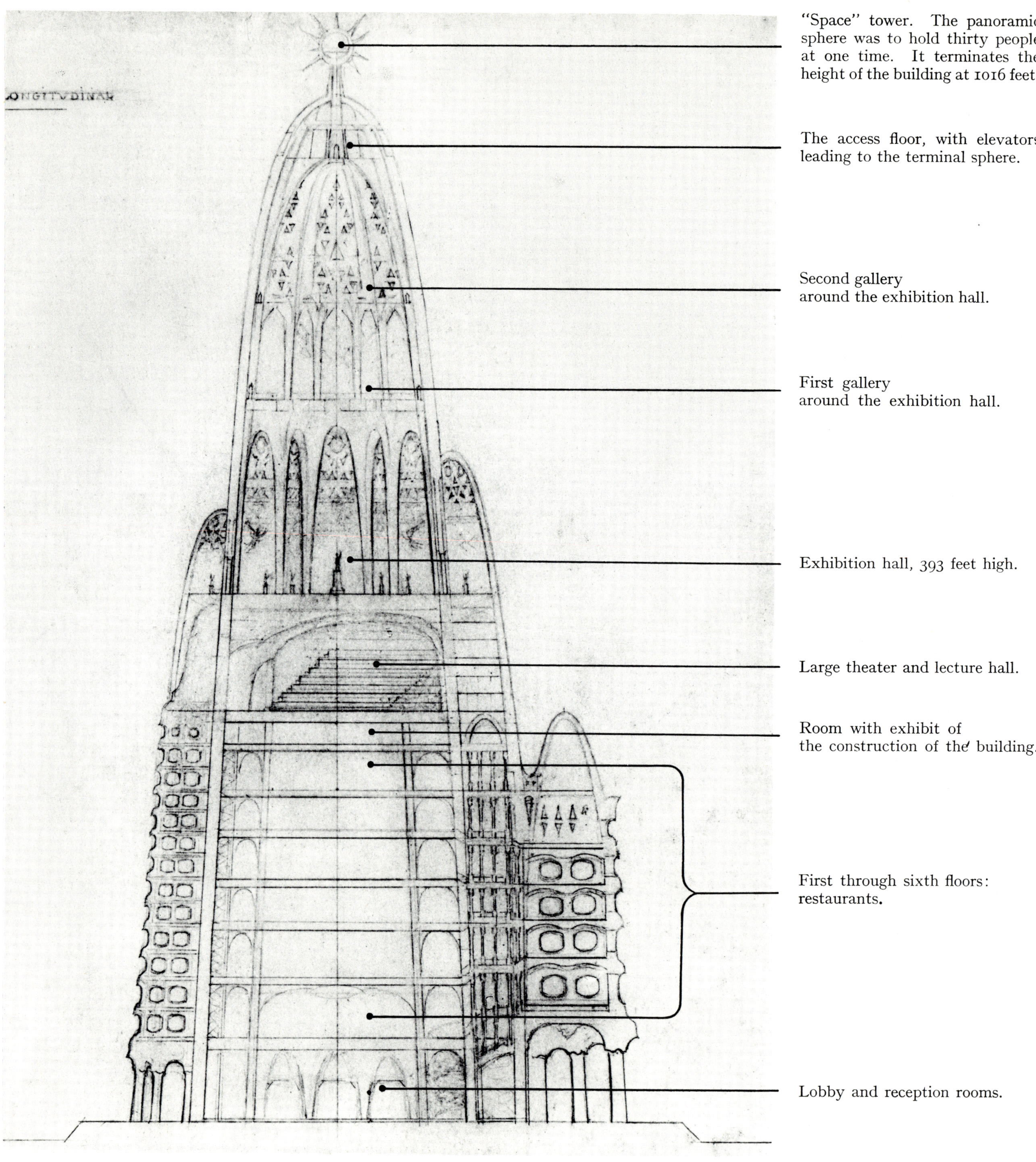
"Space" tower. The panoramic sphere was to hold thirty people at one time. It terminates the height of the building at 1016 feet.
The access floor, with elevators leading to the terminal sphere.
Second gallery around the exhibition hall.
First gallery around the exhibition hall.
Exhibition hall, 393 feet high.
Large theater and lecture hall.
Room with exhibit of the construction of the building.
First through sixth floors: restaurants.
Lobby and reception rooms.

was destined to contain the statues of all the Presidents of America. The wall surface was to be reserved for decorators, mosaic workers, and the greatest contemporary fresco artists. It was planned that the metal framework, proper to American constructions, should be double. This very flexible technique allowed the lifts to the towers, rising vertically from the lower floors, to change course later to marry and follow closely the parabolic curves of the building. Tourists would thus be carried up to the terminal viewpoint, the 'sphere of all space'. A gigantic panoramic star, inspired by the pure form of the sea urchin, was to replace the traditional cross which surmounted the majority of buildings designed by Gaudí, whether religious or secular.

The multiple towers surrounding the principal tower, of parabolic shape, contain smoking rooms, tea rooms, meeting rooms and bedrooms, and communicate with the central tower, thus allowing some of the principal rooms to be much extended.

All the towers were to be polychromed on the outside. To clothe the middle portions of the building, Gaudí, had planned to import different coloured marbles to allow a subtle change of colour. For the lower portions, in stone, it is possible that he envisaged a rhythm and treatment inspired by that of the *Casa Milá*.

In fact, nothing was decided immutably in advance. As for the *Park Güell*, the most disparate elements were to have been used — building debris, terra cotta, minerals, fragments of glass, tiles... The glittering whole, flamboyant in a thousand colours during the day, was to be

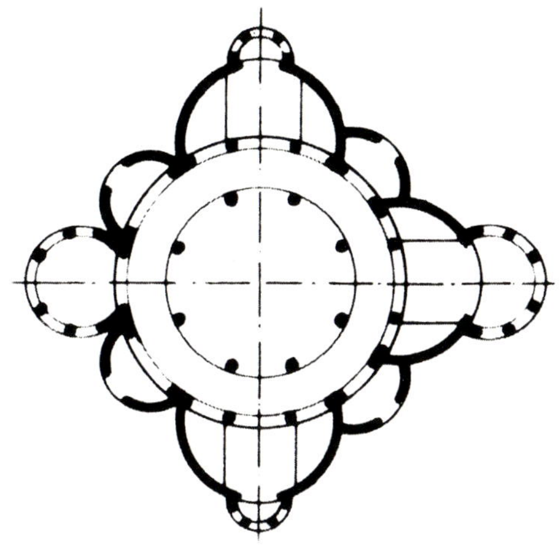

Project for the hotel: plan by Juan Matamala

GRAND HOTEL IN NEW YORK, 1908. Opposite is Matamala's general section of the building. The halls in the large central tower were to be reserved for conventions, theater, and exhibitions. Around these halls were to be lobbies, elevators, and observation galleries. The lateral towers were to be occupied by bars, smoking rooms, rooms for small meetings, and a few apartments.

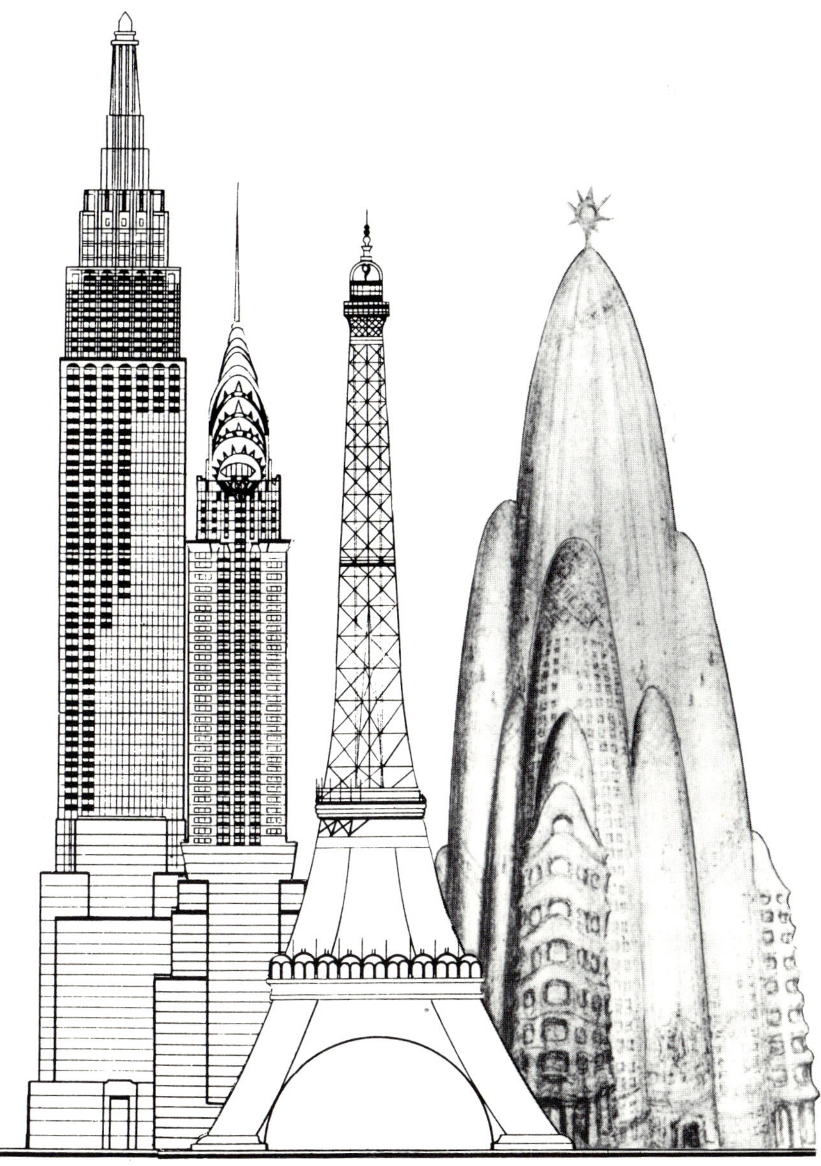

Comparative heights among various buildings; from left to right:

1931	New York	Empire State Building	1250 ft
1930	New York	Chrysler Building	1046 ft
1888	Paris	The Eiffel Tower	1024 ft
1908	New York	Gaudí's hotel project	1016 ft

The detail, opposite, from the drawing on page 194 by Matamala shows that Gaudí had considered, in addition to the polychromy, decorative sculptural motifs for the walls of the building; these would have been illuminated at night by spotlights on the highest points of the façades.

illuminated by night by powerful floodlights placed on the highest points of the façades: 'Light', specified Gaudí, 'should always fall from the sky.'

Master-builder for this enormous undertaking, Gaudí would have had to travel to the United States to oversee the works, allowing himself, as usual, to improvise on the spot. It is not known for which reasons the journey seems to have been abruptly cancelled, or for what reason nothing was undertaken or even started on the project.

Until a short time ago, an elderly gentleman in Barcelona possessed certain documents, conserving them lovingly. Some were by the hand of the great architect, others he copied or redrew from memory, since everything had burnt during the Civil War. The man was the sculptor Juan Matamala, son of Lorenzo, Gaudí's right hand. Until his recent death, Matamala was Gaudí's most active spokesman. It was he who, with passionate enthusiasm, convinced us of the exceptional importance of the *American Hotel* project, and who enabled us to devote a chapter to it here. His fervent devotion to Gaudí's legacy enabled us to imagine the prodigious influence the artist exercised over the men who surrounded him. Thus, if in certain of the plans for the *American Hotel*, the vision of Juan Matamala seems rather obvious, we can be assured that he remained faithful to Gaudí's creative spirit.

The sphere "of all space", which terminate Matamala's drawing of the hotel, recalls the platform arranged for the public in the head of the Statue of Liberty.

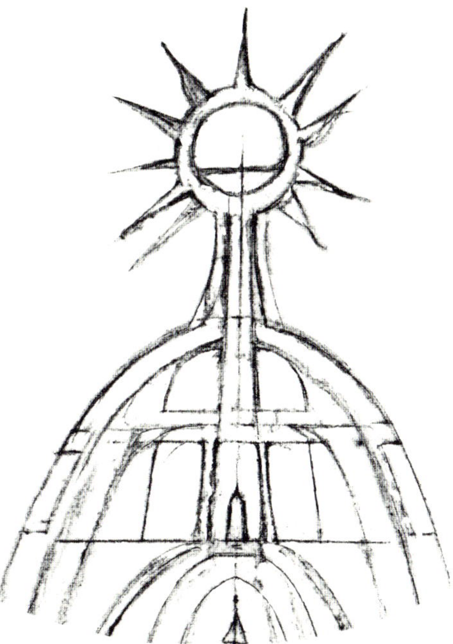

Here, in this sphere whose form was inspired by the sea urchin, thirty people could have assembled to admire the vast panorama of New York.

Francesc Pujols

Gaudí's Artistic and Religious Vision

(La visió artística i religiosa d'En Gaudí)

First published in 1927 as *feuilleton* No. 1
of the Libreria Cataloña, Plaza Cataloña 17, Barcelona

Text for the original French edition of this volume was an "instantaneous"
translation from the Catalan by Salvador Dali

Translation from the original Catalan into English by Judith C. Rohrer

Introduction by Joan Alavedra

CONCERNING FRANCESC PUJOLS

By JOAN ALAVEDRA

"Here is the most important man on earth, second only to the Eternal Father," declared a priest from Montpellier as he introduced Francesc Pujols.

He is important in the sense that the imposing Nativity façade of the *Sagrada Familia* is important. In his commentary on it in this book Pujols compares it with other existing cathedrals. And just as Gaudí's creative genius contorts architectural forms to yield a "living" church, Pujols also contorts his fantastic style to give us a literature that expresses every nuance of his thought in a "living" manner.

Both of these men devoted their lives to religion: Gaudí, the "universal architect," to the glorification of the Catholic religion by means of art; Pujols, the founder of "universal science," to the philosophical structuring of a "Catalan religion" which, extending the ideas of Ramón Lull (of whom Pujols considered himself the follower), means to demonstrate its principles scientifically to the world.

Never, perhaps, have the aim and the style of a writer so closely identified with his object of concern as in this case, because Pujols' genius, like Gaudí's, is of extraordinary form and proportion.

Monstrous and delicate, full of passion and imagination, given to a ferocious realism while simultaneously overflowing with fantasy, always inspired and yet unpublished—Pujols, with his sinuous and plastic language, inexhaustible like light or water, seeks out all the meanings and aspects of Gaudí's prodigious creation to provide us with an exhaustive analysis. As the great church was built, so was Pujol's exegesis, with the massive blocks of his paragraphs that are also "poems in stone," vibrant with emotion. And like Gaudí's church, the whole is impressive.

The Montpellier priest had known Pujols when he was a Catalan refugee following the Spanish Civil War, uprooted from his native land, poorly clothed and undernourished. How, then, could he have imagined the radiant Pujols, the elegant, refined dandy, the worldly landowner and great patron of culture, the productive writer and brilliant conversationalist, the lover of concerts, backstage, restaurants, literary circles, opera (in his impeccable tail-coat), the lecturer sought out by the notable lecture halls of his day?

The priest had before him a tall, corpulent man who walked through the streets of the old university town in a second-hand overcoat, wearing a cap with earlaps, and carrying delicately—as a memento from before the disaster—a cane with a carved golden handle in the form of a head that might possibly recall the face of Ramón Lull.

"He looked like God's chauffeur," said the philologist Pompeu Fabra.

"Or rather nature's secretary," added the poet Carles Riba.

The "Mad God," was someone's conclusion.

Pujols, an intellectual giant who evoked the idealism of the Middle Ages, the joyous culture of the Renaissance, and the scientific rigor of our own day, might well be remembered in terms he wrote himself: "A mixture of

FRANCESC PUJOLS

Barcelona, August 1882—
Martorell, February 1962.

the elegant, refined dandy, the worldly land-owner . . .

The "Torre de les Hores" at Martorell.

madness and genius has always been indispensable in accomplishing any great undertaking in the field of human activity." And perhaps he would have added: "The same might have been said about Ramón Lull!"

"Ramón Lull?" curious students would ask when they saw the veneration with which Pujols would speak of this thirteenth-century philosopher.

"Oh yes," he might reply, "Ramón Lull, my Master, the most modern of thinkers. This 'Illumined Doctor,' this 'white-bearded' Master Ramón, who more than six hundred years ago lectured at the Sorbonne in Paris and at the University in this very town of Montpellier, where right now I am in the process of completing his system."

Having lost all his possessions, suffering from such bad eyesight that he was almost unable to read or write, Pujols, the Stoic, subsisted on his mind alone. Young students took his courses. He who had already "studied all possible careers"—because "instead of working to make a living it was necessary to have money to be able to work"—continued of necessity to apply all the strength of his powerful mind to investigating the various aspects of his life's work, his *Pantologia*, or "The Science of Everything," which, by means of a cosmic synthesis, provided a logical explanation for man and the universe. When he was surrounded by an audience, anything was sufficient pretext for him to exercise his authority; one might say that the entire history of culture was reviewed at each session. Thus, when he addressed students of literature, he would cite literary examples, whereas to students of philosophy he would give philosophical examples, and to students of science, scientific examples: his extensive knowledge, solid and alert, embraced everything. Yet nothing seemed to come from books. Theories, ideas, phrases would slip from his mouth with the freshness of recent invention.

In Catalonia he had lived as a recluse, surrounded by silence, in his "Torre de les Hores" (House of Hours), at Martorell, where he "spent the summer every year," studying and working on his system. He was completely taken with the light that radiated from the "Ars Magna" by Ramón Lull, the great Catalan who was born on Majorca, "the island in the sea that is the most luminous island in the world." Pujols, a dedicated gourmet, would visit Barcelona only for a special dish in one of the good restaurants, to go to the opera, or to attend or deliver a lecture.

In exile—"the Exiliad," he would say, to give our era a Homeric resonance—he had nothing to do but to "rethink everything," and he was always at our disposal. During his stay at Prades, in Roussillon, before he left for Montpellier, I approached Pujols as would a man with a keen thirst drawing near to a fresh-water spring.

In the morning Pujols went, as he did every day, to meditate among the huge cypress trees in the gardens of the hilltop cemetery that dominates the whole town. The former poet, who had not quit poetry but who had been abandoned by it, would contemplate the elongated silhouette of the pink tile roofs, "as if they were a naked woman lying on the green grass of a meadow." At noon, after exclaiming, "I have enjoyed enough for today!" he would come down for lunch at the Grand Hotel, where he was the guest of Pablo Casals. My own great intellectual feast would begin in the early hours of the afternoon and would often continue until past midnight.

Lacking books, we had to live off our own ideas. And it was in this way that I measured the scope, depth, solidity, and precision of the knowledge of this philosopher and his fabulous faculties for analysis and synthesis. The physical as well as the cultural worlds, each so varied and multiple, were both carefully ordered in his mind, and he could detail the periods, evolution, detours, confluences, and possible developments of either world in a colorful, vivid language that was untainted by anything pedestrian or pedantic. He was an accomplished master of words and gestures, and, given his sensitive temperament, was often impressed by a revealing anecdote of a famous personality or of a historical event. He was a penetrating thinker who could grasp the sense of the basic ideas of any system. His perorations in the garden of the café across from the Grand Hotel, or in the course of a stroll through the fields around the Abbey of St. Michael of Cuxa, at the foot of the great bluish mass of Canigou, were lessons of inestimable value. The sequences were perfect, the anecdotes characteristic. Everything was logical and coherent, everything connected. The sciences, history, philosophy, religion, astronomy, medicine, politics, the arts—poetry, literature, painting, sculpture, music, architecture—all were explained with regard for their evolutions and the great men who animated them; and all was told as if it were the marvelous adventure of a humanity that advanced with difficulty and sometimes with promising step, often irresistibly deviating throughout the centuries, but eventually resuming its original direction.

With what a sense of drama he would point out the decisive moments! With what enthusiasm he would praise success! With what joyous aggressiveness he would in a single word take the wind out of the philosophical systems of the "traveling salesmen of smoke"! With a verse from Dante, a phrase from Shakespeare or Cervantes, an aphorism from Goethe, he would locate the position of each of these masterminds of literature in respect to Christianity. An analysis of the Book of Job, the first creator of doubt—translated in paraphrase by Pujols—gave new light to the meaning of Jesus' teachings. Pericles, Richelieu, Bismarck, the hegemonies of men and nations, coincidences, divergences, all furnished an occasion for a history of politics. A chance meeting on the road with a monk from St. Michael's Abbey provoked an exposition of his theory of the "Diastasis."

"Nature," he told me, "separates spirit from itself, and does so automatically. This is the foundation of my system, by which I have established, scientifically, an explanation for and the aim of evolution. I could demonstrate to this monk that, faced with the material laws of Generation, Conservation, Relation, and Nutrition, the spirit always retorts with Chastity, Charity, Reclusion, and Fasting . . ."

the ladder of life . . .

The discovery of a dead salamander on the ground recalled to him his theory of art: if the yellow markings of its back were regular, the decoration would be academic; they must be unequal because they are aesthetically alive. In the Parthenon no column is quite like the others, and the Venus de Milo has one eye larger than the other as well as a body twisted in the manner of El Greco. Life always pushes us onward, but man sometimes ignores it. And so the eras of decadence have come along. The moribund paintings, sculpture, and architecture of these centuries have provoked artists who distort—Picasso, for example, born in Malaga but formed by Catalonia—artists who contort form to awaken the vital spark, the natural aesthetic element. This is just what Gaudí did. With academic architecture everything was stillborn because it was concerned with copies. Cold cathedrals were built. It was necessary for a genius to show us a new direction . . .

Francesc Pujols followed the same path in literature. And it was this architect, according to Pujols' own declaration, who inspired his literary style, which he adapted like a glove to Gaudí's architectural style, as it is described with his exceptional unity in this present book.

young poet . . .

the flower he was wearing in his lapel . . .

This thinker who devoted his life to building a philosophical system, his *Pantologia,* which proposes to explain the ladder of human evolution, was possessed of such a universal curiosity that he wrote several books and innumerable articles on the most diverse subjects. He worked out an abridged résumé of his system in his *Manual of Hyparxiology,* which was dictated to a Catalan writer. Of the Catalan tradition, which originated with Ramón Lull and was continued by Ramón de Sibiule (a Catalan philosopher, born in Barcelona, translated by Montaigne), and which had been latent among all the Catalan philosophers who were successors to these extraordinary figures, Pujols, who incorporated this tradition into his theory, spoke at length in his *General Concept of Catalan Science.* Both in his books and in many of his articles he has referred in brief to this "ladder of life" that goes from the plant to the angel; passing through the protozoa, the animal, and man, and of which he said, in a poetic manner: "The plant is an angel who sleeps on earth. The angel is a plant that awakes in the sky."

Seriously involved in the cultural explosion called "Renaixensa" in Catalonia, the originality of Pujol's talent brought together all aspects of this great awakening of our people and, like a Proteus who possessed all the dialectical finesse of a Socrates, Pujols in the course of meetings and lectures analyzed and synthesized the various branches of knowledge in graphic formulas that have fared well in our intellectual world. Following a study of Shakespeare's influence on Goethe, for example, Pujols said: "Marguerite, the little Gretchen of Faust, is an Ophelia who remains pregnant." Speaking of Galileo's apparent abjuration and of the sacrifice of Giordano Bruno: "Truth has no need for martyrs." Summing up the meaning of socialism: "Jesus preached voluntary charity. Another Jew, Karl Marx, made it obligatory." And he concluded a scientific lecture with this extraordinarily concise definition: "All nutrition is a grafting. All generation is a tearing."

As a young poet laureate, endorsed by the patriarch of Catalan poetry, Juan Maragall, Pujols was, as was Plato, "abandoned by poetry" and, also like Plato, he was to discover that his true vocation was philosophy. Once he had entered the labyrinth of ideas, he picked up the thread of thought that Ramón Lull had discovered six centuries earlier: "If religion is true, it must be possible to prove it through science." It was at this moment that he sought refuge in the "Torre de les Hores" and began his studies.

His devoted friends, who would visit him in his retreat, were artists, politicians, and playwrights, all of whom sought his advice. Pujols, besides his own work, which he never completely set aside, translated Wilde, Maeterlinck, or Björnson for some, and for others wrote illuminating treatises on political theory, his aim being to demonstrate historically—"because history has laws as certain as biology"—Catalonia's mission of hegemony on the Iberian peninsula. He composed for the stage a *Medeia* (Medea), a tragedy in which, taking up the ancient myth, he brought together "all the poetic ideas that he had fostered in recent years"; and he published essays on painting that created a sensation among the Catalans. All this, however, was but a game which I cite to indicate the diversity of his talents. He applied his unbounded genius to the formulation of the "Catalan religion," for Catalonia, which "has to extend the liberty of the earth and of men to all of Spain, also has the great mission of extending the liberty of heaven to the whole world through universal science."

At the same time, apart from his appearances in Barcelona, he proliferated phrases and anecdotes or delivered lectures that were events in themselves. Everything he said or did was new, unexpected, pregnant with irony and layers of meaning; and everything was always expressed in a language full of the great Catalan flavor, a tongue that so well grasps thought, "with its phonetics which are as in tune and as precise as the hum of a bee." Everything for Pujols was an appropriate subject for a dissertation: the history of ways of eating, the history of the art of seduction, or of clothing, or of sinning . . . In literary circles he was listened to with the delectation reserved for a *bel esprit.* One day, however, when somebody cast doubt on one of his chance assertions, he exclaimed seriously:

"I have established laws that have never been established before and I have defined concepts—of reason and ethics, for example—which have never been defined in a satisfactory way. And now I might add," he continued with a smile, "that I know why the carrier pigeon returns to the sender, why the cat moves in the dark, why the dog returns to his home, even in the night . . . and it is not because they see it, as everybody thinks! I also know, and have explained, the 'mechanism' of both aesthetic and moral problems."

He sensed that he was not followed because he was not understood; and so he struck out with the humorous jibes for which he is celebrated and which are repeated about everywhere. In the early hours of the morning his friends accompanied him to the station on his return to Martorell. His parting gesture was to remove the flower he was wearing in his lapel, saying to the poet Sagarra:

"Here! Finish it . . ."

When, as he observed a tortoise's slow movement in the garden of the Ateneo, someone interrupted his meditation, he sighed and said:

"Today, no one does things like that any more . . ."

In Montpellier, right in the middle of World War II, a time of rationing, a lady in a restaurant offered him the remains of a bottle of wine, saying:

"This is for you, Monsieur!"

His reply: "I always had luck with women!"

He wrote in a style that he called "organic," inspired by the torrential fluidity of Wagner and Gaudí. Was this a writer's technique?

"Technique," he said, "is something that must be learned by someone who is not gifted in doing what he has to do. I am the slave of no convention. I merely follow the train of my thought, and, if I can think without interruption, I write virtually without periods and with a lot of commas. In fact, this is the *natura non fecit saltus* [nature makes no leaps] of the evolutionists, but here it is applied to prose. Prose, however, like cooking, always needs seasoning, even if only a pinch of salt." As a result of this principle, a typical paragraph, which often fills two full pages, is seasoned with sayings, popular expressions, and vivid images that give his long and serious dissertations a human vitality that is often colorful as well.

After our exile we both returned to Catalonia, and several times I went to visit him at Martorell. He had taken up his former way of life. His income allowed him to live comfortably.

"Life is so sad, and to boot, one's living has to be earned!" he said, thinking of those who had to work.

He would get up at two o'clock in the afternoon. Always a big eater, he would have an enormous breakfast, followed by a brief rest. Then he would go out for a walk around the town or receive a visitor. He was by himself when the sun set for the day. He would take hold of "the fishing rod of my meditation, cast it into the spaces of thought, and then wait for the ideas to bite." In the silence of his room, into the early hours of the morning, he would think about his catch—from time to time drinking

This face recalls Goethe's . . .

. . . Stendhal's

. . . Pope John XXIII's

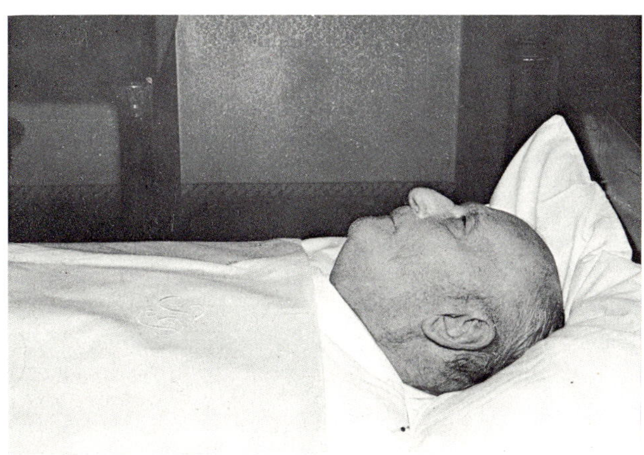

a glass of white wine, wine produced from his own vineyard. With the first light of dawn he would get into bed, and even make a few notes.

"In fact, I work all night long and in bed, like the whores."

Sometimes his catches were extraordinary. For example, one day, as we were setting the table for dinner, he said, "Yesterday, I caught the Holy Ghost. I will tell you about it after the meal . . ."

He offered us a roast capon, which, the moment it was carved and served, was replaced by a whole new one.

"The Sultan Soliman served his generals in this way. He understood that for guests to be able to have the same part of the capon next serving, it is necessary to have an entirely new beast at one's disposal."

"Yes, of course," I replied, "but this obliges you to . . ."

He then rose from the table and led me over to a glass door that opened onto a courtyard filled with fowl, and exclaimed: "Just look at all I have left!"

And then, quite resigned, he added:

"And to think that I have to eat them all!"

The afternoons and the nights—we inevitably left his house at about five o'clock in the morning—always passed very quickly. He once asked my wife to play Beethoven's First Piano Sonata, which she had already played for us at Prades. He ceremoniously offered her his arm and led her into the little music room. He listened with devotion, his eyes closed, and when she had finished, he accompanied her back to her armchair. Then, all of a sudden, he asked her if she would play it all over again. He repeated the same ceremony, and afterward, in the room dominated by the portrait of him by Canals, "painted with the light of the moon," he spoke, as always, at length and with spirit, until dawn.

He died in 1962, when he was almost eighty years old. On his deathbed his face, which in a photograph taken at Montpellier recalls Stendhal's, and which in another photograph of Pujols with Dali evokes Goethe's, now resembled the face of Pope John XXIII. I studied the curve of his temple and what he called his "imperial" nose, and noticed that his eyes were not completely closed. The eyelids were partially open, as if he still hoped to see something. One of his aphorisms came to mind at that moment: "Nothing is definitive, not even death." And then I suddenly remembered the line by Marius Torres which harmonizes so well with the theory of this philosopher: "This twilight of the angel that comes from behind prevents me from stopping."

Pujol's son Faust asked me to deliver the funeral oration. In front of the casket of the friend who had been a master I tried to sketch an image of the man and his work; and in the gentle evening, as we went into the cemetery in the middle of the fields, I recited a poem written by Pujols in his youth, a poem of "fra-angelical" simplicity and purity.

He told us that Gaudí, interred in the crypt of the *Sagrada Familia,* had his stone dream "over his head, like a canopy," and I now think that Francesc Pujols, buried at Martorell, has "over his head, like a canopy" the dream contained in the unpublished books and manuscripts that perpetuate his memory. Each of the two Titans who are brought together in this present work directed the flamboyant towers of a great unfinished work toward the sky of the soul. When and who will finish their work?

Gaudí, smiling, spoke of centuries. He was working for God. "My client is not in a rush."

Sure of himself, Pujols said: "I am not even a hundred yet!"

JOAN ALAVEDRA

I

THE POETICS OF GOTHIC HELLENISM AND THE SAGRADA FAMILIA

. . . those glassy blue eyes of his, so like the marbles that children play with . . .

Although many people will be surprised that in the midst of our articles on literary matters we speak of the great architect of Catalonia—whom we call the great architect of the universe for reasons that we have stated and will state in this and other critiques and commentaries which we have dedicated and perhaps will dedicate to the architectural work that Gaudí has left to us on passing to the other world—they will not find it so strange when they see that in contributing to the treasury of anecdotes, sayings, and recollections which everyone has been compiling as a result of his death, we plan to bring out his brilliantly illuminating and ardently comparative ideas about classic and romantic literature, set forth in a memorable conversation held in the shadow of the apse of the Temple of the *Sagrada Familia*—a conversation we will never forget as long as we live and a conversation that we hope will always be remembered by Catalonia, however many centuries may pass, for in it Gaudí set forth one of his finest visions, a vision as grand as the visions that he made of stone and cemented with the blood of his soul.

THE GOTHIC ORESTEIA

We recall speaking with that enlightened thinker from the Campo de Tarragona—he told us that as long as he saw people dying he would believe in immortality, that he enjoyed seeing the sea from the land because in that way he could see heaven twice, once in the air and again in the water, and he went on to talk of Greek art, the only art in the world which is and forever will be classic (a point on which we agree)—as if the conversation were taking place today, and as if we were still listening to him and watching him as he said that we had only to compare Aeschylus' Orestes with Shakespeare's Hamlet and we would see (here he demonstrated that literary vision which marks the separation between classical and romantic art) that Hamlet was nothing but a Gothic Orestes (this phrase so beautifully composed and spoken was his own); Shakespeare's great genius in conceiving Hamlet, his greatest creation, was not in the creation of a new character as many people believe and maintain, but rather in the deformation of an ancient Greek character who had long existed in poetry and legend.

that enlightened thinker from the Campo de Tarragona . . .

The village of Reus, where Gaudí was born, is located between the sea and the mountains, about nine miles inland from Tarragona.

. . . he enjoyed seeing the sea from the land . . .

"Mediterraneans are people of space . . ."

(Gaudí)

The difference between the Aeschylean vision of the *Oresteia* and Shakespeare's vision of Hamlet (both ancient and modern tragedy center on the same divine and human mission to avenge the death of the father by killing the mother who had assassinated him in order to marry her brother-in-law, the brother of the dead man, who sought and indeed did capture the crown by gaining control of the wife and queen) was, according to Gaudí's artistic vision, the same difference as that which exists between the Greek temple and the Gothic cathedral.

Orestes, like the Greek temple, has an external light that shines far and wide and can be seen by the spectator in his seat high above the stage just

. . . like bread soaked with oil . . .

At any hour of the day Catalans like to nibble at a chunk of their bread—among the best of the world—rubbed with garlic and onion or tomato, and then sprinkled with olive oil.

as sailors can perceive Greek mountain temples from the sea, and in order to comprehend the tragedy we need only contemplate the character who represents it (Gaudí explained this, taking in everything around us with those glassy blue eyes of his, so like the marbles that children play with), but Hamlet, like the Gothic cathedrals, carries his light within, and in order to appreciate and comprehend the tragedy he embodies, one has to delve into the corners of the soul and the character, like one who walks through the nave of a cathedral and approaches the altars of the chapels, where the light of the windows mixes with the light from the oil of the lanterns that anoints the brightness of the day—like bread soaked with oil, we said, adding a bit of our own style to that of Gaudí.

GREEK ART AND FORMAL PURITY

It is clear as spring water that Gaudí read and admired Shakespeare, just as he admired and visited daily the Cathedral of Barcelona—the cathedral whose light is most anointed with shadow (as if the shadow were the oil of the lanterns and the light the bread)—but he always preferred the Cathedral of Tarragona, which he and his disciple Jujol (who is also from Tarragona and is worth as much as the master) knew as well as if they had constructed it themselves (Jujol's pencil had caught its every corner, and Gaudí must certainly have sketched it too); it is also clear that he admired above all other artistic visions the Hellenic concept which had succeeded in discovering the definitive forms for the art of all mankind, however much other lands of the world may have or possibly could have surpassed Greek art in vital expressive intensity; as we ourselves have said so many times, the expression of life—the essential secret of all aesthetics according to our own Milá—has been known by all peoples from the most savage to the most civilized, but pure form was only discovered by Greece, and all peoples who have wanted to obtain and possess it have had to copy from her; whereas all other peoples have developed their artistic conceptions from their religion, Greece developed her religion from her artistic conception, for the Greek religion presided over by Venus and Apollo was, as we all know, a work of art, as was the work of science left to us by Plato's homeland.

. . . his disciple Jujol . . . worth as much as the master . . .

ORESTES AND HAMLET

Thinking back after so many years on Gaudí's artistic vision (at least nineteen or twenty years have passed since that conversation: as we now write these lines, we are forty-four years old, and then, at the most we must have been twenty-four or twenty-five) and recalling the words of that art critic who, good architect that he was, compared the characters of the tragedies of all periods with the temples and cathedrals in the architecture of all times, it occurs to us now, as we write and evoke the artistic and religious visions of Gaudí, that someone might argue that the immense genius of Shakespeare did much more than deform the Orestes of Aeschylus, that he created a new character by introducing immense doubt into the soul of Hamlet, causing Hamlet to doubt—as we all know—what he had been told by his father's ghost when it appeared to him at the castle demanding revenge, causing him to doubt that there is life after death, for Hamlet—as we also know—when confronted by the closed doors of eternity, questions whether there is another life beyond this one or not, whether he should believe or ignore it, and whether it would be more worthy to kill himself or to live; similarly, he is made to doubt the extremely pure love of Ophelia, who dies in madness brought on by his doubt, and finally to doubt, with sword in hand, whether or not he should indeed revenge his father by killing his stepfather (who had killed the father as we know) when he finds him praying and fears that the criminal's soul might go to heaven and his father thus be left without the revenge which he has demanded—one of the greatest scenes ever written for the theater; such an argument might further maintain that Aeschylus' Orestes is just the opposite of Hamlet in being the embodiment of decision and fated destiny that goes directly to its goal without vacillation: the author's genius presents him to us expressly headed home and disguised so that no one will know him, determined to accomplish the fatal and inescapable vengeance, ready to do everything that he has been commanded to do and never doubting anything; this is a fair description of the situation, for there is no tragic attitude more firm and singleminded than that of Orestes, not only in Aeschylus' version but also in those of Sophocles and Euripides when they too send him to avenge the father by killing the mother; but we must not forget that it was the genius of Aeschylus as immense as Shakespeare's and as immense as Gaudí's, after clearly presenting Orestes' unvacillating determination, to have him doubt when the decisive moment arrives to strike the knife into his mother's breast and accomplish the revenge that fate has ordered: hearing his mother beg him to recall that hers was the breast that suckled him and that she is after all his mother, Orestes with his knife in hand—condensing into one single instant all of the doubts in Shakespeare's tragedy which occupy five acts and a multitude of scenes—turns to his good friend Pilades, who is always at his side (the two being constant companions), and asks what he should do; Pilades answers that he should carry out the fated revenge, and so Orestes does; we need hardly comment that it is precisely when Orestes—who is decision personified, just as Hamlet is the personification of doubt—is made to doubt for just an instant that the characterization is elevated to the highest peak of tragic sublimity: we see the man who will stop at nothing to accomplish his fate stand paralyzed by doubt and indecision (like Hamlet before the gates of eternity and before the love of Ophelia).

. . . at the most we must have been twenty-four or twenty-five . . .

GREEK EXTERNALIZATION AND GOTHIC INTERNALIZATION

Doubt, then, which constitutes the sublime soul of Hamlet, likewise constitutes the sublime moment of Aeschylus' *Oresteia,* and consequently the very element which might seem to disprove Gaudí's comparison of these two characters of the ancient and modern theater serves instead to substantiate and reinforce it: we see clearly that the doubt of Hamlet is like a cathedral filled with light and shadow—a mixture of the brightness of day and the light of the lanterns, which are also the brightness of night, for they burn by day and by night—and the doubt of Orestes', like the brightness of lightning, which paralyzes those who contemplate it—a doubt like a Greek temple, sustained by decision as if by columns, and surrounded by the light of day without a single shadow that might otherwise dim its sublimity; indeed, even the doubt that might seem to be the radical difference between Orestes and Hamlet substantiated Gaudí's vision, for, as we have seen and said, he held that the difference between Orestes and Hamlet was the same as that between a Greek temple and a Gothic cathedral, and here we see that in the doubt of these two personages as well, the same difference obtains and the same comparison can be made, for just as light surrounds the Greek temple and makes its lines stand out, doubt surrounds the decision of Orestes, who doubts because of outside circumstances rather than because of what he carries within him, and just as the Gothic cathedral contains its light within—in its core, which is the choir—thus also is Hamlet's doubt born of his very own soul (like the light from the lanterns) and his doubt is constant—the opposite of Orestes, who doubts only in the decisive moment of the tragedy, when sublimity steals, or is made to steal, the scene.

And thus not only is the conception of the character Hamlet a deformation of the conception of Orestes—as Gaudí pointed out—but also Hamlet's doubt is the deformation of the doubt of Orestes, that prototype of the completely decided man; similarly, the Gothic is nothing more than a deformation of the classic, for despite the greater and more intense expression of the fundamental, vital aesthetic element which this deformation may have or could have produced, it is evident that never has an artistic form been discovered superior to that of Hellenic art, which both we and Gaudí admired for its uniqueness.

Just as the classic can be considered as an aesthetic externalization, and the Gothic an internalization (for where the classic points out and explains, the Gothic seems to hide and collect), the external and shining doubt of Orestes becomes the internal and shaded doubt of Hamlet, which goes beyond the form to the innermost depths, supporting what Gaudí told us on that memorable day when he compared ancient and modern tragedy to the classic and Gothic temples—a conversation which we hereby bequeath to the intellectual treasury of Catalonia.

THE GOTHIC HELLENISM OF THE SAGRADA FAMILIA

Confronted with this literary and artistic vision which so radically set apart this man who built flaming and living cathedrals in an age that is everywhere else building them cold and dead, Gaudí being the only architect in modern times who gives life to the architecture of his time—an architecture dead to the world—confronted with this graphic vision which gave us Hamlet as the glassmaker's Orestes, painted in the colors of the stained glass that filters light into the naves of the Gothic temples, all of the artist's architectural ideas shook as if there had been an earthquake; it was then that we ourselves, personally, standing there in front of the apse, asked him why such a determined and convinced admirer of the art of the Greeks (the *unique* art of the Greeks) had conceived and constructed the temple of the *Sagrada Familia* as a Gothic cathedral, and we heard from his lips that response which was to be both disconcerting and enlightening at the same time—that which was published in the newspapers when he died—as he maintained that his temple was Hellenic.

. . . just as light surrounds the Greek temple . . .

THE GREEK CANON: DEFINITIVE ARTISTIC FORMS

This paradoxical statement by our architect (a man of the baroque and a worshipper of the Greeks, as we are) who could give any architectural monstrosity all of the grace in the world, was based—as he himself explained when he saw our surprise and that of our friends who listened to him, half-bewitched and half-confused—on Gaudí's belief that his style was that which the Greeks would have developed had they continued to thrive until our time; needless to say, we did not and do not believe this, for we are convinced—like Gaudí—that before dying off and disappearing from the face of the earth, the Greeks left behind the definitive models for every art form, developing an exclusive classicism, and it would seem natural that they would have continued to work within this style until this day, or however long they lasted, repeating the same definitive forms once they had flowered and born fruit, for if they had continued to live and had also changed radically, they would not have shown the ability to surpass their own artistic visions as contained in the eternal aesthetic forms, but would only have demonstrated their capacity to decay and to forget the definitive artistic vision that was once their own—a vision that humanity was to forget centuries later: after having produced the Greco-Roman civilization, mankind fell into obvious decadence and had to await the centuries of the Italian Renaissance before realizing once more that the canonic forms were those discovered by the ancients, and not by men of the Byzantine, Romanesque, or Gothic periods, which preceded the Italian Renaissance, men who opened the eyes of the founders of our modern civilization; in founding their civilization the men of the European Middle Ages overlooked the Greek temples, the Roman arches, and those statues that remained from ancient times and had not been buried for centuries, passed over the land of the vines, the fields, and the cities without seeing that those stones contained the eternal edifice of the only complete artistic vision known in the history of mankind, until finally they achieved sufficient cultural development to understand it; once the statues were dug up from the vineyards and from the foundations of the Gothic houses, the artistic canons of Greco-Roman antiquity were rehabilitated under the conviction that neither the Gothics nor the Asians, neither Africa nor the newly-discovered America, had developed an artistic canon which could compare with that of the Greeks.

. . . his masterpiece, the Casa Milá *on the Paseo de Gracia . . .*

II

GAUDÍ AS THE ARCHITECT OF LIFE

The witnesses to that conversation with Gaudí, who listened in wonder and ecstasy—my friends the late Montoliu and the still living Obiols and Grau, who will bear me out—can testify to the emotion we felt in the presence of that man who had used architecture, the art of organizing inorganic forms, to create works that disorganize organic forms—as can be seen quite clearly in his masterpiece, the *Casa Milá* on the Paseo de Gracia at the corner of the Calle de Provenza; they must still remember, as we ourselves do, that as the conversation and the discourse continued on the excellence of Greek art (whose praises he sang and exalted), we, who all admired his work, congratulated him in chorus on the rich quality of the stone in the *Sagrada Familia* façade and especially in the four bell towers which bind in the portals—to which he replied that the stone was not to be admired, for the towers would be painted from top to bottom.

. . . the whole Sagrada Familia *was nothing but hens and roosters . . .*

(drawing by José María Jujol)

COLOR AND LIFE

"It was the Romans," he told us to support his intention of hiding the marvelous aesthetic quality of the stone (which must be familiar to all of our readers), "who showed off and reveled in the richness of stone and marble, leaving it bare so that everyone would see it, for the Romans were not artistic, and their only trait was vanity and love of ostentation and luxury; the Greeks always painted their stone, even if it was marble, so that nothing of it could be seen—and it was color that attracted everyone's eye, even above the architectural or sculptural forms which were intended to be seen and admired from near and far."

"It surprises everyone that I plan to polychrome the façade of the *Sagrada Familia,* because people are surprised at anything," Gaudí told us with his

. . . Brilliantly illuminating ideas . . . set forth in a memorable conversation held in the shadow of the apse of the Sagrada Familia . . .

Gaudí is recognizable in the center of these visitors with his white beard and his hands held behind his back.

. . . the figures of fowl . . .

luminous half laugh, which was brighter than an out-and-out laugh and which demonstrated the naturalness and the ease with which he did and said the strangest things, far removed from ordinary ways of thinking (this can also be seen in the effortless way that he realized his most complicated buildings), "but the other day, one of the many visitors who come said, on seeing the figures of fowl which decorate the sides of the entrance portal, that the whole *Sagrada Familia* was nothing but hens and roosters, and though his intentions were perhaps not the best, I consider the phrase to be highly significant," he said this laughingly, "because it demonstrates that in the bare stone that you are now admiring, the visitor already saw the red of the comb and the wattle on the roosters and the hens, and the yellow, blue, green, white, black, and all the colors of the beak, the eyes, the feathers, and the legs which will be there when the work is completely ready and fully colored."

. . . on Majorca, that golden island . . .

THE GREAT CARILLON FOR BARCELONA

This great architectural builder, who has been rightly called the poet of stone, could also be called a musician—not only because of the silence that accompanies his architecture and the wind that sings in the original lines of his stone edges and walls with a sound very different from that of the buildings of the other modern architects, Gaudí's disappearing contemporaries, but also because he told us that he had devised a system of tubular bells which were to be played by means of a keyboard and occupy all of the 15 or 20 bell towers of the temple, making melodies and harmonies to be heard by all of Barcelona in the morning, at noon, and in the evening; he could also be called the sculptor of architecture, because besides including many figures from the organic world (which properly belong to sculpture, as the inorganic goes with architecture), he gave—as we have said before and will repeat—an organic quality to both the over-all conception and the details of the buildings that he erected, especially his later ones; and he could also be called a painter, not only because of his stated plans to polychrome the entire temple, but also because—as we all know—the color combinations which he used in decorating his buildings were extremely pure and refined—colors that melt in the eyes at a glance, much like sugar in the mouth; he was the architect who, loving and adoring Greek art throughout his lifetime as few others have, could leave behind a building such as the *Sagrada Familia,* of which a coachman could say (turning to the visitor he was accompanying and who was observing that sublime fragment of Gaudí's cathedral from his seat in the coach pulled up in front) that the façade was made entirely out of stone cut out by hand with the hammer; we ourselves heard him say this on one of the many visits we have made, still make, and will make to that piece of temple façade which perhaps is never to be finished, and which sings in the silence of the Field of the Harp (which is where the modern temple is located); Gaudí, using a language as concrete as it was symbolic, called this the Portal of the Life or the Nativity, and there he placed the roosters and hens, as if at the door of a country house; the other lateral façade, on the opposite side of the temple, was to contain the Portal of Death [or the Passion] and that of the middle—the principal entrance to the church—the Portal of the Resurrection; Gaudí could describe them with such vivid detail that they seemed already finished, as if one could walk in and out of them, because for him (as we have said and we will repeat here as the end of this discussion of his artistic vision and before going on to the religious vision) everything was quite uncomplicated, and when he had thought something through it was as good as done and finished.

. . . the story which the illustrious Rusiñol tells with such good humor . . .

. . . he could also be called a musician because he told us that he had devised a system of tubular bells . . . to be heard by all Barcelona . . .

A project for the organ towers of the Façade of the Glory or of the Resurrection.

. . . the opposite side . . . was to contain the Portal of Death [or the Passion] . . .

THE BIRTH OF A CATHEDRAL

Since we have decided to take advantage of this opportunity to set down all the anecdotes that we know about Gaudí, and since in ending our evocation of this great architect's artistic vision we have mentioned that the temple of the *Sagrada Familia* may never be completed—something which constantly worries those of us who contemplate, admire, and adore it because we feel that it would be a shame if a work such as this, so well begun, should not be finished—we can cite another anecdote which reveals Gaudí's religious vision as well as the one mentioned above illustrates his artistic ideas; it is the story which the illustrious Rusiñol tells with such good humor in recalling a conversation with Gaudí, concerning the *Sagrada Familia*, on Majorca, that golden island that reminds one of the temple which, when one arrives by sea, rises up like a golden architectural island in the midst of the silver sea of houses of our beloved city of Barcelona; they talked at length, and touched on the problem of the termination of the *Sagrada Familia*, begun by the architect del Villar (father of our friend del Villar, who was also an architect and author of the present façade of the church of the Monastery of Montserrat, he died only a few days ago in Geneva, and his funeral was held here in Barcelona, as we were writing this article; his extremely lovely wife Rosa, who also died, was queen of the Floral Games in the third year of this century, when we won the natural flower which is the first prize—the prize of honor and courtesy—in that annual literary competition responsible for the revival of Catalan poetry, and it was to her—in gratitude—that we had the honor of dedicating our first and last book of poetry, which was published on that day).

THE ARCHITECTS OF THE SAGRADA FAMILIA

It must be admitted, in spite of the close friendship and respect which we held for our defunct and distinguished friend del Villar, that the work of his father, who was, as we said, the first architect of the *Sagrada Familia* and author of the crypt—that crypt which now serves as Gaudí's tomb and preserves the brain which harbored the artistic and religious visions that we evoke in this article, illuminated by the brilliance of the visions of death which now shoot up above the crypt like flames above wood, because the crypt is dry as wood, and Gaudí's work burns like fire—was the beginning of a cold cathedral which, had he been able to finish it, would not have any of the life that Gaudí has given to the continuation, because it was born dead (and in this case buried, for the crypt is underground, and can be considered dead like all of the modern cathedrals in the world); now they are all dead—he, his son, his daughter-in-law, who was queen of the festival, and Gaudí, who is buried in the building; just as the death of del Villar, the first architect, meant life for the cathedral, now the death of Gaudí, the second architect, could signal its death should it once again fall into the hands of an architect like del Villar—even though now the impulse and the life injection which Gaudí gave it would carry the architectural conception along for many years, setting the new architect's mind on fire even if it were naturally as cold as ice; and of course, the life that Gaudí has instilled in it could continue to thrive and grow if only the cathedral were placed (as we have already insisted in *La Veu de Catalunya*) under the direction of Jujol or of some other Catalan architect who, however different in school and style from Gaudí, would have a concept of architecture as vivid and flaming as that of the architect whose tomb lies at the base of the temple which he inspired with life.

. . . the first architect of the Sagrada Familia *. . .*

The initial project of Francisco del Villar. The cornerstone was laid on March 19, 1882; on August 11 of the same year Francesc Pujols was born.

. . . needless to say, we are interested in the problem of the completion of the temple on the Field of the Harp . . .

. . . The *Sagrada Familia,* still under construction.

. . . the crypt . . . was the beginning of a cold cathedral . . .

The work of Francisco del Villar.

We have, then, within our lifetime (the *Sagrada Familia* is a temple that was begun in exactly the same year that we were born) already seen two architects, and we will see three the day that it is announced who is to continue the work, if such an announcement is ever to come; needless to say, we are interested in the problem of the completion of the temple on the Field of the Harp, as was Rusiñol, in those moments in Majorca when he spoke with Gaudí and asked him if he hoped to finish it himself, for at that hour, which has now passed into history, there was still time to hope that the great genius Gaudí could completely deliver that cathedral of which he had already produced an extremely large fragment—a fragment which emerged from his genius like an infant from the belly of its mother.

. . . *in* La Veu de Catalunya . . .

The journal *La Veu de Catalunya*, or The Voice of Catalonia, promoted Modernista ideas and publicized the archeological discoveries that supported the thesis of a Greek Catalonia.

THE LAST GREAT CATHEDRAL BUILDER

Gaudí knew perfectly well how the great cathedrals of the Middle Ages had been constructed as the daughters of the faith, hope, and charity of generations of Christians who spent their days on earth hoping for heaven and put all effort into the construction of the house of God (which was often larger than all of the houses in the town put together) in the middle of the village to pull together the aspirations of all of the souls into one single stone inspiration that climbed up to the heavens through the bell towers, where the bells—being so high—seemed more the tongues of heaven than the tongues of the earth; these were cathedrals built with gigantic quantities of gold and of work, with those who could not offer gold offering their labor, and built over long periods of time; they were begun in one style, continued in another, and terminated in yet another, as we can see in the cathedrals which began as Romanesque, became Gothic, and ended up in the Renaissance or the Baroque and Neoclassic styles, which actually return them to the stage previous to the Romanesque, because—as we know—the Greeks and the Romans were first in historical order, and seem to be last in the artistic; he who knew all of these facts so well answered Rusiñol with his stock response to this question about the termination of the *Sagrada Familia*, saying that neither he nor anyone now living would finish it, because it is a known fact in the history of architecture that all cathedrals have taken three or four centuries to build; at this, Rusiñol, with characteristic irony, asked him if he believed that there would still be religion three or four hundred years from now.

We need not tell those who knew Gaudí and know how he thought and how he felt, that on hearing this question from the great Rusiñol, who was never one to mince words and would always speak his mind because he scoffed at everything, the great architect of the universe fell as silent as a corpse, as silent as he is now, for as we all know, he had a blind faith in religion, even though—as likewise we all know—his convictions were those of Catholicism, which dims the religious vision of all who profess it, because instead of making the vision scientific or dialectic, they make it a moral or ethical one—completely disfiguring the general picture of the religious reality that swaddles and contains us all; he lowered his eyes and closed his lips, as if he were mentally praying, while his shoulders drooped, not knowing what to say or do; Rusiñol must have continued to look on in amusement, contemplating Gaudí's solemn reaction, which intensified in a manner as comical as it was mystical; as in every case when he heard someone speak against religion, he was disconcerted to the point of being speechless: a reaction that demonstrates his moral and ethical conception of religion, for if his concept had been scientific like ours, he would have been able to laugh along with those who laugh at it, and to follow the joke of the painter-poet—a man completely free of such mystical preconceptions alt-

. . . *a blind faith in religion* . . .

Gaudí receives communion during a religious ceremony held in the open air.

hough he was the author of *El Místic*—who left Gaudí without an answer. The architect of the temple of the *Sagrada Familia,* which rises up from the Field of the Harp like the harp of the field, sculpted his religious vision there in those stones which represented the height of his artistic vision, as if he were playing the harp of the field that today is filling with houses; just as a religious preacher or a sacred orator sculpts his religious vision in artistically envisioned words of discourse or propagandistic sermons as if plucking the harp of sacred oratory, he puts art at the service of religion instead of putting religion at the service of art—a feat which (as we have said) only the Greeks have achieved in all history.

To raise doubts about the eternity of that religion which Gaudí professed and preached in words of stone—hammer-hewn by hand as the coachman said—was like interrupting a sacred orator in the midst of the silence of those who listen; if the orators that preach with words within the cathedrals of stone are left mute and disconcerted by thoughtless interruptions in the moment of their most inflamed oratorical propaganda, it goes without saying that he who preached not only with the stones of the cathedral but also with the cathedral itself from the outside and from within (his discourse being the cathedral, and his words the stones which are heard from the sea, from where the towers are visible) was left all the more mute and disoriented by the several doubting words of Rusiñol, which broke in on Gaudí's orations and faith like a crack in the façade of the temple under construction, which could have destroyed everything, for while Gaudí was more than sure that neither the Catholic religion nor the church that he dedicated to it would fall, he saw that if his religious vision were destroyed, his artistic vision would also be shaken, and if snuffed out like a candle whose flame is gone, only the wax would remain, for in the *Sagrada Familia,* Gaudí consubstantially united his religious vision with his artistic vision, making them into one single conception and one single realization, because the stones—as we have already said—are words, and the words are the sermon of the Field of the Harp, delivered in the midst of Barcelona in defense of the religion of the King of the Jews and his family.

Many years later, when Rusiñol no longer remembered the question that had left the daring and luminous genius of Gaudí without an answer (he who was never without a reply and always came out on top, who always had the brilliant last word, had had his flame put out with one breath—as the candles are snuffed out on the altar—and had withdrawn like a snail into his shell) the great Catalan humorist, master of everything and author of *The Happiness that Passes Away*—a work which will never pass on itself but will always belong to the age in which it was written and acted out—accompanied the director of the Carmen Cobeña theatrical company (who was also the husband of the actress for whom the company was named) on a visit to the *Sagrada Familia* to see for himself the marvels that he had heard so much about—the marvels which nest the entire year in those stones like the birds of spring.

Rusiñol, with the distinction and grace that were his hallmark, introduced the architect and the visitor, like a minister bringing together two who are to be married, and also acted as their interpreter—for, as is well known, Gaudí did not understand Castilian very well and Oliver did not know any Catalan at all, despite his indigenous surname; the visitor immediately began to wonder, as is natural, about the eternal question which concerns us all: whether or not the *Sagrada Familia* will be finished, and when.

Rusiñol, with his special irony, interpreting and faithfully translating from Castilian to Catalan the words of Oliver as he asked the question which every one of us is asking, told Gaudí that he wanted to know if the *Sagrada Familia* would be finished; it was then, needless to say, that the great architect who dedicated cathedrals that were to last for centuries to his artistic and religious beliefs—finding the perfect manner and opportunity to respond to that question with which Rusiñol had confronted him so many years before, leaving him without an answer in a conversation on the island of Majorca—told him to answer that all cathedrals had taken three or four centuries to be finished, and that this would be no different, despite some people's belief—he added this with purposefulness, straightening those shoulders which had drooped on that day so long before—that there would be no religion three or four hundred years from now.

III

THE CATALAN RENAIXENSA

Rusiñol, when faced with this response to his own question as evoked in the words of Gaudí's answer, neither flinched nor laughed, but simply—with complete seriousness and without letting the visitor in on the secret—translated Gaudí's words from Catalan to Spanish with a literal fidelity and precision; for in spite of the fact that he confused the Catholic religion with the True religion, the architect had spoken a truth as grand as a cathedral or, perhaps better, two truths as grand as two cathedrals: it is true that cathedrals are always the work of several generations and never the work of one alone, and it is true that in most likelihood there will be religion three or four hundred years from now—with these truths Gaudí passed the ball back to Rusiñol; not only will there be a religion, but by then all false religions will be gone, and in their stead will be the true religion, as we call it—we who have for so many years dedicated ourselves to the study of the religious question from a scientific point of view; instead of dedicating cathedrals to our religion, as he whom we call the great architect of the universe did to his, we dedicate and will continue to dedicate books to it, for we are convinced that it can better be supported by arguments than by stones, for whereas stones cannot support arguments, arguments can be found to support stones—even stones as weighty as those that comprise the bell towers rising above the portals of the Expiatory Temple of the *Sagrada Familia;* to those of us who know that religion and morality are two very different things in eternity, this name is a misnomer, for this temple with all of its artistic quality and all of its possible religious significance has nothing to do with expiation: humanity is not subject to a dominant moral order that sends us to expiate in the eternal life (as prisoners are sent to prison), despite what most of the established religions teach; instead, the only moral order—as we ourselves will demonstrate in a head-on confrontation with all established religions that will prove them wrong—is the natural, logical, and necessary manifestation of that cosmic force which carries humanity on to the other life beyond this one (just as this one came after the many levels of humanity that came before us on the biological scale of organic being, forming, as we do, steps on the ladder of life which climbs from earth to eternity), which may or perhaps may not be represented and symbolized in the cathedrals of the future, which would do well to obtain at any cost an artistic value as deeply rooted and profound as that contained in this fragment of Gaudí's cathedral—a value that would characterize the entire cathedral had he been able to complete it, or if its termination should be entrusted to Jujol, who has the ability to take up the work where Gaudí left off, in that temple humbly dedicated to the Holy Family of Jesus, Mary, and Joseph (the son, the mother, and the father), which, no matter what the Catholics say, is less important than the ladder of life which climbs from earth to heaven; we all know that this was a family of Jews—carpenters

. . . either ignore or disparage the methods invented by Ramón Lull in the thirteenth century . . .

Lull, the philosopher who was called "the Illuminated Doctor," was born on Majorca and was stoned to death in 1315 at Bougie, Algeria.

Sanctuary of Montserrat at Montferri; south elevation. A project by José María Jujol, 1928.

. . . the cathedral . . . entrusted to Jujol, who has the ability to take up the work where Gaudí left off . . .
The *Sagrada Familia* in 1906—a watercolor by José María Jujol.

and shopkeepers, to be exact—who, according to legend (and we have no way of knowing how true the story is, for we were not there to check it), conquered all of Europe with Israelite ideas, subdued the Roman Empire, and placed a wooden cross above the Holy Book of the people of Israel (the Bible or Holy Scriptures), nailing their son to it by his hands and feet, and placing a crown of thorns on his head with a scroll above which said, or is said to have said, Jesus of Nazareth, King of the Jews, in Hebrew, Greek, and Latin; after he was dead and buried he was declared the Son of God, King of Heaven and Earth, the Right Hand and Factotum of the Divine Being conceived in the folklore of Judea, which has dominated twenty centuries of European civilization for the simple reason that those who specialize in religion and general science studies either ignore or disparage the methods invented by Ramón Lull in the thirteenth century, and therefore all Catalan philosophy to this day, instead of studying reality, has studied the Bible—that book which our Gaudí wanted to glorify with the Expiatory Temple of the *Sagrada Familia,* which may never be finished because, as Rusiñol jokingly put it so well, there will be no religion (if we are referring to the Catholic) three or four hundred years from now; but if it were finished, and even if it were finished by Jujol (as we suggest), who is as Catholic as Gaudí, it might be possible to find the means and the manner of dedicating it to the True religion, which, as we prophesy, preach, and maintain, will destroy the religion of the Jews, and which, as we also maintain despite the derisive laughter that we hear, will be based on the Universal Catalan Science founded by Ramón Lull.

Now we know that this subject which we have brought up and touched on so many times, and which we now bring up and touch upon once again in speaking of Gaudí's religious vision is a theme that bothers and anguishes not only many of those Catalans who still maintain a façade of Catholicism, but also those who are indifferent to religion or, more than indifferent, contrary, while more or less disguising themselves in the cape of indifference, and who consider us to be the secret agent of the Catholics or a fantastic reactionary and a visionary who does not know what he is saying and is lost in his daydreams—especially when we reveal the mission that we assign to Catalonia.

THE CATALAN GENIUS

Leaving scientific arguments and proofs to our scientific works where they belong, we will now permit ourselves—in these solemn moments dedicated to recalling and setting forth the artistic and religious visions of our Gaudí, who in art was Hellenic, and in religion Catholic, Apostolic, and Roman—to bring to light certain arguments which, without proving anything, show that Catalonia, which is so degraded and considered as less than nothing by those Catalans who publicly mock our missionary prophecies, is a land which produces giants and geniuses among men, such as Gaudí himself, in whom the people cannot believe even though he was here before their eyes and under their noses, and they all saw him place stone upon stone in plain sight of all Barcelona, for no one has written his legend; we ourselves were able to see him, even though we did not pay any attention to who he was and what he represented, because he all alone—like the painter Fortuny, or General Prim, who were sons of Reus as he was, and like other people whom we could mention who are not from Reus, even though they seem to be—is proof enough, and a living and unquestionable indication of the force of the people's plenitude, for gigantic geniuses like Gaudí are not produced by accident, without some sort of relationship to the earth from which they are born—a relationship such as that which our Gaudí had with his sorely unappreciated Catalonia.

BILLETE N.° 2221 DEL EXPOSITOR
D. Antonio Gaudi

CONDICIONES Á QUE ESTÁ SUJETO ESTE BILLETE

1.ª Este billete es rigurosamente personal. Si lo usare otra persona que aquella á favor de la cual va extendido y por quien está suscrito, será inmediatamente recogido é inutilizado y se someterá el caso á la acción de los Tribunales.

2.ª Da derecho á entrada y permanencia en la Exposición durante los días y las horas de apertura reglamentaria.

3.ª En los días de grandes solemnidades, sólo dará derecho á permanecer junto á las instalaciones del expositor, sin perjuicio de otras disposiciones que sobre el particular pueden dictarse por la Comisión Directiva de la Exposición.

4.ª Los expositores han de entrar en la Exposición, exclusivamente por las puertas y pasos que al efecto se señalen.

No se expiden duplicados en caso de extravío.

Barcelona, Abril de 1888.

El Delegado General,

Imp. Suc. Ramírez

Catalonia . . . is a land which produces giants and geniuses among men such as Gaudí . . .

Gaudí in 1888—his exhibitor's pass to the Universal Exposition of Barcelona.

. . . like the painter Fortuny . . .

Mariano Fortuny was one of the most celebrated Spanish painters in the latter half of the nineteenth century; he died in Rome in 1874 at the age of 36, at the height of his fame.

The "Battle of Tetouan" is the most famous of Fortuny's paintings. The canvas represents one of the outstanding events of the Moroccan campaign; it shows General Prim leading the Spanish troops to victory.

THREE GENIUSES OF REUS: GAUDÍ – PRIM – FORTUNY

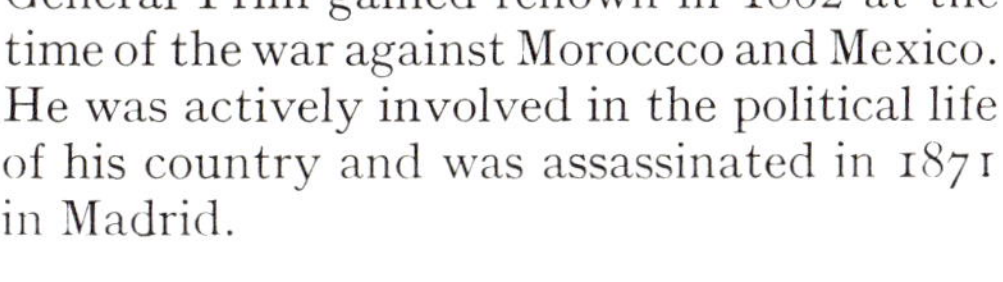

General Prim gained renown in 1862 at the time of the war against Moroccco and Mexico. He was actively involved in the political life of his country and was assassinated in 1871 in Madrid.

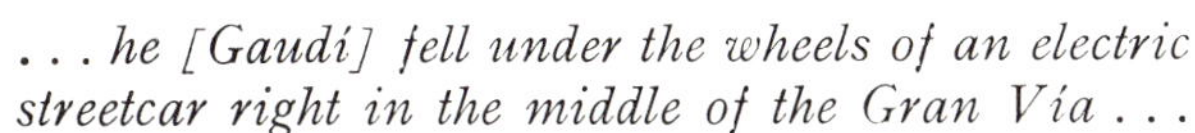

. . . he [Gaudí] fell under the wheels of an electric streetcar right in the middle of the Gran Vía . . .

left:
Barcelona, the Gran Vía.

right:
General Prim and his family.

Those who consider us exaggerated and chauvinistic can say what they please, for so long as one stone stands above another in the buildings that he left to us as his testament in stone, we will have a mute witness (the best kind, for they can never be silenced) to that which we describe as respect for the present-day glory of our land, and it will testify to our honesty and clearly demonstrate to future generations how right we are when we declare publicly, without fear or error, that Gaudí's vision is a vision worthy of comparison to the Vedic visions of India, to the Homeric visions of Greece, and to the Gothic visions of medieval Europe which covered our continent with cathedrals.

When, in those days that our architect still lived, designed, and worked among us—those days before he fell under the wheels of an electric streetcar right in the middle of the Gran Vía to be taken to his death in a public hospital, his greatest desire in life—we used our conversations and writings to proclaim that he was the greatest artist of our time, not only because of the works he accomplished and now has left to us (representing only a minimal part of what he was capable of accomplishing), but also because he alone in his genius, doing what other artists had done in other media and in other countries, revived for architecture that vital aesthetic element which, as we have said and as is known to all, had been lost to the world and especially to those populations and countries which today so gloriously lead our modern civilization; when we did this, we were considered crazy as he—or even more so; throughout his lifetime everyone (except the Catholics, who forgave him everything because he belonged to the clan) considered him fantastical from the moment he began the house for Güell on the Carrer Nou off the Ramblas, until he placed the highest stone on the only completed bell tower of the Nativity of Life façade only a few hours before arriving at the gates of death, opened to him at the Hospital de la Santa Cruz, as if placing a crown on life before entering the eternal realm of death; they say that when he was building the house on the Carrer Nou—the first palace he had ever done—he one day took his friend Güell aside (the two had become close friends, and Güell was one of the few who loved, admired, and defended him throughout his life, as is proven by the commission to develop the Park Güell) and confided that he had found only two people who liked his palatial residence: Güell and himself.

Let us say then, for the sake of informing those Catalans who still don't know it, that this man is unique in the history of modern art, and that he alone, unaccompanied by anyone from beyond our Catalan borders (in Catalonia we probably could find others, or at least one, as good) will occupy the chapter of modern times dedicated to architecture, which will include all of his works and will feature the beginnings of the Cathedral, which—as we say and we repeat—was born alive in a moment when cathedrals everywhere around the world were being born dead; these works will bear witness to the fact that Catalonia in the late nineteenth and early twentieth centuries gave its all in the effort to return life to architecture which by then had lost all vitality, just as all of the other arts which have also had to be fragmented and tortured into taking on once again that vital quality which they had exhibited in all previous periods of history.

. . . he [Count Güell] trusted him completely in the construction of the Park Güell . . .

A portico in the *Park Güell* in 1904.

WAGNER AND THE CASA MILÁ

As long as our beloved Catalan soil can produce such giants as Gaudí (it is not we who speak, but rather the stones of his poems), who raise cathedrals and build houses like the *Casa Milá* on the Paseo de Gracia, which, despite the manifest influence of modern German art that informs it in an ostensible and obvious manner, has a life and an aesthetic palpitation equaled by no

. . . considered him fantastical from the moment he began the house for Güell . . .

The salons of the Palacio Güell in 1927.

. . . Gaudí confided that he had found only two people who liked his palatial residence : Güell and himself . . .

Count Eusebio Güell, a friend and admirer of Gaudí.

other house in today's world or in ancient times—it is as if in this unique house all the aesthetic vitality of the past had been concentrated and condensed to blossom forth in the very midst of the mortal frigidity of modern architecture, which has discovered new styles without re-encountering the fountain of life, in the same way that the "Twilight of the Gods" (the last part of Wagner's tetralogy, which does indeed resemble the *Casa Milá*, for the "Twilight of the Gods" and the *Casa Milá* have the same colossal and monstrous forms, the same enormous and undulating rhythm which unites line with form, as Wagner joins the melodic line with the harmonic forms) presents in a condensed and concentrated form all of the essential aesthetic vitality of past music in the very midst of the mortal coldness of modern music, for music before Wagner had become as cold and as dead as architecture before Gaudí—something which had never been known to occur in either of these arts or in any other of the fine arts, which had always been alive and vital in the past—and Wagner did in music what Gaudí did in architecture, the one working with violins, flutes, trumpets, trombones, and tympani, and the other with the hammer and chisel, cutting into the stone as if he too were creating music in the same way as Wagner, who was caricatured as hammering away at the eardrum with a hammer and chisel; she (we speak of Catalonia, in case the readers have become lost after this long digression dedicated to comparing Gaudí with Wagner—a comparison which has never before been made and which, though it would have pleased Wagner very little, would have pleased Gaudí even less, and which can now be made only because both are dead and gone) must have blind faith in herself and her capabilities, for our dead architect represents one of the most significant arguments that can be set forth by the Catalan nation in favor of her present and future potential; Gaudí had a blind faith in Catalonia, and when those who denied the glorious future of our land would confront him with the fact that the country had done nothing in modern times, Gaudí would cite that very fact as positive proof of what could be done, for he always maintained—and rightly so—that those who have not done anything are precisely those with things left to do; this was told to us by the divine Nogués, who heard him say so one day—the same Nogués who, at this very moment, as we are writing these lines, is creating with his brush numerous painted divinities on the walls of the salon of the Plandiura house; there he paints those figures which are better than any that are being painted anywhere in the world today, yet are completely ignored and unrecognized by everyone—the Catalans ignore them, for they know as little as the foreigners about what is going on in Catalonia (the exception being our friend Carles, another great Catalan painter who brings prestige to our land—who, indeed, let the truth be told, is not a great admirer of Gaudí's work—and who first brought our attention to the capital importance of the mural paintings in the salon of our illustrious Plandiura, that inspired visionary and protector of Catalan pictorial art); we take great pride and always will take pride at having recommended Nogués to do the decoration of the main hall of that house, which is located in the Born and dedicated to being a museum of ancient and modern Catalan art; Nogués, that glory of Catalonia, who here with his work has converted the house into a palace of fine arts, so that the phrase *"roda el mon i torna al Born"* has a special meaning for those Catalans who travel around the globe seeking out artistic marvels, he too was one of the few consistent admirers of Gaudí—both of the man and of his work—and we found ourselves in agreement every time that we happened to speak of the great artist of the universe.

. . . comparing Gaudí with Wagner . . .

Caricatures: Gaudí in front of the *Casa Milá*. Below, Gaudí's Wagnerian architecture.

. . . *"roda el mon i torna al Born"* . . .

A Catalan saying that may be translated: "You wander around the world but return to the Born." The Born is a district of Barcelona.

THE VATICAN AND CATALONIA

Well then, the Catholics and those who without being Catholic, nor Apostolic, nor Roman are concerned with the religious question in Barcelona and in Catalonia will ask us how is it, and especially how can it be, that this land has the mission that we so flatteringly assign to it—that of bringing the True religion into the world and of destroying the Catholic one—Gaudí chose to spend his time building cathedrals—and living cathedrals, at that (as we ourselves confess, and as we have just affirmed here in developing our aesthetic criticism)—and churches dedicated to the exaltation, glorification, vivification, and ignition of this religion which we include among the false, saying that it will fall victim to Catalan Science founded by Ramón Lull in the thirteenth century and die at the hands of Catalonia, just as it was born at the hands of the Jews, in a Jewish family which was precisely the one to become the Holy Family to which the Expiatory Temple in question was dedicated—a church that burst forth flaming from the hands of that Catalan genius just as the True religion will burst forth flaming from the genius of our people; and if he did not make it grow more quickly, and did not build the temple in four days, as all of those who see the *Sagrada Familia* and all those who would like to see it finished demand, it is—as we have said—because the glitter of the gold and of the bank notes which represent it in the marketplace had become scarce, as if in times of drought, and the Church was at the point of breaking apart and of drying up because the golden spring of the fountain of the Catholic religion, better known as the fountain of Saint Peter, does not even glitter in the fountain of Saint Peter's in Rome—as the Vatican is well aware, and can see at very close range; we were told this not long ago by a completely reliable friend of ours who knows the Vatican inside and out; we were discussing the desperate state of the Vatican finances, which, unable to find money in Europe because of the many expenditures of the 1914 war when Germany hoped to conquer the world and was forced to content herself with that hope—the only thing she did not lose—publicized itself in America by celebrating Eucharistic congresses which we have seen lately; Pope Benedict XV had a similarly brilliant, grandiose, and original idea when he tried to rebuild the unity of Christ's Church by suppressing the use of Latin (the universal tongue of Catholicism) and by granting extensive ritual freedom and autonomy to the different Christian sects or churches in the different states or nations of the earth—an attempt to see if perhaps in building up the exhausted Vatican treasury a sort of Christian unity might also be accomplished, the logical double dream of every pope since both these things had been lost; when he was still a cardinal, the present pope was sent to Warsaw by the great Benedict XV (who could also be called Benedict the Great), and it is said that he was reluctant to go; when he had told his papal predecessor his private motives for not going, Benedict XV asked him the day of his departure, and at that point the present Pious XI, reverencing the sanctity of the father of the faithful, announced that he would leave on whatever day the Pope wished; the purpose of his mission was to study the religious state of the Slavic countries and of the schismatic sects in Russia and the other nations of Eastern Europe from the archiepiscopal seat of Poland, and we are certain that the completion of this religious mission was what earned him his present status as Pope, even though, according to reports which can now be confirmed by the facts, it was a mission that failed completely: they had been counting on Russia, who, because of the social revolution, had lost its visible head of the Church—the Czar—and they felt certain that the Pope in Rome would be needed to fill the vacuum (with ritual autonomy granted, of course), but things did not work out the way they planned, and they were left with nothing more to do, without a hope in the world, for only the example of Russia would have attracted the other states and re-established that Catholic unity so long desired and dreamed of; and only then would they have been able to aspire to dominate all of Christianity, would their hope have been justified that they could encounter a way of extending Catholicism all over the globe, even into the continents which had never before allowed it, such as Asia, which already had a religion that was superior in many important ways to the Catholic; thus they would have had universal dominance, which is and always has been the supreme and natural aspiration of the Catholic, Apostolic, and Roman Church, just as it is, has been, and will be the dream and the aspiration of other religions, of other peoples, of other empires, and of other captains, as well as of other thinkers who have wanted, want, and will want, so long as they live, to dominate the world with ideas (as Ramón Lull wanted), while the peoples, the empires, and the captains rule, or want to rule, with arms; for once the union of all Christian sects or churches is achieved and religious harmony is established between states and nations that are now divided politically and economically opposed, the Vatican would have triumphed not only in the spiritual order of faith but also in the material and temporal order, and it would have accomplished the dream of Benedict XV (before he died in a flu epidemic), who, as far as ecclesiastical dreams are concerned, could be considered as one of the greatest popes in history, but he found himself without the means to realize his dreams; the present pope, Pius XI, has practically recognized the fact that the papal crown has not been able to conquer the universe; it is up to Catalonia to vie for this prize and dispute the crown, though most of us who are here now will probably not live to see the Catalan triumph, but will then be long dead and buried.

Pope Benedict XV

Pope Pius XI

GAUDÍ AS THE ARCHITECT FOR CATALANISTA CATHOLICISM

The question, then, that we Catalan Catholics and non-Catholics must ask ourselves—returning to the theme that we left in order to discuss for a moment the general religious and political state of the Catholic Church, which is destined to die right here in Catalonia and which Gaudí glorified in his sermon of stone—a question, needless to say, capable of disquieting even the most serene among us (even he who is fully aware of the deteriorating state of the sinking Church)—is a very difficult question, not only because of the fact that Catalonia has dedicated a cathedral to the family of the founder of the Catholic religion, but also because of the equally grave or graver fact that the greatest genius in our country today, whom we have presented in support of our point as the most significant and typical representative of the force of the Catalan soil which is rooted in the minds of her sons, maintained a religious vision that was firmly and solidly Catholic—a vision that he was even able to translate into living stone, erecting an apse and four bell towers that were to sustain, exalt, and celebrate that false religion which Catalonia is destined to combat, if we are not mistaken (although this is possible, it is highly unlikely).

Indeed, one must confess that this question, which deserves an answer, gets to the very heart of the problem, and the fact that the hottest and brightest flame of Catalan and Catalanista Catholicism resided in the greatest Catalan genius of the day makes the answer to the question very difficult; for it is very hard to explain why a land that has the mission which we assign to Catalonia should exalt, elevate, and glorify Catholicism with precisely the most important and the most significant man that it has pro-

. . . *Bishop Torras* . . .
a good friend of Gaudí's, the Bishop of Vich, Torras y Bages, was the most zealous and ardent reviver of Catalan spirituality.

duced, as smoke from the fire emerges from the highest point of the house At any rate, we, as our readers can imagine, encounter difficulties of this sort at every step of the way and at every moment; to the point that they are now no longer new to us because we are used to them; reality is funny in that when it wants to simplify things, it makes them more difficult than ever by virtue of the law of paradox, which regulates all things in this world, as can be seen in the fact that Gaudí's religious vision, which inflamed his genius that was unique in Catalonia and beyond, does not definitively demonstrate that our land must each day become more Catholic—as both Bishop Torras and Gaudí himself maintained in confusing the modern mission of Catalonia with the ancient mission of Castile; not only does it fail to demonstrate this in a conclusive manner, but also it leaves much ground to be covered, and large as the difficulty which it creates may be, it still backfires in the face of the very people who hope to capitalize on it; we, availing ourselves of the very enormity of the circumstances, and without definitively proving anything (for our opponents have not proven anything against us, either) will show what consequences can be deduced from the situation that has presented itself in the question raised—consequences that can and will be used in proving the mission of Catalonia (though not beyond a doubt, for in questions of mission the sciences are still not refined enough, and we can only establish general laws which might possibly refer to the specific case—as we now propose to do, following the system that we have already used in other writings).

THE CATHEDRAL OF THE POOR AND THE NEW JERUSALEM

The religious vision of Gaudí burst into flame in the very midst of Catalonia, burning as brightly as the Life or the Nativity façade of the temple on the Field of the Harp, which sings beneath the hands of the harpist in the field in praise of the God of the Jews and His family, right in that very field which is no longer a field because it is fast becoming one of the most modern working-class neighborhoods of Barcelona—and as a neighborhood of the working class, we need not mention that it is not at all Catholic, because due to another of those paradoxes of life, Catalan Catholicism is primarily supported by our rich people and not by our poor, because in the basic ideas of society the first are as wrong as the second; the rich, as we have observed so many times, believe that their social order can be better sustained in the legend of Israel than in science, and the poor think that their order can be obtained more through science than through legends, while the truth is exactly the opposite: in some ways the Christian religion can be said to support the Communist concept of society based on a maximum expression of charity, whereas science can only be used to support the conservative social organization maintained by the ruling classes, who are those who benefit most from the social realities because they can take advantage of all of the laws that result from human progress.

So then, the religious vision of Gaudí, petrified in those four towers that rise so suddenly from the ground like a crag above the water of our Catalan Costa Brava, toward Gerona, was born and raised not only in the very midst of the land destined to destroy the Catholic religion, but also in the very midst of the most modern working-class neighborhood in Barcelona (for that reason it is also referred to as the Cathedral of the Poor), takes on the nature of a reaction or of a retaliatory response on the part of Christ's religion, which, on feeling itself mortally wounded here in our country and in this neighborhood of the Field of the Harp, as if on a field

. . . like a crag above the water of our Catalan Costa Brava, toward Gerona . . .

This is a montage of two photographs showing the relationship between the rocks of Cap Creux (above) and a detail of the "geological decoration" of the *Sagrada Familia* (below). The figure in the rocks, to indicate scale, is Salvador Dali.

of battle, rebounds and kicks, like a beast that has been wounded and ensnared by the hunter, within the soul of Gaudí—the most elevated soul in Catalonia, to assure that the rebound will be high—and the result consists of those four flames which are the four bell towers of stone; although they are mute and cannot sing, being without their bells and therefore without tongues, it cannot be denied that these are the four fingers of the prophets of Israel, which pluck the harp of the field (just as they plucked the harp of David before the coming of Jesus Christ), which continues to sing in the very midst of the workers' neighborhood; the people do not pay it any heed and do not wish to listen, for such songs are made for the ears of the rich man who listens to them while he eats and then digests his food in bed, lying at the side of a nude and famous woman, shut up in palaces filled with furniture and ancient *objets d'art*, beneath the paintings and in the shadow of the sculptures, surrounded by his gardens and great factories, his country estates and his urban properties—it is in such environs that one hears best the singing of the psalms and the hymns of the prophets—the best lyric poetry of all times and all places which we (being devotees) will never tire of hearing, especially when so well accompanied as by the harp of the field in that modern Barcelona neighborhood, plucked by Gaudí, whom we have compared to Aeschylus, to Shakespeare, and to Wagner, when speaking of Orestes, Hamlet, and the "Twilight of the Gods" (which was the twilight of Wagner's orchestral riches), and whom we can compare as well to such biblical prophets as Isaiah and Jeremiah (who, when the people mocked his preaching, said that the word of God was his opprobrium), for they were prophets who erected lyrical columns of hymns to Jehovah, placing word upon word as Gaudí placed stone upon stone in praise of God—not only to the one who was invoked by the armies in the battles fought on the pages of the Bible to contest the empire of the world, but also the God of peace and justice, whose Son conquered Europe and was placed on church altars everywhere—for each tower of the Nativity or Life façade of the *Sagrada Familia* is one of David's psalms, translated into Latin—as is indicated by the letters of the words sculpted in the stone which climb the bell towers proclaiming "Sanctus, Sanctus, Sanctus"—and the entire façade is little more than an occidental echo of the oriental prophets who sing to us from the pages of the Bible in the shade of the willows; the difference is that the prophets of Israel, like all of the other prophets, sang while looking into the future, but Gaudí, the prophet who constructed cathedrals and manipulated stones like words, sang looking backward to a past as mute as a bell tower without bells; in the temples which he dedicates to the Catholic religion, he confesses that he has nothing to add to the prophets, because for the Catholics those visionaries have said everything that there is to say, and one can only repeat their words over and over and await that which they foretold; it could be said that there is more history than prophecy involved in Gaudí's creation of the *Sagrada Familia.*

It is logical that cathedrals should be stillborn in all of those nations and states whose mission is other than that of destroying Catholicism, for there is nothing in the atmosphere of such places to excite the cathedral builders: they are produced like any other building, as if they were flour mills to bring nourishment to the body, or soap factories to keep it clean; it also seems logical that precisely in Catalonia, which is where the Catholic cathedrals will meet their final resting place—as all things must in this world—that a cathedral should be born alive, brought into the world by the only architect of modern times who was capable of giving it life, as if he were performing a miracle.

. . . Balmes who . . .

Jaime Balmes y Urpia was a Spanish philosopher of the nineteenth century. A defender of the doctrine of St. Thomas Aquinas against German philosophy, he was one of the last great Iberian scholastics.

CARLIST WAR AND CATALAN HEGEMONY

Examples of these typical biological reactions are quite frequent and well known, and there is nowhere that they cannot be found; we need go no further than Balmes, who, as we noted in our *Historiá de l'hegemonia catalana* (a book filled with examples of this sort of reaction), stated that the reason that the Carlist War in Catalonia—where absolute monarchy and the Catholic religion were defended with greater vigor and constancy than in any other region of Spain in the last century—took root and lasted longer than anywhere else was precisely because Catalonia was also the most liberal region in Spain, and that which—as we all know—most steadfastly defended the liberal or constitutional monarchy and religious freedom, suppressing the Inquisition, which the Carlists defended with fire and blood; we, in the above mentioned book, have similarly pointed out that the supreme effort made by the tradition of our Universal Science (which will scientifically explain the religious laws that involve and envelop us before this life and afterward, as well as while we are in this world, from the time that we are born until the time that we die and they bury us in the earth from whence we came) was able to take root and have an effect in the mind of that very Balmes—who was as Catalan, as Catholic, as fanatic, and as exalted as Gaudí ever could have been, and who dedicated to the architect a book which is itself a veritable cathedral—to the point that, inverting what we are saying, the brightest flame of Catalan Catholic thought shone in the very brain which developed the scientific method that would be used to expose the laws employed by the Catholic religion, just as the four bell towers of the *Sagrada Familia* façade rise up in the midst of the most modern neighborhood of Barcelona; it is as if the flesh and the soil of Catalonia were the oil of the lantern or the wax of the candle, and the flame the Catholic religion, which is to be snuffed out in the lantern's oil or the candle's wax.

Regarding the particular case of Gaudí, the religious vision, which we are using as a basis for what we are saying, revealing it as we are, and having compared the Catalan Temple of the *Sagrada Familia* with the Carlist War, which was ignited with weapon fire in the very midst of Catalan nineteenth-century liberalism, let us say (laying aside the thesis of those who maintain that it was not Gaudí who made the cathedral Catholic, but rather the cathedral that made Gaudí Catholic, because even though those who say that they knew him before he was a Catholic deserve our fullest attention, they cannot explain how this religious evolution came about, and it is something that we can never be sure of, because not only is he dead and buried, but even if he were still alive, we would not be close enough or friendly enough to ask him about it directly) that there is nothing strange or extraordinary in the fact that it should be this giant of the Catalan genius who would clearly demonstrate what we Catalans are and what we can be in that last intense and brilliant blaze of the religion that is to be destroyed right here in Barcelona, just as it was born in Jerusalem; similarly, the Carlist War—of which we have here expressly recalled Balmes' version—shone bright and effusive in the breast of those who defended the absolute monarchy and the Catholic religion (the ideals of that Castile of the sixteenth and seventeenth centuries that reigned as queen and mistress of the world and founded the long-forgotten Castilian Empire); the war lit up the Catalan mountainside, just as the four bell towers of Gaudí's cathedral light up the Field of the Harp, and Catalonia in the midst of the nineteenth century seemed to the rest of the world as the last European region to defend the Roman, Catholic, and Apostolic Church with weapons and with men, bringing religious war to our continent at a time when seemed unthinkable.

Anyone who read the newspapers in those days and saw the news of Catalonia would have thought that our land was the most Catholic in the world, because it killed and was killed in a war without rest or quarter in which even the prisoners were shot, including the wounded who were carried to their fate on stretchers; nevertheless, the Catholic Balmes, priest of the Roman Church, sheds light with his explanation that if Catalonia went to war for Catholicism, it was not because the Catalans wanted these ideals to triumph, but rather because their extreme liberality—so much greater than in the other regions of Spain—caused fury in the hearts of the Catholics who put lives and money on the line in defense of the theory of the Jews —a clever people who knew how to cover their tracks and found fanatics who defended their ideas and still defend them, as in the Carlist War.

Without wishing to compare the architectural genius of Gaudí, who arranges stones to give an artistic and religious form, with the strategic genius of General Cabrera, leader of the Apostolic forces in the first and second Carlist Wars (who, they say, was a prodigy and earned the name of "Tiger"), we will state that all that we have said in discussing the Catalan religious wars could also be related to the temple of David's harp, which, once placed on the Field of the Harp, became the temple of the harp of the field; just as the war cries of the mountain guerillas that made all of the Catalan countryside resound with the three words "God," "Country," and "King" were the last words of the Christians who went down fighting like those first martyrs who allowed themselves to be killed, so too the religious vision of Gaudí—as brilliant as his artistic vision and his architectural vision—bids farewell to the religion based on that greatest book in the history of literature (as Milá put it so well in his aesthetic studies), which is a book read more by the religious than by the artists—a situation that should be reversed, for we artists should read it to savor the aesthetic essence it contains, and the religious folk should not even look at it, for we all know that the true religion is contained in science, and not in legends.

The curious coincidence, then, that Catalonia, who must carry out her mission by destroying Catholicism, should be the only nation in the world capable of producing a living cathedral like those of the most fiery days of the Catholic faith which it glorifies and symbolizes, is explained, or can be explained, by the biological laws of action and reaction that control all things; we have seen that in this manner we can explain the Carlist War (or the last European religious war), which, needless to say, was a war as alive as Gaudí's cathedral; just as the Castilians say so wisely that there is no worse wood for making a mast than the wood of the boat itself, we can also say that there is no stronger and livelier Catholicism than that found in the land of Universal Science, which will drown it in the sea of time and history.

Don Carlos de Bourbon, pretender to the Spanish throne, was the cause of the three so-called Carlist Wars, the last of which ended in 1876 in favor of Alfonso XII.

THE NOURISHING MYSTIQUE OF CATALONIA

Without wishing to offend the Catholic religion (which—as our readers know—we respect most highly and consider to be among the best that exist today), it seems to us that when Catalonia (the very land assigned to destroy it) dedicates not only cathedrals but the most fundamentally artistic cathedral in the world to Catholicism, we have the case of those who, in calling the pigs to the slaughter, give them everything possible to fatten them up and get them to weigh what they should at the moment of death, when they are prepared to be eaten by man, following the laws of antagonistic symbiosis, which dictate that we organic beings must live off one another; and we all know that every last bit of the pig is edible: as the Catalan refrain referring to the laws of nutrition and regeneration—whose truth we can observe in the bodies of all living beings—tells us, "in the pig as in the woman, every part is delicious."

. . . the strategic genius of General Cabrera . . .

Ramón María Cabrera y Griño was one of the most ardent of Don Carlos' generals; he was knighted as the Count of Morella.

The name "Carlist" was applied in Spain to all those who refused to recognize the legality of the law by which Ferdinand VII modified, in 1830, the succession of the throne in favor of his daughter Isabella and to the detriment of his son Don Carlos and his descendants. Those who supported Don Carlos were mostly members of the clergy and the peasantry, people largely hostile to liberalism and centralization. The satirical period drawing illustrated below ridicules the partisans of Don Carlos by transforming them into tools of the Inquisition.

IV

VIGOR AND SUPREMACY OF BAROQUE AND FANTASTIC FORM

When there no longer exists any trace or recollection of this reactionary Catalan Church which the Catholics call their Expiatory Temple, when humanity, educated in Catalan Universal Science, realizes that it has nothing to expiate because there will be no expiation in eternity, and when the mountain of stones has disappeared from the debris which is all that will remain in the Field of the Harp, which, having lost its harp, will once again be only a field—if at that time these words which we are writing now should still exist (although everything is bound to disappear, words can always last longer than stones, for words have wings and are carried by the wind), let all who read this know that the artistic vision of Gaudí, fused in one mass and concentrated in those four flames of a fire more intense than ice, created something unique in architecture, giving Barcelona something extraordinary to see without leaving Barcelona, by erecting that façade which, with all the luminous exteriority of the Hellenic art that Gaudí so admired and adored, also embodied—according to the architect himself—all the structural daring of the Gothic which erected bell towers above portals in the Gothic cathedral of Barcelona (where Gaudí went every day), just as he erected the four bell towers of the *Sagrada Familia* above the portals of the Nativity façade; the whole and even the details were enveloped in a monstrous grandiosity that recalled at a distance the great architectural conceptions of India, with which Gaudí would have nothing to do, despite the inescapable relationship: universal genius that he was, he not only had relatives in all places and in all times, but also benefactors from whom he accumulated inheritances to carry into the streets of Barcelona.

Having mentioned this grand mixture of styles which produced the confused, baroque, and monstrous style of Gaudí's architecture, we will say that there are very few of us who admire the aesthetic power of this Catalan genius of our time (who would have no rival if all men were equally sensitive) and there are many thousands who do not like it, who can't bear it—something that we can understand perfectly well, for only those of us who seek in art the aesthetic essence which is the substantial and universal basis of all artistic work, and who can feel and admire it when it is there, only we are not afraid to experience the earthquake that comes with it.

And if our style—like that of Gaudí—is confusing, baroque, and monstrous (as those who read this very literary composition dedicated to the great architect of Catalonia and those who have read our other works can testify), we, like him, recognize and declare that there is no other classic and definitive style but the Greek style in architecture, sculpture, and poetry—and we only omit music because the music of that artistically privileged people is not well known enough, nor did it produce figures comparable to those in the other arts.

The result of this similarity between Gaudí's style and our own (comparing the two at a respectful distance) is that it can somewhat rightly be said of both of us that whereas we are, or could be, more or less important, and we have more or less personal artistic and literary significance (in spite of the many defects attributed to us), we are, on the other hand, generally a plague and a misfortune to our people, because, instead of contributing to the creation and formulation of a pure and unsullied collective style, we undo and monsterize it; the case is similar when water from the clouds, instead of falling gently as in a winter rain, falls all at once, as the rain of summer which comes with lightning and thunder.

. . . in the pig as in the woman, every part is delicious . . .

"This is worthy of Homer! It's communion! What a grandiose thing and what colossal dialectic!"—uttered by Salvador Dali as he dictated his "instantaneous" translation of Pujols into French.

Period caricatures that make fun of the *Casa Milá*, from the periodical *En Patufet.*

. . . there are very few of us who admire the aesthetic power of this Catalan genius . . .

A UNIVERSAL VISIONARY STYLE

Those who say this are more than right, for both of us (in this case we permit ourselves to stand proudly at Gaudí's side, within the limits of modesty), being avid admirers of Greek art and composing in the artistic style that we do, must recognize that it is a style which disintegrates everything and makes people dizzy (even those with a good head on their shoulders must tilt it in order to get the picture straight), and many do not even want to bother to turn their eyes to look at Gaudí's buildings or to glance at the pages of our writing; it is a style that cannot and never will have the model and canonical effectiveness to educate and direct the artistic taste of a people or of a collective; nor will it smooth the paths for those who will come later and follow in our footsteps, and we must admit that however much we admire the Greeks, who produced the eternal artistic guidelines and are the educators of the collectives and the peoples, we do not preach by example, nor does our style have anything to do with that of those unique and ancient people, for Gaudí—like the architects of India and the Gothic times, like the Vedic hymns, the Bible, and like us, who (in spite of our modesty) aspire in our field to something greater than all of them—uses his work as a means of expressing his real or fantastic, retrospective or prophetic, profane or religious, historic or invented, legendary or scientific vision, placing—as we have said before—the artistic vision at the service of his great ideals, as opposed to the Greeks, who, as we have also said before, place their ideals at the service of their artistic vision; thus, whereas the work of Greece which subordinated everything to its artistic conception—taking even its religious vision from the artistic—can be and will be the eternal model for artists and admirers of art (for Greece was born and lived until she accomplished her artistic mission, just as Rome accomplished her juridical mission, and Catalonia will carry out her scientific mission—as we have maintained so so many times), the artistic work of other peoples, however inspired and elevated, will always be subordinate to their mission: India, Israel, Gothic Christianity, Gaudí in the Temple of the *Sagrada Familia,* and we ourselves to a certain extent subordinate our art to a religious mission—these peoples and races and Gaudí because they seek in it a proper religious end, and we indirectly seek the same, for we know that the mission of Catalonia is scientific, and that science contains the laws of religion within its universal objective; thus we do what the others do and what the architect of our people did in subordinating the artistic to the religious vision, by taking our visions of art from the conventions of our scientific or religious visions.

ATHENS, JERUSALEM, AND BARCELONA

Like the Hindus, like the Hebrews, like the Gothics, and like the architect of the modern Catholic temple of Catalonia, we, poets or architects that we may be, are not truly artists as the Greeks were; the Greeks were nothing else, while we are propagandists or preachers of our ideas or the ideals of our people, as were those immense and unequaled poets Jesus of Nazareth (the greatest poet we have ever read) and the prophets who came before Him and announced His coming; they did not set out to make works of art, nor did the poets of the Vedic hymns propose to do so; whereas the Greeks created the eternal models of aesthetics, we, like the others mentioned, want to create the eternal models of ethics or of dialectics, and we concern ourselves with religion or science—a task, needless to say, quite different from that of Greece, whose only mission on earth was to light the aesthetic light and make Athens the artistic capital of the world, just as the Jews made Jerusalem the religious capital of medieval Europe, and just as we hope to make Barcelona the scientific capital of the earth, even though the thought horrifies the Catalans and though men of other countries will not listen to us (but they will listen eventually, while the Catalans continue to be horrified, because it always happens that way: when those outside are convinced, it is they who must convince those at home).

GREEK ART AND THE CASA MILÁ

Whereas we recognize that our style has nothing to do with Hellenicism, and that the two cannot be even vaguely compared, because whatever we lack in academicism we make up for in deformation, it happened that Gaudí—as is well known—claimed to be a pure Hellenic, and thus, as we have seen, he was able to tell us face to face what the Greeks would be doing today had they continued to thrive in our times.

We feel, taking into account the reckless Germanisms that he included in his masterpiece, the *Casa Milá*—a work much more vital aesthetically speaking than all the modern art that has come out of the Germany that Gaudí imitated—that he was completely mistaken; when we saw how it angered him when they said that his style was artistically moribund, we did not dare console him by saying that they said the same of our work, afraid that he might think that in comparing the moribund overtones that we both evidently share in the artistic field, we meant to compare similarly his creative potential with ours, which is so inferior to his that it does not even reach the sole of his shoe.

THE WILL TO POWER IN MODERN ART

Nevertheless, leaving our style aside (it is basically nothing more than propaganda, full of that holy insistence counseled many years ago by our admired d'Ors on scientific ideas and the basic ideals of Catalonia), we will say that it is evident that if a city had been designed and constructed under Gaudí's architectural vision and based on his grand, monstrous, baroque, and contorted style, the result would have been a city which was just as monstrous, baroque, and contorted with streets, squares, buildings, and gardens, just as monstrous, baroque, and contorted as the *Park Güell*, the *Casa Milá*, and the *Sagrada Familia;* but it cannot be denied that this would have been the most aesthetically alive of all modern cities which, for the most part, are constructed mathematically and mechanically like a work of science to be cities of the scientific age that they are, without seeking anything but the most academic artistic façade; to those who say that a Gaudían city would have been horrible and out of tone, and then shut their eyes to the marvelous artistic vision that this idea evokes, we say that we can't imagine why they should be surprised that a modern city contorts and deforms its architectural style to rediscover the living and flaming essence of the fundamental aesthetic emotion in precisely this modern age which has—as all of us know—contorted poetry, music, painting, and sculpture to rediscover the mentioned aesthetic element which had been lost by the cold and regulated application of academic canons taken from other styles, leaving Gaudí alone to do in architecture what the age as a whole had done collectively and successfully in the four other fine arts.

. . . propaganda full of that holy insistence counseled by our admirable d'Ors . . .

A writer and art critic, Eugenio d'Ors had said to Pujols: "You will be the Aristotle of Catalonia, and I will be the Plato." This portrait of Eugenio d'Ors was drawn by Ramón Casas Carbó.

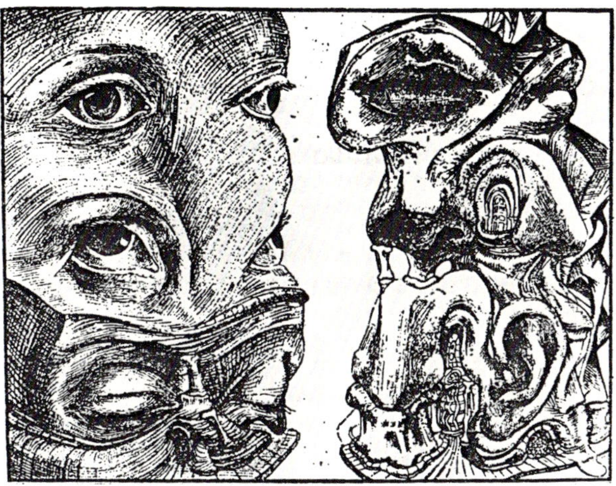

. . . *his masterpiece, the* Casa Milá . . .

"An architectonic project dated 1929, a time when I defended Gaudí's sublime genius against the Protestant Le Corbusier"—words and drawing by Salvador Dali.

In the epoch of Wagner and of Cézanne, who distorted established musical and pictorial ideas, breaking the canons of Italian music and painting respectively, and in the epoch of Strauss and Stravinsky and Picasso—not to mention their followers and imitators in poetry and in sculpture, two arts which, in this specific period, have not taken the initiative in deforming the canons and have been limited to following the lessons and the practical examples of painting and music which took the lead in the artistic adventure of modern times—those people who cannot accept as natural and logical a city like that which Gaudí would have conceived and built, if he had been allowed to, are the same who would not find it natural in the midst of primitive civilization when art produced the deformations and monstrosities which we all know and have seen in the history of art—in the burning creations of the primitive peoples who, although we maintain that they produced as they did because they did not know any better, created an art like that of the paintings and the drawings and the writings of the children of today who have still not emerged from their innocence; this primitive deformation, which came about as a result of difficulties and ignorance, gave a powerful amount of vital aesthetic expression to that art—the same quantity and quality that the artists of today seek in tearing everything apart, twisting and deforming with no pity or compassion whatsoever, whatever pleases them; their artistic conception is not meant to please, and they know that it provokes deep reactions: these artistic contortionists are concerned with that sensitive minority which is perhaps able to achieve some sort of live emotion, the element they seek, hoping to find and pass it on; some do so grandly, like Wagner, Cézanne, and Gaudí, who are the Homeric creators and deformers that destroy the sublime harmony of this great Greek poet—the greatest classic who ever has and ever will live—but they keep his magnitude and grace; and others do so delicately, as if writing or painting with an insect's antennae—those sensors which feel reality like the human sense organs should feel the artistic visions that reach our soul. Wagner, Strauss, and Stravinsky sought new forms in music by turning to primitive artistic conceptions, employing a sharper refinement in order to get closer to the primitive quality, on the theory that the two ends meet; Wagner deformed the canonical framework of Italian music—as we have said—Strauss augmented the sonority and made it more strident, while Stravinsky broke sharply through the melodies and the harmonies to get at their inner bowels; while Cézanne deformed figure and landscape to intensify the life of his pictorial vision, and Picasso made his paintings with genial feline marks and skill (triumphing in Paris after having spent the first years of his life in Barcelona, where his parents lived although they were not Catalans), Gaudí, as mute as stone, silently did the same, following the same tragic pattern of modern artistic revolution by returning to the fundamental principles of all peoples—without leaving Barcelona and without knowing Wagner, Strauss, Stravinsky, Cézanne, or even Picasso, or anyone (just as they did not know him or know who he was): he did as they did, and in this way Catalonia—without leaving Barcelona and without presenting herself on the universal market of modern art—was incorporated into the artistic fever of our times in that single branch of art which the other countries had left alone and subjected to the classic canons of antiquity or to the needs of modern construction, which twists iron like straw and makes stones out of the very cement that used to serve to join and unite stones with one another.

As a final point to these considerations regarding the history of art and its characteristics in modern times, we might add that Wagner, Cézanne, and the other revolutionary innovators who sought the live aesthetic of basic sensitive emotion—all worked at the top of a mountain of artists who had themselves worked slowly and with minor innovations, preparing the way for the artistic revolution of the nineteenth and twentieth centuries and the explosive triumph of the aesthetic essence over the canonical debris of the pure forms that had lost their life in our eminently scientific times, which dried the greenest leaves of the aesthetic tree; for the wind of science was not very favorable to the aesthetic harvest, which needed the light of a new sensitivity attuned to this age that is so much more scientific than any in history—a sensitivity that would remake the essential vision of the work of art; Gaudí, contrary to Wagner, Cézanne, and the others, began his revolution alone in Barcelona, without precedents here or anywhere, for the modern styles that he admired and imitated—like those he admired from ancient times—were not styles that sought that aesthetic essence which was the supreme aspiration of nineteenth- and twentieth-century sensitivity, irritated by the scientific death of artistic work; and so it happens that Gaudí situated Catalonia in the history of art, just as we might locate it geographically on the map, accomplishing with his genius that which the other geniuses of other lands and of other branches of art did by collecting and perfecting the efforts of the artists who had preceded them.

V

GAUDÍ'S TESTAMENT: IN DEFENSE OF TOTAL ART

Although it is very difficult, if not impossible, to present in writing the ideas and images which Gaudí set forth in his constructions or in his own words aided by the pencil in his hand, outlining his words in the whiteness of the paper, we can say that "The Temple Being Born" *(El Temple que naix)*, as Maragall called it in his article, or the New Temple as we could call it, dedicated to the family of Jesus (had it been finished, Barcelona would have become a city of two cathedrals, the old and the new, like Lérida, whose old cathedral, sung by the poet Morera, is the most ardent and alive of the Catalan cathedrals, and whose new one is the coldest, saved only from death by the slightest trace of neoclassic life), or the temple of the Field of the Harp, as we poetically do call it, just as we also call it the temple of the harp of the field, or the harp of the field of the temple when we want to suggest an idea that approximates the musicality which emanates from that architectural structure, which, breathing the air of the heavens, seems not only like a harp but also like an organ that can be played by either the fingers or the lips; one could almost say that the area is called the Field of the Harp because there is a temple there that seems like the harp of the field, and which plays the same tunes and makes the same harmonies as the harp of David, which, turning its back on Asia, resounded through all of Europe and America, just as Israel left behind the continent which served as her cradle and sang to the continent which served as her empire, and will eventually be left behind in her Catalan tomb; but returning to what we were saying, it was a cathedral dedicated to the Jewish family which had been consecrated the Holy Family—an explosive encounter between the architecture of India, Greece, and Northern or Gothic Europe (the culture that produced the tragedy of Hamlet and those cathedrals of Doubt which are so much taller than all the cathedrals of Faith, for they rise up like questions to eternity, filled with phrases which illuminate the shadows of life—just as the lanterns of the naves illuminate the shadows of cathedrals—as

. . . Maragall in his article . . .

Maragall's article, "El Temple que naix," appeared in the *Diario de Barcelona* of December 19, 1900.

if illuminating the very shadows of eternity that were questioned by Hamlet), a baroque and confused reunion of architectural styles representing the artistic and religious visions of humanity—all of which burn with a flame kindled in the debris of the structures from architectural history, ignited and burning in the fire of time, which destroys and consumes everything; it is as if all the history of architecture had been exhumed and summarized and made to flower and thrive in the present, when all it represents is dead, decayed, fallen, and buried; at the same time, it was also a meeting place for the fine arts: because poetry, music, sculpture, and painting, joining hands as if dancing the Catalan *sardana*, had arranged to meet in the Field of the Harp, to build there together a work of architecture, and all those who can imagine this ardent and intensive fusion of the fine arts—hot from the oven and fresh as a rose—will have an idea, vague and fuzzy though the image may be, of the artistic vision of our Gaudí—a vision which incarnated, condensed, and petrified his religious vision, and was the last blush of Catholicism in the world, in that very land which, as our readers in times to come will understand more clearly, was the country assigned to kill it, to push it beneath the wheels of science just as the wheels of the scientific electric streetcar on the Gran Vía would kill Gaudí, who spent more than thirty years building and singing Jerusalem's hymn to Barcelona as he chipped away at the stone and put the cement in place—like the day-laborers and working men who sing while they work—without being able to see that his own Barcelona was the Jerusalem of the future; for although Gaudí—as we have said and we repeat—madly loved Catalonia and sang with the harp of stone which he himself was building, his eyes were on the past and he sat with his back to the future like the blind man who sings in the street and sees nothing more than that which he saw when he had eyes; instead of being—as it deserved to have been for all that it represented—the first flame of the true religion which must rise up from our land to illuminate the world, it became the last flame of the fire that had been kept burning for twenty centuries by the creative peoples of modern civilization, and instead of being the architect of the first cathedral of the true religion, Gaudí had the misfortune of being the architect who was unable to complete the last cathedral of the greatest of the false religions; and what is even sadder for a Catalanista such as he, who so loved Catalonia, he was the architect of the last temple to the religion of the Jews, when he could have been the builder of the first temple of the religion of the Catalans, serving the true rather than the false, which was destined to die like all religions no matter how true they may be (for when the hour arrives, not even truth can save their lives—as will be demonstrated by Universal Catalan Science, which will provide the basis for the true religion), because religions decay and pass on just as cathedrals do; although it is the religion that sustains the cathedrals and not the cathedrals that sustain the religion, all come to the same end—just as we and all that has been born, is born, and will be born in this life, which serves as a road to the other; just as Hamlet—the man of doubt—vacillated after questioning if we will be or will not be after we are dead, saying "to be or not to be, that is the question" (the words which begin the most famous soliloquy in this work or any other), daring to add those words "to die, to sleep, perchance to dream," which are the only response to his question, which resounds in the cathedral of Doubt like the Psalms of David and the songs of the prophets in the cathedrals of Europe and America; as we have said in speaking of the comparison that Gaudí made with Aeschylus' *Oresteia*, *Hamlet* is a tragedy in five acts and numerous scenes, all filled with that half-light which fills the Gothic cathedrals illuminated by the light of the lanterns like gold and precious stones; he noted this with a sparkle in his eye—that art critic who was able to sculpt his religious visions into an artistic vision of architecture, the author of the temple of the *Sagrada Familia* who is now in heaven and

. . . just as the wheels of the scientific electric streetcar on the Gran Vía . . .

The first streetcar circulated in New York in 1852, the year of Gaudí's birth.

who, if he could recall this life in the other (something that is completely impossible, as we will demonstrate among the many other things that we propose to demonstrate), he would see that—as we have already said in this article and as we repeat in closing so that everyone will remember it—the Holy Family was nothing more than a family of Jews, however securely enveloped in the sumptuous folds of the mantle of legend, which crackles when folded and unfolded like the mantles of the kings, and it was the family that produced the most Jewish of Jews—He who was able to summarize all of the Bible in a single chapter by dying on the cross after supping with his companions; He demonstrated with His toast (wine cup in one hand and bread in the other), which referred to the sacrifice that He would make and did make, that He was the greatest and most refined poet that had ever walked the earth, and that He was a poet of speech and of action—of words and of deeds; while other poets take inspiration from legends, He was a sublime poet who, without writing a word or leaving a single written phrase behind, inspired a legend (as if He were the legend and the legend the poet) which said all that Jesus said, even when no one could hear Him such as when He stood alone and isolated on the Mount of Olives while the Apostles slept, and spoke those still unequaled words in preparation for the sacrifice which would deliver the kingdom of heaven and earth—pure and elevated words that only legend could hear and pass on to us; it was legend that inspired Gaudí's Nativity or Life façade for the temple, dedicated to Him who died awaiting glorious resurrection—the king of the world—who did indeed live again in the very legend that later gave birth to Him at the portal of Bethlehem, surrounded by angels, shepherds, and kings guided by the stars, and nineteen centuries later he dedicated the Portal of the Nativity or the Life to the family of the poet who inspired the legend, planning also to dedicate to Him the Portal of Death and, especially, that of the Resurrection (which was to have been the principal entrance, as we have already said) in glorification of the son of the Family to whom the legend gave birth, death, and life after death; these doors figured in the general plan of the building left behind by Gaudí after he was begged and persuaded to do so: this prophet of the past, who had always declared and maintained that no plan was necessary in the building of a cathedral, was finally convinced to draw one up—as if he were leaving a will—by those who never tired of telling him that, should he die, his artistic vision (and the religious vision it contained) would not be finished and completed after he had begun it so well.

As we are speaking of the death of Gaudí and are also contributing all the anecdotes that we can to the intellectual treasury of our land, and as we have now come to the end of this article with the death of the architect, who—as we have said and as everyone knows—was run over by a streetcar belonging to the Barcelona Streetcar Company, we must evoke as our last recollection the beautiful anecdote relating to his work on the tribune of the cathedral in Palma de Majorca; since he was a specialist in cathedrals, the bishops and canons of the chapter of that marvelous Gothic cathedral—as golden as the golden island on which it stands—whose interior is entirely similar to that of the Church of Santa María del Mar in Barcelona (another marvel of our medieval centuries), contracted Gaudí to restore the interior tribune of the purest Gothic cathedral ever to emerge from the sea.

As was the case with all of the great Gaudí's works, no one was pleased with the results, yet no one wished to tell him so face to face, for his style was imposing even to those who did not like it (as we are recounting anecdotes we are reminded of the typical case of the Batlló couple, husband and wife, who commissioned him to remodel their house on the Paseo de Gracia—a marvel of color; when the greatest Catalan architect in the history of art showed them what he had decided and explained what he planned to do, they told him that it was just fine, but when he was out of sight, man

The polychrome-mosaic façade of the *Casa Batlló* on the Paseo de Gracia in Barcelona.

Interior of the *Casa Batlló*

. . . the Batlló couple, husband and wife, who commissioned him to remodel their house on the Paseo de Gracia—a marvel of color . . .

Portrait of Felio Batlló y Barrera.

. . . with great truth and aesthetic insight that even a streetcar could be very beautiful . . .

The tribune of the Cathedral of Palma de Majorca.

and wife looked at each other and mutually confessed that they didn't really like it at all); and so it was that the canons of the Cathedral of Palma de Majorca told Gaudí that his tribune was just fine, waiting until he was out of sight to express their feeling that it really looked more like a streetcar; someone revealed to Gaudí the secret opinion of the cathedral chapter—which, as a chapter, approved the work and, as canons, disapproved of it—and it was then that the architect of the temple of the *Sagrada Familia*, glorifying many years ahead of time the streetcar that was to be his death, responded with great truth and aesthetic insight, that even a streetcar could be very beautiful; it was as if he could see that streetcar which, sending him to the Hospital de la Santa Cruz, would then take him on from this world into the other; as if Gaudí, who always traveled everywhere on foot (he said it was healthier that way), chose to catch a streetcar to eternity—but instead it was the streetcar that caught Gaudí, to take him on the only trip that he ever wanted to take (as is demonstrated by his mystical archi-

. . . is entombed in the crypt of the temple of the Sagrada Familia . . .

Gaudí's funeral; the cortège enters the church grounds on June 12, 1926.

tecture) and that he had dreamed of taking so often in the shadow of that very temple which he was unable to finish but handed over to the inspiration of the centuries to come.

All glory, then, to the Catalan land which, by producing a man like Gaudí and a cathedral like the temple of the *Sagrada Familia* in the Field of the Harp, a work unique in modern religious architecture, representing the artistic and religious vision of the great architect of the universe of our times, announces the future that awaits her and that we hope will be hers for many centuries—a future that will not come in the life of those now present, but after we all are long dead and buried, like Gaudí, who, as we have said and we repeat to end once and for all, is entombed in the crypt of the temple of the *Sagrada Familia*—his lifelong dream, which went with him to his death and closed his eyes—lying there in his tomb and crowned by his dream (which even though of stone is as light as the smoke of dreams) a man who sleeps with his dream over his head like a canopy.

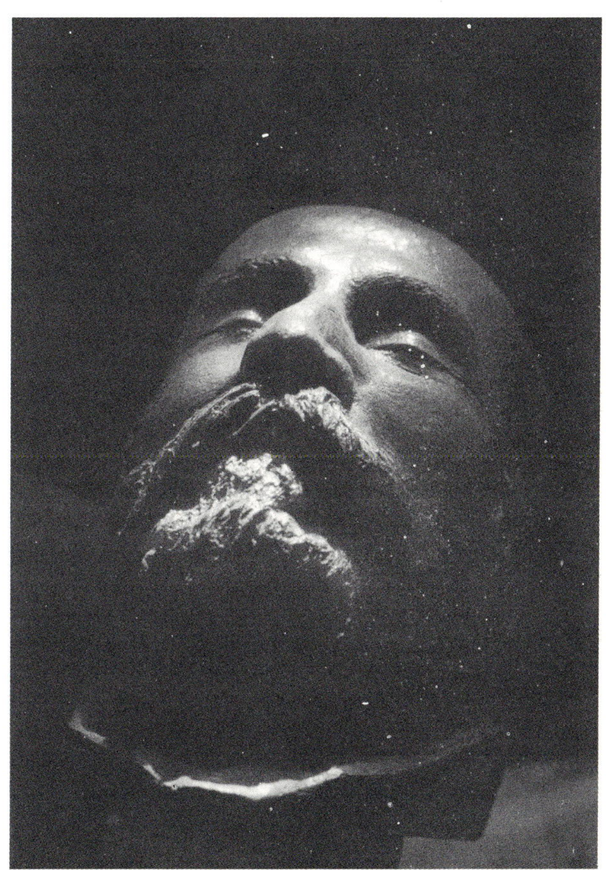

. . . a man who sleeps with his dream over his head like a canopy.

Gaudí's deathmask, cast by Juan Matamala.

INDEX OF NAMES

NOTES ON SOURCES

[1] Bergós, *Antonio Gaudí, l'home i l'obra* (see Bibliography).

[2] Cirici-Pellicer, "La escultura de Gaudí en la Sagrada Familia," in *Cuadernos de Arquit*, 1952 (see Bibliography).

[3] Guillermo Forteza, "Parlant amb en Gaudí d'En Prat de la Riba i l'actual moment de Catalunya", in *Vila-Nova*, Dec. 15, 1917.

[4] Gaudí, Youthful diary, published in Martinell, *Gaudí: su vida, su teoria, su obra*, Barcelona, 1967, Appendix 5 (see Bibliography).

[5] Martinell, *Gaudí i la Sagrada Familia* (see Bibliography).

[6] Manuel de Montoliu, "Una anecdota de Gaudi," in *Diario de Barcelona*, June 29, 1952.

[7] Puig i Boada, *El Templo de la Sagrada Familia* (see Bibliography).

[8] Ráfols, *Gaudí* (see Bibliography).

[9] Frederico Ratera, "Aspectos internos del Templo: un colaborador de Gaudí", in *Templo*, Aug.-Sept. 1949.

[10] Vicente Salaverri, "Un revolucionario de la arquitectura," *La Actualidad*, July 2, 1914.

ACKNOWLEDGEMENTS

The authors and the publisher are grateful to all the curators, museum and library directors, the people who worked with Gaudí, and Gaudí's friends who made this book possible. Particular thanks go to: Monsieurs Juan Matamala, Alfredo Opisso, and Faust Pujols for private papers and information which they were kind enough to contribute; also to Jean-Christophe Averty, Juan Bassegoda, Luis Bonet, Maria Luisa Borras, Enrique Casanelles, M. Cardonne, Société Cavisa, Joan Cuyàs, Alfredo Darnell, José Maria Garrut, Marie Gatard, Renato du Four, Madame José Maria Jujol, Madame Lancelot-Ney, Elizabeth Lanz, Xavier Llobet, Jordi Maragall and family, César Martinell, Jaime Miravillès, Juan Prats, Paco Rabane, Ramon Roca Sastre, Henri Roig, Gonzalo Serraclara, José Maria de Sucre, Jean Pierre Sudre, Juan José Tharrats, R. Tobella, Francesc Vicens, Dr. Salvador Villaseca, Francisco Villamartin Canadell.

PHOTOGRAPHIC CREDITS

The following abbreviations have been used: A = above; B = below; R = right; L = left; C = center.

The illustrations come from the following sources: Amigos de Gaudí, Barcelona: Pages 41, 42 A and BR, 44 A, 53, 63, 99 BR, 101 R, 127 A and B, 132, 140 R, 157 A, 166 R, 215 A, 219 B, 222 B, 223, 243 A; municipal administrative archives, Barcelona: Pages 162-163; Mas Archives, Barcelona: Pages 16, 22, 23, 26, 27 A and B, 51, 59 AL, 99 A, 100 L and R, 101 L, 104 AR, C and B, 128, 131 A and B, 143, 152 BL, 214 A, 215 B, 225 L, 226, 227 L and R, 242; Archives of the Temple the Sagrada Familia, Barcelona: Pages 54, 57 L and R, 58 L, 217 R, 219 A, 244 A and B; Archives of the Colonia Güell, Barcelona: Pages 29, 129; Branguli, Barcelona: Pages 42 BL, 48 BL, 49; College of architects of Catalonia and Baleares, Barcelona: Page 218; Robert Descharnes, Paris: Pages 58-59 B, 106, 107, 108, 109, 110, 111, 112, 113, 114, 115, 116, 157 B, 192, 213, 222 A, 230 A, 231, 235 A, 239; destroyed documents, copy in Ráfols "Gaudi" (see bibliography): Page 60 AR and AL; Ferran, Barcelona: Pages 125, 136, 137; Arts Gazette, Barcelona: Pages 124, 133; Municipal Institute of History, Barcelona: Pages 25 L and R, 39, 47 BR, 48 AL and AR, 102 B, 126 A and B, 216 B, 220, 228 A and B, 235 B, 236 A and B, 243 B, 245 A; Widow Jujol, Barcelona: Pages 211, 214 B; Man Ray, Paris: 152 A; Helena and Jordi Maragall, Barcelona: Page 46 R; César Martinell, Barcelona: Page 156 A; Juan Matamala, Barcelona: Pages 97, 98 A and B, 122-123, 135 B, 146, 147 A, 148 L and R, 149 L and R, 150 L, 156 C, 158 B, 159 L, 160 A, 166-167, 193, 194, 196-197, 198, 199 L, 200, 201; Museum of Modern Art, Barcelona: Pages 224 B, 225 A, 238; Alfonso Opisso, Mataro: Pages 43, 44 BR, 46 L, 47 AL, AR and BL, 96, 99 BL, 102 A, 103 AL and AR, 104 AL, 120, 121, 134 AL, AR and B, 135 AL and AR, 138 L, 139 R, 141 A, 210; Clovis Prévost, Nesle-la-Vallée: 64, 138 AR, 139 AL, 140 AL, 141 B, 147 BR, 151, 156 B, 158 A, 159 R, 161 R and L, 185, 186 L and R, 187 A and B, 199 BR; Faust Pujols, Martorell: Pages 204, 205 AL, AR and B, 206, 207 A and B, 208, 209 A and B, 212; Reus Museum, Reus: Pages 150 R, 224 A, 225 BR; René Roland, Paris: Pages 30, 31, 32, 33, 34, 35, 36, 188, 189, 190, 191; Roger Viollet, Paris: Pages 160 B, 216 A, 230 B, 234; Zerkowitz, Barcelona: Pages 8, 24, 52, 59 R, 147 BL, 152 BR, 217 L.

SELECTED BIBLIOGRAPHY

prepared by George R. Collins

(In each group, titles are arranged in the order of their appearance.)

General monographs on Gaudí:

José F. Ráfols and Francisco Folguera, *Gaudí, el gran arquitecto español,* Barcelona, 1928 (in Catalan), 1929 (in Spanish). The first and basic monograph. Complete bibliography and chronology.

J. F. Ráfols, *Gaudí, 1852-1926,* Barcelona, 1952, 1960. Briefer, with supplementary bibliography. In Catalan.

Juan Bergós, *Gaudí: l'home i l'obra,* Barcelona, 1954. Currently being translated into Spanish.

Henry-Russell Hitchcock, *Gaudí,* New York City, 1957. Catalog of the exhibition at the Museum of Modern Art.

George R. Collins, *Antonio Gaudí,* New York City, 1960. Annotated bibliography; chronology. Somewhat updated in Spanish (Barcelona, 1961) and German (Ravensburg, 1962) editions.

Jordi Elías, *Gaudí, assaig biogràfic,* Barcelona, 1961. No illus.

Roberto Pane, *Antoni Gaudí,* Milan, 1964. Bibligraphy supplements that of Collins.

César Martinell, *Gaudí; su vida, su teoría, su obra,* Barcelona, 1967. Encyclopedic, the last word; 555 illus. English edition in preparation.

Juan Bassegoda and José M. Garrut, *Guía de Gaudí,* Barcelona, 1970. Handy guidebook to Gaudí in all Spain; Spanish, Catalan, English, and French sections. Map.

Books of Illustrations:

Collection Fotoscop Gomis-Prats (various publishers, all Barcelona): Alexandre Cirici Pellicer, *La Sagrada Familia,* 1952. Le Corbusier, *Gaudí,* 1958. Carola Giedion-Welcker, *Park Güell de A. Gaudí,* 1966. A. Cirici Pellicer, *1900 a Barcelona,* 1967. José L. Sert, *Cripta de la Colonia Güell de A. Gaudí,* 1969. All are multilingual.

Juan E. Cirlot, *The Genesis of Gaudían Architecture,* New York City, 1967.

Joan Perucho, *Gaudí, una arquitectura de anticipación,* Barcelona, 1967. Spanish, English, French, and German.

Lara V. Masini, *Antoni Gaudí,* Florence, 1969.

Critical writings:

J. E. Cirlot, *El Arte de Gaudí,* Barcelona, 1950, 1954.

C. Martinell, ed., *Gaudí,* Barcelona, Centro de Estudios Gaudianistas, 1966. A collection of 12 essays.

James J. Sweeney and J. L. Sert, *Antoni Gaudí,* New York City, 1961. Revised edition 1970.

Enrique Casanelles, *Antonio Gaudí: a Reappraisal,* Greenwich, Conn., 1968. Originally, Barcelona, 1965.

(The many articles of this nature are not cited; references to them are to be found in the monographs.)

Useful Sources of Gaudí's sayings:

(See also Notes on Sources, page 245)
See Ráfols-Folguera, above.

C. Martinell, *Gaudí i la Sagrada Familia comentada per ell mateix,* Barcelona, 1951. An anthology now published in Spanish, as *Converšaciones con Gaudí, 1969.*

See Bergós, 1954, above.

Gaudí's Structural Theory:

Juan Rubió Bellver, "Dificultats per a arribar a la sintessis arquitectònica," *Anuario de la Asociación de Arquitectos de Cataluña,* 1913, pp. 63-79.

Domingo Sugrañes, "Disposició estàtica del Temple de la *Sagrada Família*"' in same *Anuario,* 1923, pp. 17-36. Reprinted in part in Spanish in Ráfols-Folguera (see above), pp. 172-190.

Francesc de P. Quintana, "Les formes guerxes del temple de la Sagrada Família," *Ciutat i la Casa* (Barcelona), 1927, No. 6. Reprinted in Spanish in Ráfols-Folguera (see above), pp. 190-203.

Santiago Rubió, *Cálculo funicular del hormigón armado*, Buenos Aires, 1952. Application of Gaudí's theories to reinforced concrete.

J. Bergós, *Materiales y elementos de construcción*, Barcelona, 1953.

Buenaventura Bassegoda y Musté, *Bóvedas tabicadas*, Madrid, c. 1957. The Catalan vaulting method in general.

G. R. Collins, "Antonio Gaudí: Structure and Form," *Perspecta 8*, (Yale University), 1963, pp. 63-90.

J. Bergós, *Tabicados huecos*, Barcelona, 1965. Practical experience, related to Gaudí's methods.

G. R. Collins, "The Transfer of Thin Masonry Vaulting from Spain to America," *Journal of the Society of Architectural Historians*, XXVII, No. 3, October 1968, pp. 176-201. Includes complete bibliography on Catalan vaulting methods.

Gaudí as Sculptor:

Joaquín Folch y Torres, "Arquitecte Gaudí," *Gaseta de les arts*, (Barcelona), III, 1 July 1926. Photos of his studio.

Idem, "Gaudí escultor," *Destino*, (Barcelona), 11 June 1955, pp. 3-4.

A. Cirici Pellicer, "La escultura de Gaudí en la Sagrada Familia," *Cuadernos de Arquitectura*, No. 20, 1956, pp. 21-24.

Eugene Santomasso, *Antonio Gaudí as Sculptor*, unpublished master's essay, Department of Art History and Archaeology, Columbia University, 1965.

Gaudí and City Planning:

D. Sugrañes, "Gaudí i l'urbanisme," *El Matí*, (Barcelona), 31 July 1932.

Manuel Ribas Piera, "Gaudí i la Cooperativa Obrera de Mataró," *Serra d'Or*, (Barcelona), VII, No. 12, December 1965, pp. 54-57.

Idem, "La planificación urbanística en España," *Zodiac 15*, (Milan), 1965, pp. 145-164.

Idem, "Consideraciones sobre Gaudí a través de sus obras urbanísticas," *Cuadernos de Arquitectura*, No. 63, 1966, pp. 20-33.

Monographs on Individual Buildings:

Palacio Güell:

Joseph Puiggarí, *Monografía de la Casa Palau y Museu del Excm. Sr. D. Eusebi Güell y Bacigalupi*, Barcelona, 1894. Brief, but of the period.

Park Güell:

Salvador Sellés, "El Parque Güell: Memoria descriptiva," in the *Anuario* cited above, 1903, pp. 47-67. Brief. Still available as an offprint from the Amigos de Gaudí of Barcelona.

See Giedion-Welcker, above.

Colonia Güell:

See Sert, above.

Sagrada Familia Church:

Isidro Puig Boada, *El Temple de la Sagrada Família*, Barcelona, 1929, 1952. The second edition is enlarged and is in Spanish. This book is fundamental.

C. Martinell, *Gaudí i la Sagrada Família...*, 1951, see above.

Idem, *La Sagrada Familia*, Barcelona, 1952.

A. Cirici Pellicer, *La Sagrada Familia*, 1952, see above.

Francisco Camprubí Alemany, *Die Kirche der Heiligen Familie*, Barcelona, 1959. A doctoral dissertation at Munich on the iconography.

Also useful are the issues of the periodical *El Propagador de la Devoción a San José*, 1867-1936, 1943-48, and its successor *Templo*, since 1948. Material is mainly devotional but occasionally articles of architectural interest appear.

Catalan Background, General:

Gerald Brenan, *The Spanish Labyrinth*, Cambridge University, 1943, 1950, revised 1960.

J. F. Ráfols, *Diccionario biográfico de artistas de Cataluña*, Barcelona, 3 vols., 1951-1954. Data on all periods.

Idem, *El arte romántico en España*, Barcelona, 1954. Unique on the subject.

Jaume Vicens Vives, *Els catalans en el segle XIX*, Barcelona, 1958.

Raymond Carr, *Spain: 1808-1939*, Oxford History of Modern Europe, Oxford University, 1966.

Antoni Jutglar, *Els burgesos catalans*, Barcelona, 1966.

The Renaixensa and Modernismo:

Francisco Rogent y Pedrosa and L. Domenech y Montaner. et al. *Arquitectura moderna de Barcelona*, Barcelona, c.1897, Valuable pictorial survey with data on individual buildings.

J. F. Ráfols, *El arte modernista en Barcelona*, Barcelona, 1943. Much enlarged as *Modernismo y modernistas*, Barcelona, 1949.

A. Cirici Pellicer, *El arte modernista catalán*, Barcelona, 1951, 1960. Basic; more than 500 illus.

Jean Cassou, Emile Langui, Nikolaus Pevsner, *Les Sources du Vingtième Siècle*, Paris, 1961. Council of Europe exhibition of the Art Nouveau throughout Europe.

Phoebe Pool and Anthony Blunt, *Picasso, the Formative Years; a Study of His Sources*, Greenwich, Conn., 1962. The years 1897-1906.

A. Cirici Pellicer, *1900*.... See above.

Rafael Tasis, *La Renaixença Catalana*, Barcelona, 1967. Literary background.

Oriol Bohigas, *Arquitectura Modernista* (Photos Pomés), Barcelona, 1968. Wide range of illus. and data.

Juan Ainaud de Lasarte, Joaquín de la Puente, A. Cirici Pellicer, J. Bassegoda, *El Modernismo en España*, Madrid, 1969. Catalog of the big Madrid exhibition. Valuable biographical data.

This book, published by Edita S.A., Lausanne, was
created under the direction of Claude Prévost, Marc Audouin,
and Jacqueline Lorch.

Printed by GEA, Milan
Bound by Maurice Busenhart, Lausanne

Printed in Italy